Funded by a State Legislature Grant
Senator Suzi Oppenheimer

Bloom's Classic Critical Views

HENRY DAVID THOREAU

Bloom's Classic Critical Views

Bloom's Classic Critical Views

HENRY DAVID THOREAU

Edited and with an Introduction by
Harold Bloom
Sterling Professor of the Humanities
Yale University

BLOOM'S
LITERARY CRITICISM
An imprint of Infobase Publishing

Bloom's Classic Critical Views: Henry David Thoreau

Copyright © 2008 Infobase Publishing

Introduction © 2008 by Harold Bloom

Bloom's Literary Criticism
An imprint of Infobase Publishing
132 West 31st Street
New York NY 10001

Library of Congress Cataloging-in-Publication Data
Henry David Thoreau / edited and with an introduction by Harold Bloom.
     p. cm. — (Bloom's classic critical views)
  Includes bibliographical references and index.
  ISBN 978-1-60413-141-3 (hardcover)
  1. Thoreau, Henry David, 1817–1862—Criticism and interpretation. I. Bloom, Harold.
II. Title. III. Series.

  PS3054.H38 2008
  818'.309—dc22

                                            2008022014

Contributing editor: Luca Prono
Series design by Erika K. Arroyo
Cover design by Takeshi Takahashi
Printed in the United States of America
Bang EJB 10 9 8 7 6 5 4 3 2 1

This book is printed on acid-free paper.

All links and Web addresses were checked and verified to be correct at the time of publication. Because of the dynamic nature of the Web, some addresses and links may have changed since publication and may no longer be valid.

Contents

WORKS   169

Series Introduction

Bloom's Classic Critical Views is a new series presenting a selection of the most important older literary criticism on the greatest authors commonly read in high school and college classes today. Unlike the Bloom's Modern Critical Views series, which for more than 20 years has provided the best contemporary criticism on great authors, Bloom's Classic Critical Views attempts to present the authors in the context of their time and to provide criticism that has proved over the years to be the most valuable to readers and writers. Selections range from contemporary reviews in popular magazines, which demonstrate how a work was received in its own era, to profound essays by some of the strongest critics in the British and American tradition, including Henry James, G.K. Chesterton, Matthew Arnold, and many more.

Some of the critical essays and extracts presented here have appeared previously in other titles edited by Harold Bloom, such as the New Moulton's Library of Literary Criticism. Other selections appear here for the first time in any book by this publisher. All were selected under Harold Bloom's guidance.

In addition, each volume in this series contains a series of essays by a contemporary expert, who comments on the most important critical selections, putting them in context and suggesting how they might be used by a student writer to influence his or her own writing. This series is intended above all for students, to help them think more deeply and write more powerfully about great writers and their works.

Introduction by Harold Bloom

I have been so ardent an Emersonian since 1965 that only belatedly have I come now to a fuller appreciation of Thoreau. Ruggedly his own person, Thoreau nevertheless began as Emerson's disciple, even as Walt Whitman did. *Walden* remains a very Emersonian book, and so does *Leaves of Grass* (1855), and both works are American masterpieces. The influence of Emerson was and is liberating, perhaps because the Concord sage legislates against influence.

Thoreau arrived late at canonical status, as did Whitman, whom Thoreau visited and greatly admired. Now, in the twenty-first century, it seems almost odd that Thoreau, Whitman, and Herman Melville were accepted only in the earlier twentieth century as luminaries of the American Renaissance, joining Emerson and Hawthorne in the pantheon of classic American imaginative literature.

The importance of Thoreau is multiform, and I want here to center only on his foundational status as the vitalizing precursor of contemporary American ecological writing. You can argue that, historically considered, the Thoreau of "Civil Disobedience" must take precedence over the Thoreau of saving-the-earth since both Gandhi and Martin Luther King, Jr. took their starting point from the Concord woodsman who chose jail in preference to paying poll tax to a society that refused to abolish black slavery and that waged imperialistic war against Mexico. Yet the long-range effect of Thoreau as ecological prophet is likely to be even greater.

My reflections are moved by a remarkable new Library of America anthology, Bill McKibben's *American Earth: Environmental Writing Since Thoreau*. After selections from Thoreau, we are given a thousand pages of those in his wake, including John Muir, Theodore Roosevelt, John Burroughs,

Rachel Carson, Gary Snyder, John McPhee, Wendell Berry, Annie Dillard, Jonathan Schell, W.S. Merwin, Al Gore, and Rebeccca Solnit. In a far broader sense, Thoreau's master, Emerson, fostered almost all of American imaginative writing, frequently by dialectical recoil, as in Hawthorne, Melville, Dickinson, Henry James, T.S. Eliot, but more fecundly by direct inspiration: Whitman, Thoreau, William James, Robert Frost, Wallace Stevens, Gertrude Stein, Hart Crane. Thoreau's influence, more specialized, has an immediate urgency now, when the planet is in jeopardy: air, water, soil, food, weather. His lonely eminence would not have either surprised or gratified the self-reliant Thoreau.

One great paragraph of *Walden* always stays in my mind as the center of Thoreau's vitalism:

> Let us spend one day as deliberately as Nature, and not be thrown off the track by every nutshell and mosquito's wing that fall on the rails. Let us rise early and fast, or break fast, gently and without perturbation; let company come and let company go, let the bells ring and the children cry,—determined to make a day of it. Why should we knock under and go with the stream? Let us not be upset and overwhelmed in that terrible rapid and whirlpool called a dinner, situated in the meridian shallows. Weather this danger and you are safe, for the rest of the way is down hill. With unrelaxed nerves, with morning vigor, sail by it, looking another way, tied to the mast like Ulysses. If the engine whistles, let it whistle till it is hoarse for its pains. If the bell rings, why should we run? We will consider what kind of music they are like. Let us settle ourselves, and work and wedge our feet downward through the mud and slush of opinion, and prejudice, and tradition, and delusion, and appearance, that alluvion which covers the globe, through Paris and London, through New York and Boston and Concord, through church and state, through poetry and philosophy and religion, till we come to a hard bottom and rocks in place, which we can call *reality*, and say, This is, and no mistake; and then begin, having a *point d'appui*, below freshet and frost and fire, a place where you might found a wall or a state, or set a lamp-post safely, or perhaps a gauge, not a Nilometer, but a Realometer, that future ages might know how deep a freshet of shams and appearances had gathered from time to time. If you stand right fronting and face to face to a fact, you will see the sun glimmer on both its surfaces, as it were a cimeter, and feel its sweet edge dividing you through the heart and

marrow, and so you will happily conclude your mortal career. Be it life or death, we crave only reality. If we are really dying, let us hear the rattle in our throats and feel cold in the extremities; if we are alive, let us go about our business.

This is the great Thoreau, whose motto was: "In wildness is the preservation of the world." His later *Journals* sadly show him dwindling into a mere recorder of natural facts, numbering all the streaks of the tulip, as Dr. Samuel Johnson warned against those who forsook the generalizing intellect. But before he began to fall away, Thoreau had joined Emerson and Whitman as the true prophets who understood that there is always more day to dawn upon America. *Walden* ends: "The sun is but a morning-star."

BIOGRAPHY

HENRY DAVID THOREAU
(1817–1862)

Henry David Thoreau was born on July 12, 1817, in Concord, Massachusetts, where he spent most of his life. He entered Harvard in 1833, and after graduating in 1837 returned to Concord, where he attempted to support himself by teaching, first for a few weeks at public schools, then at a successful private school, which he and his brother John maintained from 1838 to 1841. In 1839 Thoreau and his brother took a trip along the Concord and Merrimack rivers, which Thoreau later recorded as a memorial to his brother, who died in 1842. Sometime before this expedition, in 1836 or 1837, Thoreau first became acquainted with Ralph Waldo Emerson. He lived with the Emerson family from 1841 to 1843. During those two years, Thoreau helped Emerson edit his literary periodical, *The Dial,* to which Thoreau had been contributing poems and articles since 1840. He was not, however, able to support himself through these literary activities and was eventually forced to earn a meager living by carrying on his father's trade as a pencil maker.

On July 4, 1845, Thoreau moved into a cabin he had built near Walden Pond, in a wooded area purchased by Emerson in 1844. There he hoped finally to be able to compose his memorial tribute to his brother. While he did produce the account, published in 1849 as *A Week on the Concord and Merrimack Rivers,* Thoreau also kept a journal while there. After two and a half years of living alone in extreme simplicity, Thoreau left Walden Pond in 1847 and began transforming his journals into what was to become his masterpiece, *Walden* (1854). In 1849 he published the essay "Civil Disobedience" (originally titled "Resistance to Civil Government"), which argued the right of the individual to refuse to pay taxes when his or her conscience so dictated. In 1846 Thoreau himself had been briefly jailed for not paying the Massachusetts poll tax, a gesture of protest against the Mexican War and the institution of slavery. He died in Concord on May 6, 1862.

Both *Walden* and "Civil Disobedience" were largely ignored during Thoreau's lifetime. In the years following his death, however, Thoreau's reputation grew and he is now considered one of America's greatest writers and thinkers. His *Journals* (14 vols.) were first published in 1906, and a new edition of his *Writings* began publication in 1971.

PERSONAL

"The true Thoreau," writes Robert Louis Stevenson in the second of his two essays included in this section, "still remains to be depicted." Stevenson clearly points out Thoreau's elusiveness, a characteristic that haunts the different contributions gathered here. Rose Hawthorne Lathrop, for example, records her contrasting reactions to Thoreau. At first, she was dreadfully frightened by "his enormous eyes, tame with religious intellect and wild with the loose rein." Yet, her heart subsequently softened toward him. As for the people who knew him, Thoreau also proved an enigma for literary critics, which probably accounts for the slow development of his fame. Although he is now considered a classic American literary icon—the solitary thinker walking in the woods and the ultimate individualist—during his lifetime, Thoreau was considered little more than a disciple of Emerson and was often unfavorably compared to his friend. The publication of his abolitionist essays immediately after the Civil War secured him a small readership in the North. The appearance of his journals at the turn of the twentieth century began to increase his reputation as a cantor of the American wilderness. His ascension to the American literary canon, however, had to wait until the 1930s, when antimodernists found in his writings nostalgic pleas for simple living.

The writings of this first section all contributed to establish Thoreau's reputation as a hermit and a recluse. In many of the recollections that follow, Thoreau is described as an iconoclast who lived a solitary existence within the woods around Walden Pond. Authors such as Louisa May Alcott, Emerson, and Rose Lathrop go as far as identifying Thoreau with natural elements. Emerson explicitly uses the words "hermit" and "iconoclast" to characterize his friend and explains that Thoreau preferred to "keep his solitary freedom at the cost of disappointing the natural expectations of his family and friends." It is undeniable that Thoreau was irritable, blunt, at times misogynistic, and that, in his last years, he was confined to his home by illness. Yet, in spite of their characterization of Thoreau as a hermit who lived a "simple and hidden life" (again Emerson's words), these personal reminiscences also tell a different and opposite story that contrasts with their own portrayals. Through them, we learn of Thoreau's social and political life. He kept regular contacts with other transcendentalist writers based in Concord such as William E. Channing, Orestes Brownson, Bronson Alcott, Nathaniel Hawthorne, Margaret Fuller, and, obviously, Ralph Waldo Emerson. With them, Thoreau shared a critique of American materialism and an active involvement in the many reform movements of the nineteenth century.

It was while living at Walden Pond from 1845 to 1847 that Thoreau spent a night in the Concord jail for failing to pay his poll tax. This act was Thoreau's way of rejecting a state government that he found complicit with the institution of slavery, which Thoreau vigorously condemned. Thus, it was only logical to condemn the government that fostered and perpetuated the institution. While the night spent in jail is one of the most widely known facts about Thoreau's life, it was by no means an isolated event but was the result of the author's lifelong interest in abolitionism. He was shaped from an early age by his mother and sisters, an influence that is seldom acknowledged, and soon took an active role in abolitionist causes. He wrote for the antislavery newspaper *The Liberator*. His essays "Civil Disobedience" (1848, or "Resistance to Civil Government"), "Slavery in Massachusetts" (1854), and a series of pieces on John Brown (1859–60) were all centered in abolitionist theory. Thoreau was thus not as aloof to the social and political matters of his era as some of the biographical sketches included here portray him to be. Thoreau embodied the dual dimension of transcendentalism: the movement and its members were both deeply rooted in the cultural milieu of New England as well as modern and cosmopolitan individuals producing incisive critiques of American society. The characterization of Thoreau as a hermit detached from society, so common in the early critical pieces on the author, has thus been challenged by more modern commentators.

It is certainly undeniable that Thoreau held negative views of the dominant values of pre–Civil War America. He was deeply concerned with the destruction of the environment and rejected the likely consequences of the rise of industrialization with its attendant materialistic values. Thoreau's sharp judgments, however, imply a deep awareness of the political and economic theories of the time and of the philosophical systems of his age, particularly of Kant and Coleridge. Such an awareness is typical of an intellectual who is significantly concerned with the society in which he lives. Thoreau's writings do not simply re-create the crises of the nineteenth century, they also anticipate the social unrest of the next century. This is one of the reasons why Thoreau has become such a central literary and social figure in contemporary times. In the 1960s, for example, Thoreau's criticism of American democracy contributed to his being seen as a political radical and a forerunner of the counterculture movement. One of the most significant aspects of Thoreau's legacy—his influence on Mahatma Gandhi and Martin Luther King, Jr. and the nonviolent movements for Indian independence and American civil rights—is social and political in nature.

NATHANIEL HAWTHORNE (1842)

Mr. Thoreau dined with us yesterday. He is a singular character—a young man with much of wild original nature still remaining in him; and so far as he is sophisticated, it is in a way and method of his own. He is as ugly as sin, long-nosed, queer-mouthed, and with uncouth and rustic, though courteous manners, corresponding very well with such an exterior. But his ugliness is of an honest and agreeable fashion, and becomes him much better than beauty. He was educated, I believe, at Cambridge, and formerly kept school in this town; but for two or three years back, he has repudiated all regular modes of getting a living, and seems inclined to lead a sort of Indian life among civilized men—an Indian life, I mean, as respects the absence of any systematic effort for a livelihood. He has been for some time an inmate of Mr. Emerson's family; and, in requital, he labors in the garden, and performs such other offices as may suit him—being entertained by Mr. Emerson for the sake of what true manhood there is in him. Mr. Thoreau is a keen and delicate observer of nature—a genuine observer—which, I suspect, is almost as rare a character as even an original poet; and Nature, in return for his love, seems to adopt him as her especial child, and shows him secrets which few others are allowed to witness. He is familiar with beast, fish, fowl, and reptile, and has strange stories to tell of adventures and friendly passages with these lower brothers of mortality. Herb and flower, likewise, wherever they grow, whether in garden or wildwood, are his familiar friends. He is also on intimate terms with the clouds, and can tell the portents of storms. It is a characteristic trait, that he has a great regard for the memory of the Indian tribes, whose wild life would have suited him so well; and, strange to say, he seldom walks over a ploughed field without picking up an arrow-point, spear-head, or other relic of the red man, as if their spirits willed him to be the inheritor of their simple wealth.

—Nathaniel Hawthorne, journal entry,
September 1, 1842

LOUISA MAY ALCOTT "THOREAU'S FLUTE" (1863)

Although she is primarily known for her semi-autobiographical children's novel *Little Women* (1868), Louisa May Alcott (1832–1888) was a prolific writer who produced almost three hundred literary works during her lifetime. In her books, Alcott created positive portrayals of family life with which her young readers could easily identify. Yet she also authored sensational thrillers and gothic novels, only recently rediscovered, that presented unusually strong women for the literature of the times.

Alcott grew up in a progressive family that was actively involved in the social and political liberal causes of the day such as abolitionism, educational reform, women's suffrage, and prison reform. Louisa's father, Bronson Alcott, was a well-known educator whose methods were, however, too ahead of their times. When Bronson's experimental Temple School failed in 1839, the Alcotts moved from Boston to Concord where, virtually bankrupt, they survived thanks to the financial assistance of relatives and friends—Ralph Waldo Emerson especially. In Concord, the young Louisa grew up within the prestigious transcendentalist circle and personally met, among others, Emerson, Hawthorne, and Thoreau, who taught her botany and natural science. Thus, although Bronson was unable to provide financial support for his family, which remained in poverty and in debt until the publication of *Little Women*, Louisa benefited from a unique education. After the failure of Bronson's Fruitland, a utopian community based on a strict vegetarian diet and communal work, Louisa became the family's breadwinner. Before she attained success with *Hospital Sketches* (1863) and *Little Women*, Alcott published more than eighty pieces in a range of periodicals, searching for the literary form that best suited her voice.

Written after Thoreau's death, Alcott's poem "Thoreau's Flute" celebrates the writer as a nineteenth-century Pan, as the "Genius of the wood," walking through nature with his flute. Thoreau's loss is mourned by the natural elements as the author is identified with his eternal homage to Nature. Thus, the mourning of the elements is unjustified as Thoreau's presence will always be felt within Nature. Although Thoreau's flute will remain mute, his soul, "that finer instrument" which produced lofty tributes to the natural world, will always be heard. "Seek not for him,—he is with thee" warns the last line of the poem, which also summarizes the central role of the communion with Nature in Thoreau's philosophy and in transcendentalism as a whole.

We, sighing, said, "Our Pan is dead;
   His pipe hangs mute beside the river;—
   Around it wistful sunbeams quiver,
But Music's airy voice is fled.
Spring mourns as for untimely frost;
   The bluebird chants a requiem;
   The willow-blossom waits for him;—

The Genius of the wood is lost."
Then from the flute, untouched by hands,
        There came a low, harmonious breath:
        "For such as he there is no death;—
His life the eternal life commands;
Above man's aims his nature rose:
        The wisdom of a just content
        Made one small spot a continent,
And tuned to poetry Life's prose.
"Haunting the hills, the stream, the wild,
        Swallow and aster, lake and pine,
        To him grew human or divine,—
Fit mates for this large-hearted child.
Such homage Nature ne'er forgets,
        And yearly on the coverlid
        'Neath which her darling lieth hid
Will write his name in violets.
"To him no vain regrets belong,
        Whose soul, that finer instrument,
        Gave to the world no poor lament,
But wood-notes ever sweet and strong.
O lonely friend! he still will be
        A potent presence, though unseen,—
        Steadfast, sagacious, and serene:
Seek not for him,—he is with thee."

—Louisa May Alcott, "Thoreau's Flute,"
Atlantic, Sept. 1863, pp. 280–281

Ralph Waldo Emerson
"Thoreau" (1862)

Ralph Waldo Emerson (1803–1882) has often been invoked as the found-
ing father of American literature by such classic critics as F.O. Mathiessen
and Alfred Kazin. The chief animator of the transcendentalist movement,
Emerson made eloquent pleas in his essays and addresses for scholars
and intellectuals to give literary form to the rich material that the United
States offered them. He repeatedly proclaimed America's intellectual
freedom from tradition, in general, and European tradition, in particular.

He vitally contributed to the development of the national literature that characterized the mid-1850s and is often referred to as the American Renaissance. In his portrait of Thoreau, Emerson gives voice to his lifelong protest against the social pressures that suppress and standardize art and thought.

Born in Boston, Emerson lost his father at an early age. His childhood was marked by poverty, but he was encouraged to pursue his studies by his aunt Mary Moody. He first attended Boston Public Latin School and then Harvard on a scholarship from 1817 to 1821. After graduation, he started a career as a teacher but soon changed his mind, turning to the study of theology. In 1832, three years after becoming junior pastor of Boston's Second Church, Emerson left the ministry because of his increasing skepticism about religious dogma and sacraments. In the mid-1830s, Emerson emerged as a national figure after his decision to embark on a professional career as a lecturer. His oratorical skills and sharp intellect made him one of the most highly sought speakers of his time on such diverse topics as science, literature, education, religion, and philosophy. His three important contributions of the 1830s—the pamphlet *Nature* (1836, revised in 1849), the essay "The American Scholar" (1837), and "The Harvard Divinity School Address" (1838)—made him the most visible member of the transcendentalist community. Common to the "American Scholar" and the "Address" is the rejection of conformity, authority, and tradition. In the former essay, this rejection targets the deference to European cultural models, while, in the latter, Emerson is concerned with empty religious rites, a stance that caused him to be branded a religious radical and be barred from speaking at Harvard until after the Civil War. In spite of this ostracism and his critique of the establishment, Emerson played a decisive role in the formation of American culture and letters. He became an established intellectual, whose endorsement was sought in regard to the popular social causes of the day such as abolitionism and women's rights. Emerson generally refused political advocacy, but, during his long career, he was willing to support fellow transcendentalists such as Thoreau, Bronson Alcott, and Margaret Fuller both financially and through his network of personal connections. It was thanks to Emerson's interest that works by Thoreau, Alcott, and Fuller were published. Emerson also loaned Thoreau the property at Walden Pond that inspired the writing of *Walden*.

The following portrait of Thoreau should be viewed in the context of Emerson's lifelong quest for American models. To Emerson, Thoreau exhibits all the desirable features of a truly American intellectual, "an iconoclast" who is intent in keeping "his solitary freedom" and "securing his own independence." He pushed his quest for independence to such an extreme that no institution ever acknowledged his authority in the natural sciences. Thoreau is described as the quintessential American scholar ("No truer American existed than Thoreau") whose aversion for English and European manners almost reached contempt. In his naturalist observations, too, Thoreau preferred local indigenous plants to the imported ones. In Emerson's portrait, Thoreau also emerges as the embodiment of important transcendentalist tenets such as the organic relationship with nature. Thoreau fully understood the importance of the imagination "for the uplifting and consolation of human life" and was capable of transforming every fact into a symbol of a more profound meaning. As with other transcendentalists such as Emerson, Bronson Alcott, and Margaret Fuller, Thoreau borrowed from the idealist traditions of Platonism, neo-Platonism, and romanticism to establish correspondences between nature and the spirit. These are then perceived by a person's intuitive self.

Emerson is aware that Thoreau's deep-seated convictions made him seem at times extreme. His frankness sometimes became bluntness and alienated him from his peers. He was also, at times, too prone to paradox and antagonism. Yet, to Emerson, these partial defects were offset by Thoreau's "robust and wise" spirit.

—*⟨/⟩/⟩—   —*⟨/⟩/⟩—   —*⟨/⟩/⟩—

Henry David Thoreau was the last male descendant of a French ancestor who came to this country from the Isle of Guernsey. His character exhibited occasional traits drawn from this blood in singular combination with a very strong Saxon genius.

He was born in Concord, Massachusetts, on the 12th of July, 1817. He was graduated at Harvard College in 1837, but without any literary distinction. An iconoclast in literature, he seldom thanked colleges for their service to him, holding them in small esteem, whilst yet his debt to them was important. After leaving the University, he joined his brother in teaching a private school, which he soon renounced. His father was a manufacturer of lead-pencils, and Henry applied himself for a time to this craft, believing he could make a better pencil than was then in use. After completing his experiments, he exhibited his work to chemists and artists in Boston, and having obtained their certificates to its excellence and to its equality with the best London manufacture, he returned home contented. His friends congratulated him that he had now opened his way to fortune. But he replied, that he should never make another pencil. "Why should I? I would not do again what I have done once." He resumed his endless walks and miscellaneous studies, making every day some new acquaintance with Nature, though as yet never speaking of zoology or botany, since, though very studious of natural facts, he was incurious of technical and textual science.

At this time, a strong, healthy youth, fresh from college, whilst all his companions were choosing their profession, or eager to begin some lucrative employment, it was inevitable that his thoughts should be exercised on the same question, and it required rare decision to refuse all the accustomed paths, and keep his solitary freedom at the cost of disappointing the natural expectations of his family and friends: all the more difficult that he had a perfect probity, was exact in securing his own independence, and in holding every man to the like duty. But Thoreau never faltered. He was a born protestant. He declined to give up his large ambition of knowledge and action for any narrow craft or profession, aiming at a much more comprehensive calling, the art of living well. If he slighted and defied the opinions of others, it was only that he was more intent to reconcile his practice with his own belief. Never idle or self-indulgent, he preferred, when he wanted money, earning it by some piece of manual labor agreeable to him, as building a boat or a fence, planting, grafting, surveying, or other short work, to any long engagements. With his hardy habits and few wants, his skill in wood-craft, and his powerful arithmetic, he was very competent to live in any part of the world. It would cost him less time to supply his wants than another. He was therefore secure of his leisure.

A natural skill for mensuration, growing out of his mathematical knowledge, and his habit of ascertaining the measures and distances of objects which interested him, the size of trees, the depth and extent of ponds and rivers, the height of mountains, and the air-line distance of his favorite summits,—this, and his intimate knowledge of the territory about Concord, made him drift into the profession of land-surveyor. It had the advantage for him that it led him continually into new and secluded grounds, and helped his studies of Nature. His accuracy and skill in this work were readily appreciated, and he found all the employment he wanted.

He could easily solve the problems of the surveyor, but he was daily beset with graver questions, which he manfully confronted. He interrogated every custom, and wished to settle all his practice on an ideal foundation. He was a protestant *à l'outrance,* and few lives contain so many renunciations. He was bred to no profession; he never married; he lived alone; he never went to church; he never voted; he refused to pay a tax to the State; he ate no flesh, he drank no wine, he never knew the use of tobacco; and, though a naturalist, he used neither trap nor gun. He chose, wisely, no doubt, for himself, to be the bachelor of thought and Nature. He had no talent for wealth, and knew how to be poor without the least hint of squalor or inelegance. Perhaps he fell into his way of living without forecasting it much, but approved it with later wisdom. "I am often reminded," he wrote in his journal, "that, if I had bestowed on me the wealth of Croesus, my aims must be still the same, and my means essentially the same." He had no temptations to fight against,—no appetites, no passions, no taste for elegant trifles. A fine house, dress, the manners and talk of highly cultivated people were all thrown away on him. He much preferred a good Indian, and considered these refinements as impediments to conversation, wishing to meet his companion on the simplest terms. He declined invitations to dinner-parties, because there each was in every one's way, and he could not meet the individuals to any purpose. "They make their pride," he said, "in making their dinner cost much; I make my pride in making my dinner cost little." When asked at table what dish he preferred, he answered, "The nearest." He did not like the taste of wine, and never had a vice in his life. He said,—"I have a faint recollection of pleasure derived from smoking dried lily-stems, before I was a man. I had commonly a supply of these. I have never smoked anything more noxious."

He chose to be rich by making his wants few, and supplying them himself. In his travels, he used the railroad only to get over so much country as was unimportant to the present purpose, walking hundreds of miles, avoiding taverns, buying a lodging in farmers' and fishermen's houses, as cheaper, and more agreeable to him, and because there he could better find the men and the information he wanted.

There was somewhat military in his nature not to be subdued, always manly and able, but rarely tender, as if he did not feel himself except in opposition. He wanted a fallacy to expose, a blunder to pillory, I may say required a little sense of victory, a roll of the drum, to call his powers into full exercise. It cost him nothing to say No; indeed, he found it much easier than to say Yes. It seemed as if his first instinct on hearing a proposition was to controvert it, so impatient was he of the limitations of our daily thought. This habit, of course, is a little chilling to the social affections; and though the companion would in the end acquit him of any malice or untruth, yet it mars conversation. Hence, no equal companion stood in affectionate relations with one so pure and guileless. "I love Henry," said one of his friends, "but I cannot like him; and as for taking his arm, I should as soon think of taking the arm of an elm-tree."

Yet, hermit and stoic as he was, he was really fond of sympathy, and threw himself heartily and childlike into the company of young people whom he loved, and whom he delighted to entertain, as he only could, with the varied and endless anecdotes of his experiences by field and river. And he was always ready to lead a huckleberry-party or a search for chestnuts or grapes. Talking, one day, of a public discourse, Henry remarked, that whatever succeeded with the audience was bad. I said, "Who would not like to write something which all can read, like *Robinson Crusoe?* and who does not see with regret that his page is not solid with a right materialistic treatment, which delights everybody?" Henry objected, of course, and vaunted the better lectures which reached only a few persons. But, at supper, a young girl, understanding that he was to lecture at the Lyceum, sharply asked him, "whether his lecture would be a nice, interesting story, such as she wished to hear, or whether it was one of those old philosophical things that she did not care about." Henry turned to her, and bethought himself, and, I saw, was trying to believe that he had matter that might fit her and her brother, who were to sit up and go to the lecture, if it was a good one for them.

He was a speaker and actor of the truth,—born such,—and was ever running into dramatic situations from this cause. In any circumstance, it interested all bystanders to know what part Henry would take, and what he would say; and he did not disappoint expectation, but used an original judgment on each emergency. In 1845 he built himself a small framed house on the shores of Walden Pond, and lived there two years alone, a life of labor and study. This action was quite native and fit for him. No one who knew him would tax him with affectation. He was more unlike his neighbors in his thought than in his action. As soon as he had exhausted the advantages of that solitude, he abandoned it. In 1847, not approving some uses to which the public expenditure was applied, he refused to pay his town tax, and was put in jail. A friend paid the tax for him, and he was released. The like annoyance was threatened the next year. But, as his friends paid the tax, notwithstanding his protest, I believe he ceased to resist. No opposition or ridicule had any weight with him. He coldly and fully stated his opinion without affecting to believe that it was the opinion of the company. It was of no consequence, if every one present held the opposite opinion. On one occasion he went to the University Library to procure some books. The librarian refused to lend them. Mr. Thoreau repaired to the President, who stated to him the rules and usages, which permitted the loan of books to resident graduates, to clergymen who were alumni, and to some others resident within a circle of ten miles' radius from the College. Mr. Thoreau explained to the President that the railroad had destroyed the old scale of distances,—that the library was useless, yes, and President and College useless, on the terms of his rules,—that the one benefit he owed to the College was its library,—that, at this moment, not only his want of books was imperative, but he wanted a large number of books, and assured him that he, Thoreau, and not the librarian, was the proper custodian of these. In short, the President found the petitioner so formidable, and the rules getting to look so ridiculous, that he ended by giving him a privilege which in his hands proved unlimited thereafter.

No truer American existed than Thoreau. His preference of his country and condition was genuine, and his aversion from English and European manners and tastes almost reached contempt. He listened impatiently to news or *bon mots* gleaned from London circles; and though he tried to be civil, these anecdotes fatigued him. The men were all imitating each other, and on a small mould. Why can they not live as far apart as possible, and each be a man by himself? What he sought was the most energetic nature; and he wished to go to Oregon, not to London. "In every part of Great Britain," he wrote in his diary, "are discovered traces of the Romans, their funereal urns, their camps, their roads, their dwellings. But New England, at least, is not based on any Roman ruins. We have not to lay the foundations of our houses on the ashes of a former civilization."

But, idealist as he was, standing for abolition of slavery, abolition of tariffs, almost for abolition of government, it is needless to say he found himself not only unrepresented in actual politics, but almost equally opposed to every class of reformers. Yet he paid the tribute of his uniform respect to the Anti-Slavery party. One man, whose personal acquaintance he had formed, he honored with exceptional regard. Before the first friendly word had been spoken for Captain John Brown, he sent notices to most houses in Concord, that he would speak in a public hall on the condition and character of John Brown, on Sunday evening, and invited all people to come. The Republican Committee, the Abolitionist Committee, sent him word that it was premature and not advisable. He replied,—"I did not send to you for advice, but to announce that I am to speak." The hall was filled at an early hour by people of all parties, and his earnest eulogy of the hero was heard by all respectfully, by many with a sympathy that surprised themselves.

It was said of Plotinus that he was ashamed of his body, and it is very likely he had good reason for it,—that his body was a bad servant, and he had not skill in dealing with the material world, as happens often to men of abstract intellect. But Mr. Thoreau was equipped with a most adapted and serviceable body. He was of short stature, firmly built, of light complexion, with strong, serious blue eyes, and a grave aspect,—his face covered in the late years with a becoming beard. His senses were acute, his frame well-knit and hardy, his hands strong and skilful in the use of tools. And there was a wonderful fitness of body and mind. He could pace sixteen rods more accurately than another man could measure them with rod and chain. He could find his path in the woods at night, he said, better by his feet than his eyes. He could estimate the measure of a tree very well by his eye; he could estimate the weight of a calf or a pig, like a dealer. From a box containing a bushel or more of loose pencils, he could take up with his hands fast enough just a dozen pencils at every grasp. He was a good swimmer, runner, skater, boatman, and would probably outwalk most countrymen in a day's journey. And the relation of body to mind was still finer than we have indicated. He said he wanted every stride his legs made. The length of his walk uniformly made the length of his writing. If shut up in the house, he did not write at all.

He had a strong common sense, like that which Rose Flammock, the weaver's daughter, in Scott's romance, commends in her father, as resembling a yardstick, which, whilst it measures dowlas and diaper, can equally well measure tapestry and cloth of gold. He had always a new resource. When I was planting forest-trees, and had procured half a peck of acorns, he said that only a small portion of them would be sound, and proceeded to examine them, and select the sound ones. But finding this took time, he said, "I think, if you put them all into water, the good ones will sink"; which experiment we tried with success. He could plan a garden, or a house, or a barn; would have been competent to lead a "Pacific Exploring Expedition"; could give judicious counsel in the gravest private or public affairs.

He lived for the day, not cumbered and mortified by his memory. If he brought you yesterday a new proposition, he would bring you to-day another not less revolutionary. A very industrious man, and setting, like all highly organized men, a high value on his time, he seemed the only man of leisure in town, always ready for any excursion that promised well, or for conversation prolonged into late hours. His trenchant sense was never stopped by his rules of daily prudence, but was always up to the new occasion. He liked and used the simplest food, yet, when some one urged a vegetable diet, Thoreau thought all diets a very small matter, saying that "the man who shoots the buffalo lives better than the man who boards at the Graham House." He said,—"You can sleep near the railroad, and never be disturbed: Nature knows very well what sounds are worth attending to, and has made up her mind not to hear the railroad-whistle. But things respect the devout mind, and a mental ecstasy was never interrupted." He noted, what repeatedly befell him, that, after receiving from a distance a rare plant, he would presently find the same in his own haunts. And those pieces of luck which happen only to good players happened to him. One day, walking with a stranger, who inquired where Indian arrow-heads could be found, he replied, "Everywhere," and, stooping forward, picked one on the instant from the ground. At Mount Washington, in Tuckerman's Ravine, Thoreau had a bad fall, and sprained his foot. As he was in the act of getting up from his fall, he saw for the first time the leaves of the *Arnica mollis.*

His robust common sense, armed with stout hands, keen perceptions, and strong will, cannot yet account for the superiority which shone in his simple and hidden life. I must add the cardinal fact, that there was an excellent wisdom in him, proper to a rare class of men, which showed him the material world as a means and symbol. This discovery, which sometimes yields to poets a certain casual and interrupted light, serving for the ornament of their writing, was in him an unsleeping insight; and whatever faults or obstructions of temperament might cloud it, he was not disobedient to the heavenly vision. In his youth, he said, one day, "The other world is all my art: my pencils will draw no other; my jack-knife will cut nothing else; I do not use it as a means." This was the muse and genius that rules his opinions, conversation, studies, work, and course of life. This made him a searching judge of men. At first glance he measured his companion, and, though insensible to some fine traits of culture, could very well report his weight and calibre. And this made the impression of genius which his conversation sometimes gave.

He understood the matter in hand at a glance, and saw the limitations and poverty of those he talked with, so that nothing seemed concealed from such terrible eyes. I have repeatedly known young men of sensibility converted in a moment to the belief that this was the man they were in search of, the man of men, who could tell them all they should do. His own dealing with them was never affectionate, but superior, didactic,—scorning their petty ways,—very slowly conceding, or not conceding at all, the promise of his society at their houses, or even at his own. "Would he not walk with them?" "He did not know. There was nothing so important to him as his walk; he had no walks to throw away on company." Visits were offered him from respectful parties, but he declined them. Admiring friends offered to carry him at their own cost to the Yellow-Stone River,—to the West Indies,—to South America. But though nothing could be more grave or considered than his refusals, they remind one in quite new relations of that fop Brummel's reply to the gentleman who offered him his carriage in a shower, "But where will *you* ride, then?"—and what accusing silences, and what searching and irresistible speeches, battering down all defences, his companions can remember!

Mr. Thoreau dedicated his genius with such entire love to the fields, hills, and waters of his native town, that he made them known and interesting to all reading Americans, and to people over the sea. The river on whose banks he was born and died he knew from its springs to its confluence with the Merrimack. He had made summer and winter observations on it for many years, and at every hour of the day and the night. The result of the recent survey of the Water Commissioners appointed by the State of Massachusetts he had reached by his private experiments, several years earlier. Every fact which occurs in the bed, on the banks, or in the air over it; the fishes, and their spawning and nests, their manners, their food; the shad-flies which fill the air on a certain evening once a year, and which are snapped at by the fishes so ravenously that many of these die of repletion; the conical heaps of small stones on the river-shallows, one of which heaps will sometimes overfill a cart,—these heaps the huge nests of small fishes; the birds which frequent the stream, heron, duck, sheldrake, loon, osprey; the snake, muskrat, otter, woodchuck, and fox, on the banks; the turtle, frog, hyla, and cricket, which make the banks vocal,—were all known to him, and, as it were, townsmen and fellow-creatures; so that he felt an absurdity or violence in any narrative of one of these by itself apart, and still more of its dimensions on an inch-rule, or in the exhibition of its skeleton, or the specimen of a squirrel or a bird in brandy. He liked to speak of the manners of the river, as itself a lawful creature, yet with exactness, and always to an observed fact. As he knew the river, so the ponds in this region.

One of the weapons he used, more important than microscope or alcohol-receiver to other investigators, was a whim which grew on him by indulgence, yet appeared in gravest statement, namely, of extolling his own town and neighborhood as the most favored centre for natural observation. He remarked that the Flora of Massachusetts embraced almost all the important plants of America,—most of the oaks, most of the willows, the best pines, the ash, the maple, the beech, the nuts. He returned Kane's *Arctic Voyage* to a friend of whom he had borrowed it, with the remark, that "most of the phenomena noted might be observed in Concord." He seemed a little envious of the Pole, for the coincident sunrise and sunset, or five minutes' day after six months: a splendid fact, which Annursnuc had never afforded him. He found red snow in one of his walks, and told me that he expected to find yet the *Victoria regia* in Concord. He was the attorney of the indigenous plants, and owned to a preference of the weeds to the imported plants, as of the Indian to the civilized man,—and noticed, with pleasure, that the willow bean-poles of his neighbor had grown more than his beans. "See these weeds," he said, "which have been hoed at by a million farmers all spring and summer, and yet have prevailed, and just now come out triumphant over all lanes, pastures, fields, and gardens, such is their vigor. We have insulted them with low names, too,—as Pigweed, Wormwood, Chickweed, Shad-Blossom." He says, "They have brave names, too,—Ambrosia, Stellaria, Amelanchia, Amaranth, etc."

I think his fancy for referring everything to the meridian of Concord did not grow out of any ignorance or depreciation of other longitudes or latitudes, but was rather a playful expression of his conviction of the indifferency of all places, and that the best place for each is where he stands. He expressed it once in this wise:—"I think nothing is to be hoped from you, if this bit of mould under your feet is not sweeter to you to eat than any other in this world, or in any world."

The other weapon with which he conquered all obstacles in science was patience. He knew how to sit immovable, a part of the rock he rested on, until the bird, the reptile, the fish, which had retired from him, should come back, and resume its habits, nay, moved by curiosity, should come to him and watch him.

It was a pleasure and a privilege to walk with him. He knew the country like a fox or a bird, and passed through it as freely by paths of his own. He knew every track in the snow or on the ground, and what creature had taken this path before him. One must submit abjectly to such a guide, and the reward was great. Under his arm he carried an old music-book to press plants; in his pocket, his diary and pencil, a spy-glass for birds, microscope, jack-knife, and twine. He wore straw hat, stout shoes, strong gray trousers, to brave shrub-oaks and smilax, and to climb a tree for a hawk's or a squirrel's nest. He waded into the pool for the water-plants, and his strong legs were no insignificant part of his armor. On the day I speak of he looked for the Menyanthes, detected it across the wide pool, and, on examination of the florets, decided that it had been in flower five days. He drew out of his breast-pocket his diary, and read the names of all the plants that should bloom on this day, whereof he kept account as a banker when his notes fall due. The Cypripedium not due till to-morrow. He thought, that, if waked up from a trance, in this swamp, he could tell by the plants what time of the year it was within two days. The redstart was flying about, and presently the fine grosbeaks, whose brilliant scarlet makes the rash gazer wipe his eye, and whose fine clear note Thoreau compared to that of a tanager which has got rid of its hoarseness. Presently he heard a note which he called that of the night-warbler, a bird he had never identified, had been in search of twelve years, which always, when he saw it, was in the act of diving down into a tree or bush, and which it was vain to seek; the only bird that sings indifferently by night and by day. I told him he must beware of finding and booking it, lest life should have nothing more to show him. He said, "What you seek in vain for, half your life, one day you come full upon all the family at dinner. You seek it like a dream, and as soon as you find it you become its prey."

His interest in the flower or the bird lay very deep in his mind, was connected with Nature,—and the meaning of Nature was never attempted to be defined by him. He would not offer a memoir of his observations to the Natural History Society. "Why should I? To detach the description from its connections in my mind would make it no longer true or valuable to me: and they do not wish what belongs to it." His power of observation seemed to indicate additional senses. He saw as with microscope, heard as with ear-trumpet, and his memory was a photographic register of all he saw and heard. And yet none knew better than he that it is not the fact that imports, but the impression or effect of the fact on your mind. Every fact lay in glory in his mind, a type of the order and beauty of the whole.

His determination on Natural History was organic. He confessed that he sometimes felt like a hound or a panther, and, if born among Indians, would have been a fell hunter. But, restrained by his Massachusetts culture, he played out the game in this mild form of botany and ichthyology. His intimacy with animals suggested what Thomas Fuller records of Butler the apiologist, that "either he had told the bees things or the bees had told him." Snakes coiled round his leg; the fishes swam into his hand; and he took them out of the water; he pulled the woodchuck out of its hole by the tail, and took the foxes under his protection from the hunters. Our naturalist had perfect magnanimity; he had no secrets: he would carry you to the heron's haunt, or even to his most prized botanical swamp,—possibly knowing that you could never find it again, yet willing to take his risks.

No college ever offered him a diploma, or a professor's chair; no academy made him its corresponding secretary, its discoverer, or even its member. Whether these learned bodies feared the satire of his presence. Yet so much knowledge of Nature's secret and genius few others possessed, none in a more large and religious synthesis. For not a particle of respect had he to the opinions of any man or body of men, but homage solely to the truth itself; and as he discovered everywhere among doctors some leaning of courtesy, it discredited them. He grew to be revered and admired by his townsmen, who had at first known him only as an oddity. The farmers who employed him as a surveyor soon discovered his rare accuracy and skill, his knowledge of their lands, of trees, of birds, of Indian remains, and the like, which enabled him to tell every farmer more than he knew before of his own farm; so that he began to feel a little as if Mr. Thoreau had better rights in his land than he. They felt, too, the superiority of character which addressed all men with a native authority.

Indian relics abound in Concord,—arrow-heads, stone chisels, pestles, and fragments of pottery; and on the river-bank, large heaps of clam-shells and ashes mark spots which the savages frequented. These, and every circumstance touching the Indian, were important in his eyes. His visits to Maine were chiefly for love of the Indian. He had the satisfaction of seeing the manufacture of the bark-canoe, as well as of trying his hand in its management on the rapids. He was inquisitive about the making of the stone arrow-head, and in his last days charged a youth setting out for the Rocky Mountains to find an Indian who could tell him that: "It was well worth a visit to California to learn it." Occasionally, a small party of Penobscot Indians would visit Concord, and pitch their tents for a few weeks in summer on the river-bank. He failed not to make acquaintance with the best of them; though he well knew that asking questions of Indians is like catechizing beavers and rabbits. In his last visit to Maine he had great satisfaction from Joseph Polis, an intelligent Indian of Oldtown, who was his guide for some weeks.

He was equally interested in every natural fact. The depth of his perception found likeness of law throughout Nature, and I know not any genius who so swiftly inferred universal law from the single fact. He was no pedant of a department. His eye was open to beauty, and his ear to music. He found these, not in rare conditions, but wheresoever he went. He thought the best of music was in single strains; and he found poetic suggestion in the humming of the telegraph-wire.

His poetry might be bad or good; he no doubt wanted a lyric facility and technical skill; but he had the source of poetry in his spiritual perception. He was a good reader and critic, and his judgment on poetry was to the ground of it. He could not be deceived as to the presence or absence of the poetic element in any composition, and his thirst for this made him negligent and perhaps scornful of superficial graces. He would pass by many delicate rhythms, but he would have detected every live stanza or line in a volume, and knew very well where to find an equal poetic charm in prose. He was so enamored of the spiritual beauty that he held all actual written poems in very light esteem in the comparison. He admired Æschylus and Pindar; but, when some one was commending them, he said that "Æschylus and the Greeks, in describing Apollo and Orpheus, had given no song, or no good one. They ought not to have moved trees, but to have chanted to the gods such a hymn as would have sung all their old ideas out of their heads, and new ones in." His own verses are often rude and defective. The gold does not yet run pure, is drossy and crude. The thyme and marjoram are not yet honey. But if he want lyric fineness and technical merits, if he have not the poetic temperament, he never lacks the causal thought, showing that his genius was better than his talent. He knew the worth of the Imagination for the uplifting and consolation of human life, and liked to throw every thought into a symbol. The fact you tell is of no value, but only the impression. For this reason his presence was poetic, always piqued the curiosity to know more deeply the secrets of his mind. He had many reserves, an unwillingness to exhibit to profane eyes what was still sacred in his own, and knew well how to throw a poetic veil over his experience. All readers of *Walden* will remember his mythical record of his disappointments:—

> I long ago lost a hound, a bay horse, and a turtle-dove, and am still on their trail. Many are the travellers I have spoken concerning them, describing their tracks, and what calls they answered to. I have met one or two who had heard the hound, and the tramp of the horse, and even seen the dove disappear behind a cloud; and they seemed an anxious to recover them as if they had lost them themselves.[1]

His riddles were worth the reading, and I confide, that, if at any time I do not understand the expression, it is yet just. Such was the wealth of his truth that it was not worth his while to use words in vain. His poem entitled "Sympathy" reveals the tenderness under that triple steel of stoicism, and the intellectual subtilty it could animate. His classic on "Smoke" suggests Simonides, but is better than any poem of Simonides. His biography is in his verses. His habitual thought makes all his poetry a hymn to the Cause of causes, the Spirit which vivifies and controls his own.

I hearing get, who had but ears,
And sight, who had but eyes before;
I moments live, who lived but years,
And truth discern, who knew but learning's lore.

And still more in these religious lines:—

Now chiefly is my natal hour,
And only now my prime of life;

I will not doubt the love untold,
Which not my worth or want hath bought,
Which wooed me young, and wooes me old,
And to this evening hath me brought.

Whilst he used in his writings a certain petulance of remark in reference to churches or churchmen, he was a person of a rare, tender, and absolute religion, a person incapable of any profanation, by act or by thought. Of course, the same isolation which belonged to his original thinking and living detached him from the social religious forms. This is neither to be censured nor regretted. Aristotle long ago explained it, when he said, "One who surpasses his fellow-citizens in virtue is no longer a part of the city. Their law is not for him, since he is a law to himself."

Thoreau was sincerity itself, and might fortify the convictions of prophets in the ethical laws by his holy living. It was an affirmative experience which refused to be set aside. A truth-speaker he, capable of the most deep and strict conversation; a physician to the wounds of any soul; a friend, knowing not only the secret of friendship, but almost worshipped by those few persons who resorted to him as their confessor and prophet, and knew the deep value of his mind and great heart. He thought that without religion or devotion of some kind nothing great was ever accomplished: and he thought that the bigoted sectarian had better bear this in mind.

His virtues, of course, sometimes ran into extremes. It was easy to trace to the inexorable demand on all for exact truth that austerity which made this willing hermit more solitary even than he wished. Himself of a perfect probity, he required not less of others. He had a disgust at crime, and no worldly success would cover it. He detected paltering as readily in dignified and prosperous persons as in beggars, and with equal scorn. Such dangerous frankness was in his dealing that his admirers called him "that terrible Thoreau," as if he spoke when silent, and was still present when he had departed. I think the severity of his ideal interfered to deprive him of a healthy sufficiency of human society.

The habit of a realist to find things the reverse of their appearance inclined him to put every statement in a paradox. A certain habit of antagonism defaced his earlier writings,—a trick of rhetoric not quite outgrown in his later, of substituting for the obvious word and thought its diametrical opposite. He praised wild mountains and winter forests for their domestic air, in snow and ice he would find sultriness, and commended the wilderness for resembling Rome and Paris. "It was so dry, that you might call it wet."

The tendency to magnify the moment, to read all the laws of Nature in the one object or one combination under your eye, is of course comic to those who do not share the philosopher's perception of identity. To him there was no such thing as size. The pond was a small ocean; the Atlantic, a large Walden Pond. He referred every minute fact to cosmical laws. Though he meant to be just, he seemed haunted by a certain chronic assumption that the science of the day pretended completeness, and he had just found out that the *savans* had neglected to discriminate a particular botanical variety, had failed to describe the seeds or count the sepals. "That is to say," we replied, "the blockheads were not born in Concord; but who said they were? It was their unspeakable misfortune to be born in London, or Paris, or Rome; but, poor fellows, they did what they could, considering that they never saw Bateman's Pond, or Nine-Acre Corner, or Becky-Stow's Swamp. Besides, what were you sent into the world for, but to add this observation?"

Had his genius been only contemplative, he had been fitted to his life, but with his energy and practical ability he seemed born for great enterprise and for command; and I so much regret the loss of his rare powers of action, that I cannot help counting it a fault in him that he had no ambition. Wanting this, instead of engineering for all America, he was the captain of a huckleberry-party. Pounding beans is good to the end of pounding empires one of these days; but if, at the end of years, it is still only beans!

But these foibles, real or apparent, were fast vanishing in the incessant growth of a spirit so robust and wise, and which effaced its defeats with new triumphs. His study of Nature was a perpetual ornament to him, and inspired his friends with curiosity to see the world through his eyes, and to hear his adventures. They possessed every kind of interest.

He had many elegances of his own, whilst he scoffed at conventional elegance. Thus, he could not bear to hear the sound of his own steps, the grit of gravel; and therefore never willingly walked in the road, but in the grass, on mountains and in woods. His senses were acute, and he remarked that by night every dwelling-house gives out bad air, like a slaughterhouse. He liked the pure fragrance of melilot. He honored certain plants with special regard, and, over all, the pond-lily,—then, the gentian, and the *Mikania scandens,* and "life-everlasting," and a bass-tree which he visited every year when it bloomed, in the middle of July. He thought the scent a more oracular inquisition than the sight,—more oracular and trustworthy. The scent, of course, reveals what is concealed from the other senses. By it he detected earthiness. He delighted in echoes, and said they were almost the only kind of kindred voices that he heard. He loved Nature so well, was so happy in her solitude, that he became very jealous of cities, and the sad work which their refinements and artifices made with man and his dwelling. The axe was always destroying his forest. "Thank God," he said, "they cannot cut down the clouds!" "All kinds of figures are drawn on the blue ground with this fibrous white paint." . . .

There is a flower known to botanists, one of the same genus with our summer plant called "Life-Everlasting," a *Gnaphalium* like that, which grows on the most inaccessible cliffs of the Tyrolese mountains, where the chamois dare hardly venture, and which the hunter, tempted by its beauty, and by his love, (for it is immensely valued by the Swiss maidens,) climbs the cliffs to gather, and is sometimes found dead at the foot, with the flower in his hand. It is called by botanists the *Gnaphalium leontopodium,* but by the Swiss *Edelweisse,* which signifies *Noble Purity.* Thoreau seemed to me living in the hope to gather this plant, which belonged to him of right. The scale on which his studies proceeded was so large as to require longevity, and we were the less prepared for his sudden disappearance. The country knows not yet, or in the least part, how great a son it has lost. It seems an injury that he should leave in the midst his broken task, which none else can finish,—a kind of indignity to so noble a soul, that it should depart out of Nature before yet he has been really shown to his peers for what he is. But he, at least, is content. His soul was made for the noblest society; he had in a short life exhausted the capabilities of this world; wherever there is knowledge, wherever there is virtue, wherever there is beauty, he will find a home.

Notes
1. *Walden,* p. 20.

—Ralph Waldo Emerson, from "Thoreau,"
Atlantic, August 1862, pp. 239–249

Moncure Daniel Conway (1866)

Moncure Daniel Conway (1832–1907) was an American clergyman and an energetic abolitionist. Born in Virginia to Methodist slaveholding parents, he became a Methodist minister but later converted to Unitarianism. His abolitionism led to his dismissal from his Unitarian pastorate in 1856. His removal only reinvigorated Conway's abolitionism and his activism for that cause. He established a colony for fugitive slaves in Yellow Springs, Ohio, and, in 1862, he took up the co-editorship of the Boston antislavery paper, the *Commonwealth.* During the Civil War, he lectured throughout

England to support the Union cause. He authored more than 70 books and pamphlets on a wide variety of subjects, including a scholarly edition of Thomas Paine's works.

———————

He was short of stature, well built, and such a man as I have fancied Julius Caesar to have been. Every movement was full of courage and repose; the tones of his voice were those of Truth herself; and there was in his eye the pure bright blue of the New England sky, as there was sunshine in his flaxen hair. He had a particularly strong aquiline-Roman nose, which somehow reminded me of the prow of a ship. There was in his face and expression, with all its sincerity, a kind of intellectual furtiveness: no wild thing could escape him more than it could be harmed by him. The grey huntsman's suit which he wore enhanced this expression.

> He took the colour of his vest
> From rabbit's coat and grouse's breast;
> For as the wild kinds lurk and hide,
> So walks the huntsman unespied.

The cruellest weapons of attack, however, which this huntsman took with him were a spyglass for birds, a microscope for the game that would hide in smallness, and an old book in which to press plants. His powers of conversation were extraordinary. I remember being surprised and delighted at every step with revelations of laws and significant attributes in common things—as a relation between different kinds of grass and the geological characters beneath them, the variety and grouping of pine-needles and the effect of these differences on the sounds they yield when struck by the wind, and the shades, so to speak, of taste represented by grasses and common herbs when applied to the tongue. The acuteness of his senses was marvellous: no hound could scent better, and he could hear the most faint and distant sounds without even laying his ear to the ground like an Indian. As we penetrated farther and farther into the woods, he seemed to gain a certain transformation, and his face shone with a light that I had not seen in the village. He had a calendar of the plants and flowers of the neighbourhood, and would sometimes go around a quarter of a mile to visit some floral friend, whom he had not seen for a year, who would appear for that day only. We were too early for the *hibiscus*, a rare flower in New England, which I desired to see. He pointed out the spot by the river-side where alone it could be found, and said it would open about the following Monday and not stay

long. I went on Tuesday evening and found myself a day too late—the petals
were scattered on the ground.

—Moncure Daniel Conway, "Thoreau,"
Fraser's Magazine, April 1866, pp. 461–462

Robert Louis Stevenson
"Henry David Thoreau: His Character
and Opinions" (1880) & "Preface,
by Way of Criticism" (1886)

The Scottish essayist, poet, and novelist Robert Louis Stevenson (1850–
1894) was until recently viewed almost exclusively as an author of
children's adventure fiction. His literary reputation mainly rests on such
novels as *Treasure Island* (1883), *The Strange Case of Dr. Jekyll and Mr. Hyde*
(1886), and *Kidnapped* (1886). The last two novels brought Stevenson
critical recognition and success. Recent critical assessments have made
more problematic Stevenson's status as a children's author, emphasizing
the role of colonialism, the empire, and human corruptibility in his major
novels. Stevenson's life was marked by extensive travels, and he was
known for his adventurous nature. These personal traits and biographical elements should be taken into account when reading Stevenson's
first essay on Thoreau, in which the Scottish writer paints a far from flat-
tering portrait of the American author.

Stevenson's early life was marked by poor health, which prevented
him from having a regular education. Throughout his life, the author
suffered from bouts of ill health. His father, a civil engineer, expected
Stevenson to enter the family business. To that end, the young Stevenson
briefly attended Edinburgh University studying engineering. Yet, he soon
switched to law and was admitted to the Scottish Bar in 1875. Stevenson
never practiced law and, much to his father's discomfort, he confessed
that he wanted to be a writer. Stevenson began writing professionally in
the 1870s and was immediately praised as a talented author. However,
commercial success arrived only in the mid-1880s with the publication of
The Strange Case of Dr. Jekyll and Mr. Hyde, which became an international
best-seller. In 1888, two years after the publication of *Dr. Jekyll and Mr.
Hyde*, Stevenson was asked by Scribner's, his American publisher, to write
a book on the South Seas. The travels undertaken to write the volume
took Stevenson and his wife to the Marquesas, the Paumotus, Tahiti,
Hawaii, and, finally, Samoa, where the couple settled down and lived

until Stevenson's death. The result of this extensive traveling was *In the South Seas* (1890), a book that documents the impact of colonialism on the islands of the Pacific. Stevenson was not entirely satisfied with the book, feeling that he could not devote as much time and energy to the project as he had wished, saddled with the financial burdens incurred in buying his Samoan estate. He continued to develop his study of the effects of the empire on indigenous populations in later writings such as *The Ebb Tide* (1893).

The first of the two essays that follow focuses on the "limitations" of Thoreau's "mind and character," which, to Stevenson, are already apparent by simply looking at a bad woodcut of the author's "thin, penetrating, big-nosed face." Stevenson's judgment is a rather harsh one: "Thoreau was a skulker." Stevenson's main line of argument is that Thoreau was incapable of admitting his own weaknesses and considered himself far above the rest of mankind so that he was unable to truly sympathize with others. He was on a constant search for self-improvement, which led him to neglect human contact. Thoreau's lack of sympathy for others did not allow him to see the human intention and essence of Christianity. Thoreau "fears the bracing contact of the world." Using heavily gendered language, Stevenson disparagingly points out that this attitude is "womanish" and "unmanly." This is the first hint of a theme that will become increasingly recurrent in Thoreau criticism: that of the author as a transgressor of the gender and sexual expectations of his times. Although it is difficult to document the exact nature of Thoreau's sexuality, one of the major experts on the author, Walter Harding, has concluded that several of his writings point to a clear attraction to men. In particular, the "Wednesday" chapter in *A Week on the Concord and Merrimack Rivers* (1849) contains a homoerotic description of friendship. Thoreau's blurring of romantic love and friendship, a construct that has recently attracted interest from gay critics and queer theorists such as Jonathan Katz and Michael Warner, is precisely what makes Stevenson describe him as "dry, priggish and selfish."

Stevenson also faults Thoreau for his style as he is unable to "clothe his opinion in the garment of art." His books are increasingly concerned with a detailed materialistic treatment and end up resembling guidebooks, rather than records of inner experiences. The only aspect of Thoreau that Stevenson seems to admire in his first essay is his stance not to pay the poll tax to a slaveholding state. Although Stevenson judges Thoreau's protest a "*fiasco*," he does not deem it laughable. To Stevenson, the worth of one night's imprisonment can outweigh half a hundred voters at a subsequent election. Sadly, the protest was ultimately a failure, because Thoreau lacked the power of persuasion.

Stevenson's second and much shorter essay is, in many ways, a recantation of the first. After talking to Thoreau's personal friend, H.A. Page (Dr. Japp), Stevenson is persuaded that Thoreau was not obsessed with self-improvement and that he was capable of loving women "fairly and manfully." In this second essay, Stevenson's judgment is much more nuanced, and the piece tellingly ends with the admission that "the true Thoreau still remains to be depicted."

———————————

I

Thoreau's thin, penetrating, big-nosed face, even in a bad woodcut, conveys some hint of the limitations of his mind and character. With his almost acid sharpness of insight, with his almost animal dexterity in act, there went none of that large, unconscious geniality of the world's heroes. He was not easy, not ample, not urbane, not even kind; his enjoyment was hardly smiling, or the smile was not broad enough to be convincing; he had no waste lands nor kitchen-midden in his nature, but was all improved and sharpened to a point. "He was bred to no profession," says Emerson; "he never married; he lived alone; he never went to church; he never voted; he refused to pay a tax to the State; he ate no flesh, he drank no wine, he never knew the use of tobacco; and, though a naturalist, he used neither trap nor gun. When asked at dinner what dish he preferred, he answered, 'the nearest'". So many negative superiorities begin to smack a little of the prig. From his later works he was in the habit of cutting out the humorous passages, under the impression that they were beneath the dignity of his moral muse; and there we see the prig stand public and confessed. It was "much easier," says Emerson acutely, much easier for Thoreau to say *no* than *yes;* and that is a characteristic which depicts the man. It is a useful accomplishment to be able to say *no,* but surely it is the essence of amiability to prefer to say *yes* where it is possible. There is something wanting in the man who does not hate himself whenever he is constrained to say *no.* And there was a great deal wanting in this born dissenter. He was almost shockingly devoid of weaknesses; he had not enough of them to be truly polar with humanity; whether you call him demi-god or demi-man, he was at least not altogether one of us, for he was not touched with a feeling of our infirmities. The world's heroes have room for all positive qualities, even those which are disreputable, in the capacious theatre of their dispositions. Such can live many lives; while a Thoreau can live but one, and that only with perpetual foresight.

He was no ascetic, rather an Epicurean of the nobler sort; and he had this one great merit, that he succeeded so far as to be happy. "I love my fate to the core and rind," he wrote once; and even while he lay dying, here is what he dictated (for it seems he was already too feeble to control the pen): "You ask particularly after my health. I *suppose* that I have not many months to live, but of course know nothing about it. I may say that I am enjoying existence as much as ever, and regret nothing." It is not given to all to bear so clear a testimony to the sweetness of their fate, nor to any without courage and wisdom; for this world in itself is but a painful and uneasy place of residence, and lasting happiness, at least to the self-conscious, comes only from within. Now Thoreau's content and ecstasy in living was, we may say, like a plant that he had watered and tended with womanish solicitude; for there is apt to be something unmanly, something almost dastardly, in a life that does not move with dash and freedom, and that fears the bracing contact of the world. In one word, Thoreau was a skulker. He did not wish virtue to go out of him among his fellow-men, but slunk into a corner to hoard it for himself. He left all for the sake of certain virtuous self-indulgences. It is true that his tastes were noble; that his ruling passion was to keep himself unspotted from the world; and that his luxuries were all of the same healthy order as cold tubs and early rising. But a man may be both coldly cruel in the pursuit of goodness, and morbid even in the pursuit of health. I cannot lay my hands on the passage in which he explains his abstinence from tea and coffee, but I am sure I have the meaning correctly. It is this: He thought it bad economy and worthy of no true virtuoso to spoil the natural rapture of the morning with such muddy stimulants; let him but see the sun rise, and he was already sufficiently inspirited for the labors of the day. That may be reason good enough to abstain from tea; but when we go on to find the same man, on the same or similar grounds, abstain from nearly everything that his neighbors innocently and pleasurably use, and from the rubs and trials of human society itself into the bargain, we recognize that valetudinarian healthfulness which is more delicate than sickness itself. We need have no respect for a state of artificial training. True health is to be able to do without it. Shakespeare, we can imagine, might begin the day upon a quart of ale, and yet enjoy the sunrise to the full as much as Thoreau, and commemorate his enjoyment in vastly better verses. A man who must separate himself from his neighbors' habits in order to be happy, is in much the same case with one who requires to take opium for the same purpose. What we want to see is one who can breast into the world, do a man's work, and still preserve his first and pure enjoyment of existence.

Thoreau's faculties were of a piece with his moral shyness; for they were all delicacies. He could guide himself about the woods on the darkest night by the touch of his feet. He could pick up at once an exact dozen of pencils by the feeling, pace distances with accuracy, and gauge cubic contents by the eye. His smell was so dainty that he could perceive the fœtor of dwelling-houses as he passed them by at night; his palate so unsophisticated that, like a child, he disliked the taste of wine—or perhaps, living in America, had never tasted any that was good; and his knowledge of nature was so complete and curious that he could have told the time of year, within a day or so, by the aspect of the plants. In his dealings with animals, he was the original of Hawthorne's Donatello. He pulled the woodchuck out of its hole by the tail; the hunted fox came to him for protection; wild squirrels have been seen to nestle in his waistcoat; he would thrust his arm into a pool and bring forth a bright, panting fish, lying undismayed in the palm of his hand. There were few things that he could not do. He could make a house, a boat, a pencil, or a book. He was a surveyor, a scholar, a natural historian. He could run, walk, climb, skate, swim, and manage a boat. The smallest occasion served to display his physical accomplishment; and a manufacturer, from merely observing his dexterity with the window of a railway carriage, offered him a situation on the spot. "The only fruit of much living," he observes, "is the ability to do some slight thing better." But such was the exactitude of his senses, so alive was he in every fibre, that it seems as if the maxim should be changed in his case:, for he could do most things with unusual perfection. And perhaps he had an approving eye to himself when he wrote: "Though the youth at last grows indifferent, the laws of the universe are not indifferent, *but are forever on the side of the most sensitive.*"

II

Thoreau had decided, it would seem, from the very first to lead a life of self-improvement: the needle did not tremble as with richer natures, but pointed steadily north; and as he saw duty and inclination in one, he turned all his strength in that direction. He was met upon the threshold by a common difficulty. In this world, in spite of its many agreeable features, even the most sensitive must undergo some drudgery to live. It is not possible to devote your time to study and meditation without what are quaintly but happily denominated private means; these absent, a man must contrive to earn his bread by some service to the public such as the public cares to pay him for; or, as Thoreau loved to put it, Apollo must serve Admetus. This was to Thoreau even a sourer necessity than it is to most; there was a love of freedom, a strain of the wild man, in his nature, that rebelled with violence against the yoke of custom; and he was so eager to cultivate himself and to be happy in his own society, that he could consent with difficulty even to the interruptions of friendship. *"Such are my engagements to myself* that I dare not promise," he once wrote in answer to an invitation; and the italics are his own. Marcus Aurelius found time to study virtue, and between whiles to conduct the imperial affairs of Rome; but Thoreau is so busy improving himself, that he must think twice about a morning call. And now imagine him condemned for eight hours a day to some uncongenial and unmeaning business! He shrank from the very look of the mechanical in life; all should, if possible, be sweetly spontaneous and swimmingly progressive. Thus he learned to make lead-pencils, and, when he had gained the best certificate and his friends began to congratulate him on his establishment in life, calmly announced that he should never make another. "Why should I?" said he; "I would not do again what I have done once." For when a thing has once been done as well as it wants to be, it is of no further interest to the self-improver. Yet in after years, and when it became needful to support his family, he returned patiently to this mechanical art—a step more than worthy of himself.

The pencils seem to have been Apollo's first experiment in the service of Admetus; but others followed. "I have thoroughly tried school-keeping," he writes, "and found that my expenses were in proportion, or rather out of proportion, to my income; for I was obliged to dress and train, not to say think and believe, accordingly, and I lost my time into the bargain. As I did not teach for the benefit of my fellowmen, but simply for a livelihood, this was a failure. I have tried trade, but I found that it would take ten years to get under way in that, and that then I should probably be on my way to the devil." Nothing, indeed, can surpass his scorn for all so-called business. Upon that subject gall squirts from him at a touch. "The whole enterprise of this nation is not illustrated by a thought," he writes; "it is not warmed by a sentiment; there is nothing in it for which a man should lay down his life, nor even his gloves." And again: "If our merchants did not most of them fail, and the banks too, my faith in the old laws of this world would be staggered. The statement that ninety-six in a hundred doing such business surely break down is perhaps the sweetest fact that statistics have revealed." The wish was probably father to the figures; but there is something enlivening in a hatred of so genuine a brand, hot as Corsican revenge, and sneering like Voltaire.

Pencils, school-keeping, and trade being thus discarded one after another, Thoreau, with a stroke of strategy, turned the position. He saw his way to

get his board and lodging for practically nothing; and Admetus never got less
work out of any servant since the world began. It was his ambition to be an
oriental philosopher; but he was always a very Yankee sort of oriental. Even
in the peculiar attitude in which he stood to money, his system of personal
economics, as we may call it, he displayed a vast amount of truly down-East
calculation, and he adopted poverty like a piece of business. Yet his system is
based on one or two ideas which, I believe, come naturally to all thoughtful
youths, and are only pounded out of them by city uncles. Indeed, something
essentially youthful distinguishes all Thoreau's knock-down blows at current
opinion. Like the posers of a child, they leave the orthodox in a kind of
speechless agony. These know the thing is nonsense. They are sure there
must be an answer, yet somehow cannot find it. So it is with his system of
economy. He cuts through the subject on so new a plane that the accepted
arguments apply no longer; he attacks it in a new dialect where there are no
catchwords ready made for the defender; after you have been boxing for
years on a polite, gladiatorial convention, here is an assailant who does not
scruple to hit below the belt.

"The cost of a thing," says he, "is *the amount of what I will call life* which
is required to be exchanged for it, immediately or in the long run." I have
been accustomed to put it to myself, perhaps more clearly, that the price we
have to pay for money is paid in liberty. Between these two ways of it, at least,
the reader will probably not fail to find a third definition of his own; and it
follows, on one or other, that a man may pay too dearly for his livelihood, by
giving, in Thoreau's terms, his whole life for it, or, in mine, bartering for it the
whole of his available liberty, and becoming a slave till death. There are two
questions to be considered—the quality of what we buy, and the price we
have to pay for it. Do you want a thousand a year, a two thousand a year,
or a ten thousand a year livelihood? and can you afford the one you want?
It is a matter of taste; it is not in the least degree a question of duty, though
commonly supposed so. But there is no authority for that view anywhere. It
is nowhere in the Bible. It is true that we might do a vast amount of good if
we were wealthy, but it is also highly improbable; not many do; and the art
of growing rich is not only quite distinct from that of doing good, but the
practice of the one does not at all train a man for practising the other. "Money
might be of great service to me," writes Thoreau; "but the difficulty now is that I
do not improve my opportunities, and therefore I am not prepared to have my
opportunities increased." It is a mere illusion that, above a certain income,
the personal desires will be satisfied and leave a wider margin for the generous

impulse. It is as difficult to be generous, or anything else, except perhaps a member of Parliament, on thirty thousand as on two hundred a year.

Now Thoreau's tastes were well defined. He loved to be free, to be master of his times and seasons, to indulge the mind rather than the body; he preferred long rambles to rich dinners, his own reflections to the consideration of society, and an easy, calm, unfettered, active life among green trees to dull toiling at the counter of a bank. And such being his inclination he determined to gratify it. A poor man must save off something; he determined to save off his livelihood. "When a man has attained those things which are necessary to life," he writes, "there is another alternative than to obtain the superfluities; *he may adventure on life now*, his vacation from humbler toil having commenced." Thoreau would get shelter, some kind of covering for his body, and necessary daily bread; even these he should get as cheaply as possible; and then, his vacation from humbler toil having commenced, devote himself to oriental philosophers, the study of nature, and the work of self-improvement.

Prudence, which bids us all go to the ant for wisdom and hoard against the day of sickness, was not a favorite with Thoreau. He preferred that other, whose name is so much misappropriated: Faith. When he had secured the necessaries of the moment, he would not reckon up possible accidents or torment himself with trouble for the future. He had no toleration for the man "who ventures to live only by the aid of the mutual insurance company, which has promised to bury him decently." He would trust himself a little to the world. "We may safely trust a good deal more than we do," says he. "How much is not done by us! or what if we had been taken sick?" And then, with a stab of satire, he describes contemporary mankind in a phrase: "All the day long on the alert, at night we unwillingly say our prayers and commit ourselves to uncertainties." It is not likely that the public will be much affected by Thoreau, when they blink the direct injunctions of the religion they profess; and yet, whether we will or no, we make the same hazardous ventures; we back our own health and the honesty of our neighbors for all that we are worth; and it is chilling to think how many must lose their wager.

In 1845, twenty-eight years old, an age by which the liveliest have usually declined into some conformity with the world, Thoreau, with a capital of something less than five pounds and a borrowed axe, walked forth into the woods by Walden Pond, and began his new experiment in life. He built himself a dwelling, and returned the axe, he says with characteristic and workman-like pride, sharper than when he borrowed it; he reclaimed a patch, where he cultivated beans, peas, potatoes, and sweet corn; he had his bread to bake, his farm to dig, and for the matter of six weeks in the summer he worked at surveying, carpentry, or some other of his numerous dexterities, for hire. For more than five years, this was all that he required to do for his support, and he had the winter and most of the summer at his entire disposal. For six weeks of occupation, a little cooking and a little gentle hygienic gardening, the man, you may say, had as good as stolen his livelihood. Or we must rather allow that he had done far better; for the thief himself is continually and busily occupied; and even one born to inherit a million will have more calls upon his time than Thoreau. Well might he say, "What old people tell you you cannot do, you try and find you can." And how surprising is his conclusion: "I am convinced that *to maintain oneself on this earth is not a hardship, but a pastime,* if we will live simply and wisely; *as the pursuits of simpler nations are still the sports of the more artificial.*"

When he had enough of that kind of life, he showed the same simplicity in giving it up as in beginning it. There are some who could have done the one, but, vanity forbidding, not the other; and that is perhaps the story of the hermits; but Thoreau made no fetich of his own example, and did what he wanted squarely. And five years is long enough for an experiment and to prove the success of transcendental Yankeeism. It is not his frugality which is worthy of note; for, to begin with, that was inborn, and therefore inimitable by others who are differently constituted; and again, it was no new thing, but has often been equalled by poor Scotch students at the universities. The point is the sanity of his view of life, and the insight with which he recognized the position of money, and thought out for himself the problem of riches and a livelihood. Apart from his eccentricities, he had perceived, and was acting on, a truth of universal application. For money enters in two different characters into the scheme of life. A certain amount, varying with the number and empire of our desires, is a true necessary to each one of us in the present order of society; but beyond that amount, money is a commodity to be bought or not to be bought, a luxury in which we may either indulge or stint ourselves, like any other. And there are many luxuries that we may legitimately prefer to it, such as a grateful conscience, a country life, or the woman of our inclination. Trite, flat, and obvious as this conclusion may appear, we have only to look round us in society to see how scantily it has been recognized; and perhaps even ourselves, after a little reflection, may decide to spend a trifle less for money, and indulge ourselves a trifle more in the article of freedom.

III

"To have done anything by which you earned money merely," says Thoreau, "is to be" (have been, he means) "idle and worse." There are two passages in his letters, both, oddly enough, relating to firewood, which must be brought together to be rightly understood. So taken, they contain between them the marrow of all good sense on the subject of work in its relation to something broader than mere livelihood. Here is the first: "I suppose I have burned up a good-sized tree to-night—and for what? I settled with Mr. Tarbell for it the other day; but that wasn't the final settlement. I got off cheaply from him. At last one will say: 'Let us see, how much wood did you burn, sir?' And I shall shudder to think that the next question will be, 'What did you do while you were warm?'" Even after we have settled with Admetus in the person of Mr. Tarbell, there comes, you see, a further question. It is not enough to have earned our livelihood. Either the earning itself should have been serviceable to mankind, or something else must follow. To live is sometimes very difficult, but it is never meritorious in itself; and we must have a reason to allege to our own conscience why we should continue to exist upon this crowded earth. If Thoreau had simply dwelt in his house at Walden, a lover of trees, birds, and fishes, and the open air and virtue, a reader of wise books, an idle, selfish self-improver, he would have managed to cheat Admetus, but, to cling to metaphor, the devil would have had him in the end. Those who can avoid toil altogether and dwell in the Arcadia of private means, and even those who can, by abstinence, reduce the necessary amount of it to some six weeks a year, having the more liberty, have only the higher moral obligation to be up and doing in the interest of man.

The second passage is this: "There is a far more important and warming heat, commonly lost, which precedes the burning of the wood. It is the smoke of industry, which is incense. I had been so thoroughly warmed in body and spirit, that when at length my fuel was housed, I came near selling it to the ashman, as if I had extracted all its heat." Industry is, in itself and when properly chosen, delightful and profitable to the worker; and when your toil has been a pleasure, you have not, as Thoreau says, "earned money merely," but money, health, delight, and moral profit, all in one. "We must heap up a great pile of doing for a small diameter of being," he says in another place; and then exclaims, "How admirably the artist is made to accomplish his self-culture by devotion to his art!" We may escape uncongenial toil, only to devote ourselves to that which is congenial. It is only to transact some higher business that even Apollo dare play the truant from Admetus. We must all work for the sake of work; we must all work, as Thoreau says again, in any "absorbing pursuit—it does not much matter what, so it be honest;" but the most profitable work is that which combines into one continued effort the largest proportion of the powers and desires of a man's nature; that into which he will plunge with ardor, and from which he will desist with reluctance; in which he will know the weariness of fatigue, but not that of satiety; and which will be ever fresh, pleasing, and stimulating to his taste. Such work holds a man together, braced at all points; it does not suffer him to doze or wander; it keeps him actively conscious of himself, yet raised among superior interests; it gives him the profit of industry with the pleasures of a pastime. This is what his art should be to the true artist, and that to a degree unknown in other and less intimate pursuits. For other professions stand apart from the human business of life; but an art has its seat at the centre of the artist's doings and sufferings, deals directly with his experiences, teaches him the lessons of his own fortunes and mishaps, and becomes a part of his biography. So says Goethe:

Spat erklingt was friih erklang; Gliick und Ungluck wird Gesang.

Now Thoreau's art was literature; and it was one of which he had conceived most ambitiously. He loved and believed in good books. He said well, "Life is not habitually seen from any common platform so truly and unexaggerated as in the light of literature." But the literature he loved was of the heroic order. "Books, not which afford us a cowering enjoyment, but in which each thought is of unusual daring; such as an idle man cannot read, and a timid one would not be entertained by, which even make us dangerous to existing institutions—such I call good books." He did not think them easy to be read. "The heroic boob," he says, "even if printed in the character of our mother-tongue, will always be in a language dead to degenerate times; and we must laboriously seek the meaning of each word and line, conjecturing a larger sense than common use permits out of what wisdom and valor and generosity we have." Nor does he suppose that such books are easily written. "Great prose, of equal elevation, commands our respect more than great verse," says he, "since it implies a more permanent and level height, a life more pervaded with the grandeur of the thought. The poet often only makes an irruption, like the Parthian, and is off again, shooting while he retreats; but the prose writer has conquered like a Roman and settled colonies." We may ask ourselves, almost with dismay, whether such works exist at all but in the imagination of the student. For the bulk of the best of books is apt to be made up with ballast; and those in which energy of thought is combined with any stateliness of utterance may be almost counted on the fingers. Looking round in English for a book that should answer Thoreau's two demands of a style like poetry and sense that shall be both original and inspiriting, I come to Milton's *Areopagitica,* and can name no other instance for the moment. Two things at least are plain: that if a man will condescend to nothing more commonplace in the way of reading, he must not look to have a large library;

and that if he proposes himself to write in a similar vein, he will find his work cut out for him.

Thoreau composed seemingly while he walked, or at least exercise and composition were with him intimately connected; for we are told that "the length of his walk uniformly made the length of his writing." He speaks in one place of "plainness and vigor, the ornaments of style," which is rather too paradoxical to be comprehensively true. In another he remarks: "As for style of writing, if one has anything to say it drops from him simply as a stone falls to the ground." We must conjecture a very large sense indeed for the phrase "if one has anything to say." When truth flows from a man, fittingly clothed in style and without conscious effort, it is because the effort has been made and the work practically completed before he sat down to write. It is only out of fulness of thinking that expression drops perfect like a ripe fruit; and when Thoreau wrote so nonchalantly at his desk, it was because he had been vigorously active during his walk. For neither clearness, compression, nor beauty of language, come to any living creature till after a busy and a prolonged acquaintance with the subject at hand. Easy writers are those who, like Walter Scott, choose to remain contented with a less degree of perfection than is legitimately within the compass of their powers. We hear of Shakespeare and his clean manuscript; but in face of the evidence of the style itself and of the various editions of *Hamlet,* this merely proves that Messrs. Hemming and Condell were unacquainted with the common enough phenomenon called a fair copy. He who would recast a tragedy already given to the world must frequently and earnestly have revised details in the study. Thoreau himself, and in spite of his protestations, is an instance of even extreme research in one direction; and his effort after heroic utterance is proved not only by the occasional finish, but by the determined exaggeration of his style. "I trust you realize what an exaggerator I am—that I lay myself out to exaggerate," he writes. And again, hinting at the explanation: "Who that has heard a strain of music feared lest he should speak extravagantly any more forever?" And yet once more, in his essay on Carlyle, and this time with his meaning well in hand: "No truth, we think, was ever expressed but with this sort of emphasis, that for the time there seemed to be no other." Thus Thoreau was an exaggerative and a parabolical writer, not because he loved the literature of the East, but from a desire that people should understand and realize what he was writing. He was near the truth upon the general question; but in his own particular method, it appears to me, he wandered. Literature is not less a conventional art than painting or sculpture; and it is the least striking, as it is the most comprehensive of the three. To hear a strain of music, to see a beautiful woman, a river, a great city, or a starry night, is to make a man despair of his Lilliputian arts in language. Now, to gain that emphasis which seems denied to us by the very nature of the medium, the proper method of literature is by selection, which is a kind of negative exaggeration. It is the right of the literary artist, as Thoreau was on the point of seeing, to leave out whatever does not suit his purpose. Thus we extract the pure gold; and thus the well-written story of a noble life becomes, by its very omissions, more thrilling to the reader. But to go beyond this, like Thoreau, and to exaggerate directly, is to leave the saner classical tradition, and to put the reader on his guard. And when you write the whole for the half, you do not express your thought more forcibly, but only express a different thought which is not yours.

Thoreau's true subject was the pursuit of self-improvement combined with an unfriendly criticism of life as it goes on in our societies; it is there that he best displays the freshness and surprising trenchancy of his intellect; it is there that his style becomes plain and vigorous, and therefore, according to his own formula, ornamental. Yet he did not care to follow this vein singly, but must drop into it by the way in books of a different purport. *Walden, or Life in the Woods, A Week on the Concord and Merrimack Rivers, The Maine Woods,*—such are the titles he affects. He was probably reminded by his delicate critical perception that the true business of literature is with narrative; in reasoned narrative, and there alone, that art enjoys all its advantages, and suffers least from its defects. Dry precept and disembodied disquisition, as they can only be read with an effort of abstraction, can never convey a perfectly complete or a perfectly natural impression. Truth, even in literature, must be clothed with flesh and blood, or it cannot tell its whole story to the reader. Hence the effect of anecdote on simple minds; and hence good biographies and works of high, imaginative art, are not only far more entertaining, but far more edifying, than books of theory or precept. Now Thoreau could not clothe his opinions in the garment of art, for that was not his talent; but he sought to gain the same elbow-room for himself, and to afford a similar relief to his readers, by mingling his thoughts with a record of experience.

Again, he was a lover of nature. The quality, which we should call mystery in a painting, and which belongs so particularly to the aspect of the external world and to its influence upon our feelings, was one which he was never weary of attempting to reproduce in his books. The seeming significance of nature's appearances, their unchanging strangeness to the senses, and the thrilling response which they waken in the mind of man, continued to surprise and stimulate his spirits. It appeared to him, I think, that if we could only write near enough to the facts, and yet with no pedestrian calm, but ardently, we might transfer the glamour of reality direct upon our pages; and that, if it were once thus captured and expressed, a new and instructive relation might appear between men's thoughts and the phenomena of nature. This was the eagle that he pursued all his life long, like a schoolboy with a butterfly net. Hear him to a friend: "Let me suggest a theme for you—to state to yourself precisely and completely what that walk over the mountains amounted to for you, returning to this essay again and again until you are satisfied that all that was important in your experience is in it. Don't suppose that you can tell it precisely the first dozen times you try, but at 'em again; especially when, after a sufficient pause, you suspect that you are touching the heart or summit of the matter, reiterate your blows there, and account for the mountain to yourself. Not that the story need be long, but it will take a long while to make it short." Such was the method, not consistent for a man whose meanings were to "drop from him as a stone falls to the ground." Perhaps the most successful work that Thoreau ever accomplished in this direction is to be found in the passages relating to fish in the *Week*. These are remarkable for a vivid truth of impression and a happy suitability of language, not frequently surpassed.

Whatever Thoreau tried to do was tried in fair, square prose, with sentences solidly built, and no help from bastard rhythms. Moreover, there is a progression—I cannot call it a progress—in his work toward a more and more strictly prosaic level, until at last he sinks into the bathos of the prosy. Emerson mentions having once remarked to Thoreau: "Who would not like to write something which all can read, like *Robinson Crusoe?* and who does not see with regret that his page is not solid with a right materialistic treatment which delights everybody?" I must say in passing that it is not the right materialistic treatment which delights the world in *Robinson,* but the romantic and philosophic interest of the fable. The same treatment does quite the reverse of delighting us when it is applied, in *Colonel Jack,* to the management of a plantation. But I cannot help suspecting Thoreau to have been influenced either by this identical remark or by some other closely similar in meaning. He began to fall more and more into a detailed materialistic treatment; he went into the business doggedly, as one who should make a guide-book; he not only chronicled what had been important in his own experience, but whatever might have been important in the experience of anybody else; not only what had affected him, but all that he saw or heard. His ardor had grown less, or perhaps it was inconsistent with a right materialistic treatment to display such emotions as he felt; and, to complete the eventful change, he chose, from a sense of moral dignity, to gut these later works of the saving quality of humor. He was not one of those authors who have learned, in his own words, "to leave out their dulness." He inflicts his full quantity upon the reader in such books as *Cape Cod,* or *The Yankee in Canada.* Of the latter he confessed that he had not managed to get much of himself into it. Heaven knows he had not, nor yet much of Canada, we may hope. "Nothing," he says somewhere, "can shock a brave man but dulness." Well, there are few spots more shocking to the brave than the pages of *The Yankee in Canada.*

There are but three books of his that will be read with much pleasure: the *Week, Walden,* and the collected letters. As to his poetry, Emerson's word shall suffice for us, it is so accurate and so prettily said: "The thyme and marjoram are not yet honey." In this, as in his prose, he relied greatly on the goodwill of the reader and wrote throughout in faith. It was an exercise of faith to suppose that many would understand the sense of his best work, or that any could be exhilarated by the dreary chronicling of his worst. "But," as he says, "the gods do not hear any rude or discordant sound, as we learn from the echo; and I know that the nature toward which I launch these sounds is so rich that it will modulate anew and wonderfully improve my rudest strain."

IV

"What means the fact," he cries, "that a soul which has lost all hope for itself can inspire in another listening soul such an infinite confidence in it, even while it is expressing its despair?" The question is an echo and an illustration of the words last quoted; and it forms the key-note of his thoughts on friendship. No one else, to my knowledge, has spoken in so high and just a spirit of the kindly relations; and I doubt whether it be a drawback that these lessons should come from one in many ways so unfitted to be a teacher in this branch. The very coldness and egoism of his own intercourse gave him a clearer insight into the intellectual basis of our warm, mutual tolerations; and testimony to their worth comes with added force from one who was solitary and disobliging, and of whom a friend remarked, with equal wit and wisdom, "I love Henry, but I cannot like him."

He can hardly be persuaded to make any distinction between love and friendship; in such rarefied and freezing air, upon the mountain-tops of meditation, had he taught himself to breathe. He was, indeed, too accurate an observer not to have remarked that "there exists already a natural disinterestedness and liberality" between men and women; yet, he thought, "friendship is no respecter of sex." Perhaps there is a sense in which the words are true; but they were spoken in ignorance; and perhaps we shall have put the matter most correctly, if we call love a foundation for a nearer and freer degree of friendship than can be possible without it. For there are delicacies, eternal between persons of the same sex, which are melted and disappear in the warmth of love.

To both, if they are to be right, he attributes the same nature and condition. "We are not what we are," says he, "nor do we treat or esteem each other for such, but for what we are capable of being." "A friend is one who incessantly pays us the compliment of expecting all the virtues from us, and who can appreciate them in us." "The friend asks no return but that his friend will religiously accept and wear and not disgrace his apotheosis of him." "It is the merit and preservation of friendship that it takes place on a level higher than the actual characters of the parties would seem to warrant." This is to put friendship on a pedestal indeed; and yet the root of the matter is there; and the last sentence, in particular, is like a light in a dark place, and makes many mysteries plain. We are different with different friends; yet if we look closely we shall find that every such relation reposes on some particular apotheosis of oneself; with each friend, although we could not distinguish it in words from any other, we have at least one special reputation to preserve: and it is thus that we run, when mortified, to our friend or the woman that we love, not to hear ourselves called better, but to be better men in point of fact. We seek this society to flatter ourselves with our own good conduct. And hence any falsehood in the relation, any incomplete or perverted understanding, will spoil even the pleasure of these visits. Thus says Thoreau again: "Only lovers know the value of truth." And yet again: "They ask for words and deeds, when a true relation is word and deed."

But it follows that since they are neither of them so good as the other hopes, and each is, in a very honest manner, playing a part above his powers, such an intercourse must often be disappointing to both. "We may bid farewell sooner than complain," says Thoreau, "for our complaint is too well grounded to be uttered." "We have not so good a right to hate any as our friend."

> It were treason to our love
> And a sin to God above,
> One iota to abate
> Of a pure, impartial hate.

Love is not blind, nor yet forgiving. "O yes, believe me," as the songs says, "Love has eyes!" The nearer the intimacy, the more cuttingly do we feel the unworthiness of those we love; and because you love one, and would die for that love to-morrow, you have not forgiven, and you never will forgive, that friend's misconduct. If you want a person's faults, go to those who love him. They will not tell you, but they know. And herein lies the magnanimous courage of love, that it endures this knowledge without change.

It required a cold, distant personality like that of Thoreau, perhaps, to recognize and certainly to utter this truth; for a more human love makes it a point of honor not to acknowledge those faults of which it is most conscious. But his point of view is both high and dry. He has no illusions; he does not give way to love any more than to hatred, but preserves them both with care like valuable curiosities. A more bald-headed picture of life, if I may so express myself, has seldom been presented. He is an egoist; he does not remember, or does not think it worth while to remark, that, in these near intimacies, we are ninety-nine times disappointed in our beggarly selves for once that we are disappointed in our friend; that it is we who seem most frequently undeserving of the love that unites us; and that it is by our friend's conduct that we are continually rebuked and yet strengthened for a fresh endeavor. Thoreau is dry, priggish, and selfish. It is profit he is after in these intimacies; moral profit, certainly, but still profit to himself. If you will be the sort of friend I want, he remarks naively, "my education cannot dispense with your society." His education! as though a friend were a dictionary. And with all this, not one word about pleasure, or laughter, or kisses, or any quality of flesh and blood. It was not inappropriate, surely, that he had such close relations with the fish. We can understand the friend already quoted, when he cried: "As for taking his arm, I would as soon think of taking the arm of an elm-tree!"

As a matter of fact he experienced but a broken enjoyment in his intimacies. He says he has been perpetually on the brink of the sort of intercourse he wanted, and yet never completely attained it. And what else had he to expect when he would not, in a happy phrase of Carlyle's, "nestle down into it"? Truly, so it will be always if you only stroll in upon your friends as you might stroll in to see a cricket match; and even then not simply for the pleasure of the thing, but with some after-thought of self-improvement, as though you had come to the cricket match to bet. It was his theory that people saw each other too frequently, so that their curiosity was not properly whetted, nor had they anything fresh to communicate; but friendship must be something else than a society for mutual improvement—indeed, it must only be that by the way, and to some extent unconsciously; and if Thoreau had been a man instead of a manner of elm-tree, he would have felt that he saw his friends too seldom, and have reaped benefits unknown to his philosophy from a more sustained and easy intercourse. We might remind him of his own words about love: "We should have no reserve; we should give the whole of ourselves to that business. But commonly men have not imagination enough to be thus employed about a human being, but must be coopering a barrel, forsooth." Ay, or reading oriental philosophers. It is not the nature of the rival occupation, it is the fact that you suffer it to be a rival, that renders loving intimacy impossible. Nothing is given for nothing in this world; there can be no true love, even on your own side, without devotion; devotion is the exercise of love, by which it grows; but if you will give enough of that, if you will pay the price in a sufficient "amount of what you call life," why then, indeed, whether with wife or comrade, you may have months and even years of such easy, natural, pleasurable, and yet improving intercourse as shall make time a moment and kindness a delight.

The secret of his retirement lies not in misanthropy, of which he had no tincture, but part in his engrossing design of self-improvement and part in the real deficiencies of social intercourse. He was not so much difficult about his fellow human beings as he could not tolerate the terms of their association. He could take to a man for any genuine qualities, as we see by his admirable sketch of the Canadian woodcutter in *Walden;* but he would not consent, in his own words, to "feebly fabulate and paddle in the social slush." It seemed to him, I think, that society is precisely the reverse of friendship, in that it takes place on a lower level than the characters of any of the parties would warrant us to expect. The society talk of even the most brilliant man is of greatly less account than what you will get from him in (as the French say) a little committee. And Thoreau wanted geniality; he had not enough of the superficial, even at command; he could not swoop into a parlor and, in the naval phrase, "cut out" a human being from that dreary port; nor had he inclination for the task. I suspect he loved books and nature as well and near as warmly as he loved his fellow-creatures,—a melancholy, lean degeneration of the human character.

"As for the dispute about solitude and society," he thus sums up: "Any comparison is impertinent. It is an idling down on the plain at the base of the mountain instead of climbing steadily to its top. Of course you will be glad of all the society you can get to go up with? Will you go to glory with me? is the burden of the song. It is not that we love to be alone, but that we love to soar, and when we do soar the company grows thinner and thinner till there is none at all. It is either the tribune on the plain, a sermon on the mount, or a very private ecstasy still higher up. Use all the society that will abet you." But surely it is no very extravagant opinion that it is better to give than to receive, to serve than to use our companions; and above all, where there is no question of service upon either side, that it is good to enjoy their company like a natural man. It is curious and in some ways dispiriting that a writer may be always best corrected out of his own mouth; and so, to conclude, here is another passage from Thoreau which seems aimed directly at himself: "Do not be too moral: you may cheat yourself out of much life so . . . *All fables, indeed, have their morals; but the innocent enjoy the story.*"

V

"The only obligation," says he, "which I have a right to assume is to do at any time what I think right." "Why should we ever go abroad, even across the way, to ask a neighbor's advice?" "There is a nearer neighbor within, who is incessantly telling us how we should behave. *But we wait for the neighbor without to tell us of some false, easier way.*" "The greater part of what my neighbors call good I believe in my soul to be bad." To be what we are, and to become what we are capable of becoming, is the only end of life. It is "when we fall behind ourselves" that "we are cursed with duties and the neglect of duties." "I love the wild," he says, "not less than the good." And again: "The life of a good man will hardly improve us more than the life of a freebooter, for the inevitable laws appear as plainly in the infringement as in the observance, and" (mark this) *"our lives are sustained by a nearly equal expense of virtue of some kind."* Even although he were a prig, it will be owned he could announce a startling doctrine. "As for doing good," he writes elsewhere, "that is one of the professions that are full. Moreover, I have tried it fairly, and, strange as it may seem, am satisfied that it does not agree with my constitution. Probably I should not conscientiously and deliberately forsake my particular calling to do the good which society demands of me, to save the universe from annihilation; and I believe that a like but infinitely greater steadfastness elsewhere is all that now preserves it. If you should ever be betrayed into any of these philanthropies, do not let your left hand know what your right hand does, for it is not worth knowing." Elsewhere he returns upon the subject, and explains his meaning thus: "If I ever *did* a man any good in their sense, of course it was something exceptional and insignificant compared with the good and evil I am constantly doing by being what I am."

There is a rude nobility, like that of a barbarian king, in this unshaken confidence in himself and indifference to the wants, thoughts, or sufferings of others. In his whole works I find no trace of pity. This was partly the result of theory, for he held the world too mysterious to be criticised, and asks conclusively: "What right have I to grieve who have not ceased to wonder?"

But it sprang still more from constitutional indifference and superiority; and he grew up healthy, composed, and unconscious from among life's horrors, like a green bay-tree from a field of battle. It was from this lack in himself that he failed to do justice to the spirit of Christ; for while he could glean more meaning from individual precepts than any score of Christians, yet he conceived life in such a different hope, and viewed it with such contrary emotions, that the sense and purport of the doctrine as a whole seems to have passed him by or left him unimpressed. He could understand the idealism of the Christian view, but he was himself so unaffectedly unhuman that he did not recognize the human intention and essence of that teaching. Hence he complained that Christ did not leave us a rule that was proper and sufficient for this world, not having conceived the nature of the rule that was laid down; for things of that character that are sufficiently unacceptable become positively non-existent to the mind. But perhaps we shall best appreciate the defect in Thoreau by seeing it supplied in the case of Whitman. For the one, I feel confident, is the disciple of the other; it is what Thoreau clearly whispered that Whitman so uproariously bawls; it is the same doctrine, but with how immense a difference! the same argument, but used to what a new conclusion! Thoreau had plenty of humor until he tutored himself out of it, and so forfeited that best birthright of a sensible man; Whitman, in that respect, seems to have been sent into the world naked and unashamed; and yet by a strange consummation, it is the theory of the former that is arid, abstract, and claustral. Of these two philosophies so nearly identical at bottom, the one pursues Self-improvement—a churlish, mangy dog; the other is up with the morning, in the best of health, and following the nymph Happiness, buxom, blithe, and debonair. Happiness, at least, is not solitary; it joys to communicate; it loves others, for it depends on them for its existence; it sanctions and encourages to all delights that are not unkind in themselves; if it lived to a thousand, it would not make excision of a single humorous passage; and while the self-improver dwindles toward the prig, and, if he be not of an excellent constitution, may even grow deformed into an Obermann, the very name and appearance of a happy man breathe of good-nature, and help the rest of us to live.

In the case of Thoreau, so great a show of doctrine demands some outcome in the field of action. If nothing were to be done but build a shanty beside Walden Pond, we have heard altogether too much of these declarations of independence. That the man wrote some books is nothing to the purpose, for the same has been done in a suburban villa. That he kept himself happy is perhaps a sufficient excuse, but it is disappointing to the reader. We may be unjust, but when a man despises commerce and philanthropy alike, and has views of good so soaring that he must take himself apart from mankind for their cultivation, we will not be content without some striking act. It was not Thoreau's fault if he were not martyred; had the occasion come, he would have made a noble ending. As it is, he did once seek to interfere in the world's course; he made one practical appearance on the stage of affairs; and a strange one it was, and strangely characteristic of the nobility and the eccentricity of the man. It was forced on him by his calm but radical opposition to negro slavery. "Voting for the right is doing nothing for it," he saw; "it is only expressing to men feebly your desire that it should prevail." For his part, he would not "for an instant recognize that political organization for *his* government which is the *slave's* government also." "I do not hesitate to say," he adds, "that those who call themselves Abolitionists should at once effectually withdraw their support, both in person and property, from the government of Massachusetts." That is what he did: in 1843 he ceased to pay the poll-tax. The highway-tax he paid, for he said he was as desirous to be a good neighbor as to be a bad subject; but no more poll-tax to the State of Massachusetts. Thoreau had now seceded, and was a polity unto himself; or, as he explains it with admirable sense, "In fact, I quietly declare war with the State after my fashion, though I will still make what use and get what advantage of her I can, as is usual in such cases." He was put in prison; but that was a part of his design. "Under a government which imprisons any unjustly, the true place for a just man is also a prison. I know this well, that if one thousand, if one hundred, if ten men whom I could name—ay, if *one* HONEST man, in this State of Massachusetts, *ceasing to hold slaves,* were actually to withdraw from this copartnership, and be locked up in the county jail therefor, it would be the abolition of slavery in America. For it matters not how small the beginning may seem to be; what is once well done is done forever." Such was his theory of civil disobedience.

And the upshot? A friend paid the tax for him; continued year by year to pay it in the sequel; and Thoreau was free to walk the woods unmolested. It was a *fiasco,* but to me it does not seem laughable; even those who joined in the laughter at the moment would be insensibly affected by this quaint instance of a good man's horror for injustice. We may compute the worth of that one night's imprisonment as outweighing half a hundred voters at some subsequent election: and if Thoreau had possessed as great a power of persuasion as (let us say) Falstaff, if he had counted a party however small, if his example had been followed by a hundred or by thirty of his fellows, I cannot but believe it would have greatly precipitated the era of freedom and justice. We feel the misdeeds of our country with so little fervor, for we are not witnesses to the suffering they cause; but when we see them wake an active horror in our fellowman, when we see a neighbor prefer to lie in prison rather than be so much as passively implicated in their perpetration, even the dullest of us will begin to realize them with a quicker pulse.

Not far from twenty years later, when Captain John Brown was taken at Harper's Ferry, Thoreau was the first to come forward in his defence. The committees wrote to him unanimously that his action was premature. "I did not send to you for advice," said he, "but to announce that I was to speak." I have used the word "defence;" in truth he did not seek to defend him, even declared it would be better for the good cause that he should die; but he praised his action as I think Brown would have liked to hear it praised.

Thus this singularly eccentric and independent mind, wedded to a character of so much strength, singleness, and purity, pursued its own path of self-improvement for more than half a century, part gymnosophist, part backwoodsman; and thus did it come twice, though in a subaltern attitude, into the field of political history.[1]

Preface, by Way of Criticism.

Here is an admirable instance of the "point of view" forced throughout, and of too earnest reflection on imperfect facts. Upon me this pure, narrow, sunnily-ascetic Thoreau had exercised a great charm. I have scarce written ten sentences since I was introduced to him, but his influence might be somewhere detected by a close observer. Still it was as a writer that I had made his acquaintance; I took him on his own explicit terms; and when I learned details of his Life, they were, by the nature of the case and my own *parti-pris,* read even with a certain violence in terms of his writings. There could scarce be a perversion more justifiable than that; yet it was still a perversion. The study, indeed, raised so much ire in the breast of Dr. Japp (H. A. Page), Thoreau's sincere and learned disciple, that had either of us been men, I please myself with thinking, of less temper and justice, the difference might have made us enemies instead of making us friends. To him who knew the man from the inside, many of my statements sounded like inversions made on purpose; and yet when we came to talk of them together, and he had understood how I was looking at the man through the books, while he had long since learned to read the books through the man, I believe he understood the spirit in which I had been led astray.

On two most important points, Dr. Japp added to my knowledge, and with the same blow fairly demolished that part of my criticism. First, if Thoreau were content to dwell by Walden Pond, it was not merely with designs of self-improvement, but to serve mankind in the highest sense. Hither came the fleeing slave; thence was he despatched along the road to freedom. That shanty in the woods was a station in the great Underground Railroad; that adroit and philosophic solitary was an ardent worker, soul and body, in that so much more than honorable movement, which, if atonement were possible for nations, should have gone far to wipe away the guilt of slavery. But in history sin always meets with condign punishment; the generation passes, the offence remains, and the innocent must suffer. No underground railroad could atone for slavery, even as no bills in Parliament can redeem the ancient wrongs of Ireland. But here at least is a new light shed on the Walden episode.

Second, it appears, and the point is capital, that Thoreau was once fairly and manfully in love, and, with perhaps too much aping of the angel, relinquished the woman to his brother. Even though the brother were like to die of it, we have not yet heard the last opinion of the woman. But be that as it may, we have here the explanation of the "rarefied and freezing air" in which I complained that he had taught himself to breathe. Reading the man through the books, I took his professions in good faith. He made a dupe of me, even as he was seeking to make a dupe of himself, wresting philosophy to the needs of his own sorrow. But in the light of this new fact, those pages, seemingly so cold, are seen to be alive with feeling. What appeared to be a lack of interest in the philosopher turns out to have been a touching insincerity of the man to his own heart; and that fine-spun airy theory of friendship, so devoid, as I complained, of any quality of flesh and blood, a mere anodyne to lull his pains. The most temperate of living critics once marked a passage of my own with a cross and the words, "This seems nonsense." It not only seemed; it was so. It was a private bravado of my own, which I had so often repeated to keep up my spirits, that I had grown at last wholly to believe it, and had ended by setting it down as a contribution to the theory of life. So with the more icy parts of this philosophy of Thoreau's. He was affecting the Spartanism he had not; and the old sentimental wound still bled afresh, while he deceived himself with reasons.

Thoreau's theory, in short, was one thing and himself another: of the first, the reader will find what I believe to be a pretty faithful statement and a fairly just criticism in the study; of the second he will find but a contorted shadow. So much of the man as fitted nicely with his doctrines, in the photographer's phrase, came out. But that large part which lay outside and beyond, for which he had found or sought no formula, on which perhaps his philosophy even looked askance, is wanting in my study, as it was wanting in the guide I followed. In some ways a less serious writer, in all ways a nobler man, the true Thoreau still remains to be depicted.

Notes

1. For many facts in the above essay, among which I may mention the incident of the squirrel, I am indebted to *Thoreau: His Life and Aims*, by H.A. Page, or, as is well known, Dr. Japp.

—Robert Louis Stevenson,
"Henry David Thoreau: His Character
and Opinions," 1880, and "Preface,
by Way of Criticism," 1886, *Familiar Studies
of Men and Books* 1886, pp. 18–21

ROSE HAWTHORNE LATHROP (1897)

Rose Hawthorne Lathrop (1851–1926) was the second daughter of Nathaniel Hawthorne and his wife, Sophia. Her adolescence was marked by the death of both her parents. After an unhappy marriage to George Lathrop, an assistant editor of the *Atlantic Monthly*, she separated from her husband and moved to New York City where she trained as a nurse and established a refuge for cancer victims. In this brief sketch of Thoreau, Lathrop evokes Thoreau's organic relationship with nature comparing his sadness to that of a pine tree and detecting his presence within Walden woods every time she walked through them.

Another peculiar spirit now and then haunted us, usually sad as a pine-tree—Thoreau. His enormous eyes, tame with religious intellect and wild with the loose rein, making a steady flash in this strange unison of forces, frightened me dreadfully at first. The unanswerable argument which he unwittingly made to soften my heart towards him was to fall desperately ill. During his long illness my mother lent him our sweet old music-box, to which she had danced as it warbled at the Old Manse, in the first year of her marriage, and which now softly dreamed forth its tunes in a time-mellowed tone. When he died, it seemed as if an anemone, more lovely than any other, had been carried from the borders of a wood into its silent depths, and dropped, in solitude and shadow, among the recluse ferns and mosses which are so seldom disturbed by passing feet. Son of freedom and opportunity that he was, he touched the heart by going to nature's peacefulness like the saints, and girding upon his American sovereignty the hair-shirt of service to self-denial. He was happy in his intense discipline of the flesh, as all men are when they have once tasted power—if it is the power which awakens perception of the highest concerns. His countenance had an April pensiveness about it; you would never have guessed that he could write of owls so jocosely. His manner was such as to suggest that he could mope and weep *with* them. I never crossed an airy hill or broad field in Concord, without thinking of him who had been the companion of space as well as of delicacy; the lover of the wood-thrush, as well as of the Indian. Walden woods rustled the name of Thoreau whenever we walked in them.

—Rose Hawthorne Lathrop,
Memories of Hawthorne, 1897, p. 420

Bradford Torrey "Thoreau's Attitude toward Nature" (1899)

Bradford Torrey (1843–1912) was one of the most popular travel and outdoor writers at the turn of the twentieth century. He produced 13 books of nature writings, which mainly collected articles written for the *Atlantic Monthly*. Torrey also contributed to the dissemination of Thoreau's works. He edited a "deluxe" edition of *Walden* in the 1890s, as well as the first version of Thoreau's *Journal* in 14 volumes. This was part of the 20-volume "Manuscript Edition" of Thoreau's *Complete Works*, issued by Houghton and Mifflin in 1906. Thus, Torrey had an important role in establishing Thoreau's posthumous reputation as a classic American author. Torrey's critical parable is paradoxically opposite to that of his model. Thanks to Torrey's efforts, Thoreau's critical and commercial reputation began to rise at the beginning of the twentieth century. On the contrary, Torrey's own literary fame started to decline steadily, a process that continued after his death when his literary works suffered increasing critical neglect. The huge project of editing Thoreau's journal also mined Torrey's own creativity in the last years of his life. Torrey's dedication to the project, together with the lack of reliable biographical information on Torrey, prompted a veritable identification between the two, one being conflated with the other. After his death, Torrey was described as a Thoreau-like hermit who spent the last years of his life in an isolated cabin in California. This has proved to be untrue.

In the following essay, Torrey praises Thoreau for making the study of nature not simply an amusement or even a serious occupation for his leisure hours, but "the work of his life." Torrey's portrait of Thoreau also emphasizes his "Puritan conscience," the fact that the author of *Walden* was never fully satisfied with the result of his work and constantly tried to improve it. Yet, Torrey dismisses descriptions of Thoreau as "beset with the idea of self-improvement" and counters the critical charge that his work lacked solid scientific foundations. According to Torrey, Thoreau's work should be judged on its own terms and as enriching the world already as it stands.

———

"I wish to speak a word for Nature, for absolute freedom and wildness." So Thoreau began an article in *The Atlantic Monthly* thirty-five years ago. He wished to make an extreme statement, he declared, in hope of making an emphatic one. Like idealists in general,—like Jesus in particular,—he believed in omitting qualifications and exceptions. Those were matters certain to be sufficiently insisted upon by the orthodox and the conservative, the minister and the school committee.

In an attempt at an extreme statement Thoreau was very unlikely to fail. Thanks to an inherited aptitude and years of practice, there have been few to excel him with the high lights. In his hands exaggeration becomes one of the fine arts. We will not call it the finest art; his own best work would teach us better than that; but such as it is, with him to hold the brush, it would be difficult to imagine anything more effective. When he praises a quaking swamp as the most desirable of dooryards, or has visions of a people so enlightened as to burn their fences and leave the forests to grow, who shall contend with him? And yet the sympathetic reader—the only real reader—knows what is meant, and what is not meant, and finds it good; as he finds it good when he is bidden to turn the other cheek to the smiter, or to distribute all his living among the poor.

Thoreau's love for the wild—not to be confounded with a liking for natural history or an appreciation of scenery—was as natural and unaffected as a child's love of sweets. It belonged to no one part of his life. It finds utterance in all his books, but is best expressed, most feelingly and simply, and therefore most convincingly, in his journal, especially in such an entry as that of January 7, 1857, a bitterly cold, windy day, with snow blowing,—one of the days when "all animate things are reduced to their lowest terms." Thoreau has been out, nevertheless, for his afternoon walk, "through the woods toward the cliffs along the side of the Well Meadow field." The contact with Nature, even in this her severest mood, has given a quickening yet restraining grace to his pen. Now, there is no question of "emphasis," no plotting for an "extreme statement," no thought of dull readers, for whom the truth must be shown large, as it were, by some magic-lantern process. How differently he speaks! "Might I aspire to praise the moderate nymph Nature," he says, "I must be like her, moderate."

The passage is too long to be quoted in full. "There is nothing so sanative, so poetic," he writes, "as a walk in the woods and fields even now, when I meet none abroad for pleasure. Nothing so inspires me, and excites such serene and profitable thought. . . . Alone in distant woods or fields, in unpretending sproutlands or pastures tracked by rabbits, even in a bleak and, to most, cheerless day like this, when a villager would be thinking of his inn, I come to myself, I once more feel myself grandly related. This cold and solitude are friends of mine. . . . I get away a mile or two from the town into the stillness and solitude of nature, with rocks, trees, weeds, snow about me. I enter some glade in the woods, perchance, where a few weeds and dry leaves alone lift themselves above the surface of the snow, and it is as if I had come to an open window. I see out and around myself. . . . This stillness, solitude, wildness of nature is a kind of thoroughwort or boneset to my intellect. This is what I go out to seek. It is as if I always met in those places some grand, serene, immortal, infinitely encouraging, though invisible companion, and walked with him."

Four days later, dwelling still upon his "success in solitary and distant woodland walking outside the town," he says: "I do not go there to get my dinner, but to get that sustenance which dinners only preserve me to enjoy, without which dinners are a vain repetition. . . . I never chanced to meet with any man so cheering and elevating and encouraging, so infinitely suggestive, as the stillness and solitude of the Well Meadow field."

Language like this, though all may perceive the beauty and feel the sincerity of it, is to be understood only by those who are of the speaker's kin. It describes a country which no man knows save him who has been there. It expresses life, not theory, and calls for life on the part of the hearer.

And if the appeal be made to this tribunal, the language used here and so often elsewhere, by Thoreau, touching the relative inferiority of human society will neither give offense nor seem in any wise exaggerated or morbid. Thoreau knew Emerson; he had lived in the same house with him; but even Emerson's companionship was less stimulating to him than Nature's own. Well, and how is it with ourselves, who have the best of Emerson in his books? Much as these may have done for us, have we never had seasons of communion with the life of the universe itself when even Emerson's words would have seemed an intrusion? Is not the voice of the world, when we can hear it, better than the voice of any man interpreting the world? Is it not better to hear for ourselves than to be told what another has heard? When the forest speaks things ineffable, and the soul hears what even to itself it can never utter,—for such an hour there is no book, there never will be. And if we wish not a book, no more do we wish the author of a book. We are in better company. In such hours,—too few, alas,—though we be the plainest of plain people, our own emotions are of more value than any talk. We know, in our measure, what Thoreau—

An early unconverted Saint—

was seeking words for when he said, "I feel my Maker blessing me."

To him, as to many another man, experiences of this kind came oftenest in wild and solitary places. No wonder, then, that he loved to go thither. No wonder he found the pleasures of society unsatisfying in the comparison. There he communed, not with himself nor with his fellow, but with the Wisdom and Spirit of the Universe. And when it is objected that this ought not to have been true, that he ought to have found the presence of men more elevating and stimulating than the presence of "inanimate" nature, we must take the liberty to believe that the critic speaks of that whereof he knows nothing. To revert to our own figure, he has never lived in Thoreau's country.

Thoreau was wedded to Nature not so much for her beauty as for delight in her high companionableness. There was more of Wordsworth than of Keats in him. He was more philosopher than poet, perhaps we may say. He loved spirit rather than form and color, though for these also his eye was better than most. Being a stoic, a born economist, a child of the North, he felt most at home with Nature in her dull seasons. His delight in a wintry day was typical. He loved his mistress best when she was most like himself; as he said of human friendships, "I love that one with whom I sympathize, be she 'beautiful' or otherwise, of excellent mind or not." The swamp, the desert, the wilderness,—these he especially celebrated. He began by thinking that nothing could be too wild for him; and even in his later years, notably in the *Atlantic* essay above quoted, he sometimes blew the same heroic strain. By this time, however, he knew and confessed to himself at least, that there was another side to the story; that there was a dreariness beyond even his ready appreciation. More than once we find in his diary expressions like this, in late November: "Now a man will eat his heart, if ever, now while the earth is bare, barren, and cheerless, and we have the coldness of winter without the variety of ice and snow."

And what was true of seasons was equally true of places. Let them be wild, by all means, yet not too wild. When he returned from the Maine woods, he had had, for the time being, enough of the wilderness. It was a relief to get back to the smooth but still varied landscape of eastern Massachusetts. That, for a permanent residence, seemed to him incomparably better than an unbroken forest. The poet must live open to the sky and the wind; his road must be prepared for him; and yet, "not only for strength, but for beauty, the poet must, from time to time, travel the logger's path and the Indian's trail, to drink at some new and more bracing fountain of the Muses." In short, the poet should live in Concord, and only once in a while seek the inspirations of the outer wilderness.

What we have called Thoreau's stoicism (knowing very well that he was not a stoic, except in some partial sense of the word), his liking for plainness and low expense, is perhaps at the base of one of his rarest excellencies as a writer upon nature,—his reserve and moderation. In statement, it is true, he could extravagate like a master. He boasts, as well he may, of his prowess in that direction; but in tone and sentiment, when it came to dealing, not with ethics or philosophy, but with the mistress of his affections, he kept always decently within bounds. He had a very sprightly fancy, when he chose to give it play; but he had with it, and controlling it, a prevailing sobriety, the tempering grace of good sense. "The alder," he says, "is one of the prettiest trees and shrubs in the winter. It is evidently so full of life with its conspicuously pretty red catkins dangling from it on all sides. It seems to dread the winter less than other plants. It has a certain heyday and cheery look, less stiff than most, with more of the flexible grace of summer. With those dangling clusters of red catkins which it switches in the face of winter, it brags for all vegetation. It is not daunted by the cold, but still hangs gracefully over the frozen stream."

Most admirable, thrown in thus by the way, amid unaffected, matter-of-fact description and every-day sense, and with its homely "brags" and "switches" to hold it true,—to save it from a touch of foppery, a shade too much of prettiness. How differently some writers have dealt with similar themes: men so afraid of the commonplace as to be incapable of saying a thing in so many words, though it were only to mention the day of the week; men whose every other sentence must contain a "felicity;" whose pages are as full of floweriness and dainty conceits as a milliner's window; who surfeit you with confections, till you think of bread and water as a feast. Whether Thoreau's temperance is to be credited to the restraints of stoical philosophy or to plain good taste, it is a virtue to be thankful for.

With him the study of nature was not an amusement, nor even a serious occupation for his leisure hours, but the work of his life,—a work to which he gave himself from year's end to year's end, as faithfully and laboriously, and with as definite a purpose, as any Concord farmer gave himself to his farm. He was no amateur, no dilettant, no conscious hobbyist, laughing between times at his own absorption. His sense of a mission was as unquestioning as Wordsworth's, though happily there went with it a sense of humor that preserved it in good measure from over-emphasis and damaging iteration.

In degree, if not in kind, this wholehearted, lifelong devotion was something new. It was one of Thoreau's originalities. To what a pitch he carried it, how serious and all-controlling it was, the pages of his journal bear continual witness. His was a Puritan conscience. He could never do his work well enough. After a eulogy of winter buds, "impregnable, vivacious willow catkins, but half asleep along the twigs" (there, again, is fancy of an uncloying type), he breaks out: "How healthy and vivacious must he be who would treat of these things. You must love the crust of the earth on which you dwell more than the sweet crust of any bread or cake; you must be able to extract nutriment out of a sand heap." "Must" was a great word with Thoreau. In hard times, especially, he braced himself with it. "The winter, cold and bound out, as it is, is thrown to us like a bone to a famishing dog, and we are expected to get the marrow out of it. While the milkmen in the outskirts are milking so many scores of cows before sunrise, these winter mornings, it is our task to milk the winter itself. It is true it is like a cow that is dry, and our fingers are numb, and there is none to wake us up. . . But the winter was not given us for no purpose. We must thaw its cold with our genialness. We are tasked to find out and appropriate all the nutriment it yields. If it is a cold and hard season, its fruit no doubt is the more concentrated and nutty."

In these winter journalizings, we not only have example and proof of the earnestness with which Thoreau pursued his outdoor studies, but are shown their method and their immediate object. He wished to see nature and to set it forth. He was to be a writer, and nature was to be his theme. That he had known from the beginning. For this work he required a considerable store of outward knowledge,—knowledge classified, for convenience, as botany, ornithology, entomology, and the like; but infinitely beyond this he needed a living, deepening intimacy with the life of the world itself. For observation of the ways of plants and animals, of the phases of earth and sky, he had endless patience and all necessary sharpness of sense; work of this kind was easy,—he could do it in some good degree to his satisfaction; the vexatious thing about it was that it readly became too absorbing; but his real work, his *hard* work, the work that was peculiarly his, that taxed his capacities to the full, and even so was never accomplished, this work was not an amassing of relative knowledge, an accumulation of facts, but a perfecting of sympathy, the organ or means of that absolute knowledge which alone he found indispensable, which alone he cared greatly to communicate. There, except at rare moments, he was to the last below his ideal. His "task" was never done. His union with nature was never complete.

The measure of this union was gauged, as we have seen already, by its spiritual and emotional effects, by the mental states it brought him into; as the religious mystic measures the success of his prayers. He walked in the old Carlisle road, as the saint goes to his knees, to "put off worldly thoughts." The words are his own. There, when the hour favored him, he "sauntered near to heaven's gate."

It must be only too evident that success of this transcendental sort is not to be counted upon as one counts upon finding specimens for a botanical box. There is no comparison between scientific pursuits and this kind of supernatural history. For this, as Thoreau says, "you must be in a different state from common." " If it were required to know the position of the fruit dots or the character of the indusium, nothing could be easier than to ascertain it; but if it is required that you be affected by ferns, that they amount to anything, signify anything, to you, that they be another sacred scripture and revelation to you, helping to redeem your life, this end is not so easily accomplished."

This, then, it was for which Thoreau was ever on the alert; this was the prize set before him; this he required of ferns and clouds, of birds and swamps and deserted roads,—that they should affect him, that they should do something to redeem his life. For this he cultivated the "fellowship of the seasons," a fellowship on which no man ever made larger drafts. Even when nature seemed to be getting "thumbed like an old spelling book," even in the month that tempted him sometimes to "eat his heart," he still "sat the bench with perfect contentment, unwilling to exchange the familiar vision that was to be unrolled for any treasure or heaven that could be imagined." A new November was a novelty more tempting than any voyage to Europe or even to another world. "Young men have not learned the phases of nature:" so he comforted himself, when the fervors and inspirations of youth seemed at times to be waning. "I would know when in the year to expect certain thoughts and moods, as the sportsman knows when to look for plover."

Here, as everywhere with Thoreau, nature was nothing of itself. Everything is for man. This belief underlies all his writing upon natural themes, and, as well, all his personal dealings with the natural world. His idlest wanderings, whether in the Maine forests or in Well Meadow field, were made serious by it. To judge him by his own testimony, he seems to have known comparatively little of a careless, purposeless, childish delight in nature for its own sake. Nature was a better kind of book; and books were for improvement. In this respect he was sophisticated from his youth, like some model of "early piety." Nature was not his playground, but his study, his Bible, his closet, his means of grace. As we have said, and as Channing long ago implied, his was a Puritan conscience. He must get at the heart of things, sparing no pains nor time. His was the devotee's faith: "To him that knocketh it shall be opened." In this faith he waited upon nature and the motions of his own genius. Patience, solitude, stillness, and a quiet mind,—these were the instruments of his art. With them, not with prying sharp-sightedness, was the secret to be won. In his own phrase, characteristic in its homely expressiveness, if you would appreciate a phenomenon, though it be only a fern, you must "camp down beside it." And you must invent no distinctions of great and small. The humming of a gnat must be as significant as the music of the spheres.

Was he too serious for his own good, whether as man or as writer? And did he sometimes feel himself so? Was he whipping his own fault when he spoke against conscientious, duty-ridden people, and praised

> simple laboring folk
> Who love their work,
> Whose virtue is a song?

It is not impossible, of course. But he too loved his work,—loved it so well as perhaps to need no playtime. Some have said that he made too much of his "thoughts and moods," that he was unwholesomely beset with the idea of self-improvement. Others have thought that he would have written better books had he stuck closer to science, and paid less court to poetry and Buddhistic philosophy. Such objections and speculations are futile. He did his work, and with it enriched the world. In the strictest sense it was his *own* work. If his ideal escaped him, he did better than most in that he still pursued it.

—Bradford Torrey, "Thoreau's Attitude toward
Nature," *Atlantic*, November 1899, pp. 706–710

FREDERICK M. SMITH "THOREAU" (1900)

To-day the attempt to write about Henry David Thoreau must be prefaced with an explanation. It cannot be claimed that there is anything new to add; nor can one hope to say the old things in so taking a fashion as to make that a plea for venturing upon ground where such men as Sanborn, Channing,

Salt, Burroughs, Lowell, and Stevenson have trodden. There is, however, one excuse. To have been helped by an author is somehow to be put under obligation; and as an acknowledgment of this, it is perhaps pardonable to set down some impressions of the man's character, style, and opinions, with the hope that such impressions may show why Thoreau is to be regarded as a healthful, helpful influence, as well as wherein lies some of the fascination of his work.

It cannot be denied, I think, that Thoreau fascinates. To begin with a minor reason: he is blunt. He attracts a young man because he is an iconoclast. He is no respecter of persons, and he says what he thinks. Often we find that he thinks things we should like to think if we only dared. He is very plain-spoken with his reader. In life such treatment would not be tolerated; in a book it is, on the whole, pleasant. The free-handed way in which he criticises the world and the conventions it has learned to work with is delicious. He has no time to waste upon the things most persons have been taught they have to do. He says those things are unnecessary, and he proceeds to do as he pleases. A man who has found time to do that in this world is to be listened to. It does not matter whether what he pleases is what we please; it does not even matter whether his ways are the best ways or the practical ones; so long as he has the courage of his convictions he is an inspiration. But there are men in plenty who have such a possession and are bankrupt at that. With Thoreau one soon begins to find that the better things lie deeper.

Perhaps his chief trait (and it is a good sign when you find it in a man) was what he called his yearning toward wildness. He felt this, I think, not because he was a rover, but because he had the soul of a poet; and no better appellation can be found for him than that given by his friend Channing. He is above all things the "Poet-Naturalist."

His business seems to have been to get close to Nature. Man somehow failed to interest him, and he tried flowers and bees. As he smelt, tasted, saw, and heard better than most men, he recorded the slightest impressions that animated nature made upon him with as much care as though they were factors in a mathematical proposition. At whatever cost he must get the thing accurately and always get everything,—so that he even "waked in the night to take notes." Yet it is not so much the fact that he is after as the truth behind the fact. Fond as he is of mere measurement, the poet gets the better of him, and though he starts in with cold figures he often ends in rhapsody. He is so precise that one feels moved to acknowledge that he has traits of the scientist—and at the same time he is as open-minded and delicate as the poet. The outward look of the world appeals to him,—the shapes of things, the play of light, and the splash of color. There is something almost oriental in his love of sensation. He revels in pure color, and loves to press poke-berries that he may see the red juice stain his fingers. When carried to that extreme, it is a note which seems almost out of place in such an austere character as we fancy him.

In a way, it is out of place, as, for the greater part, Nature is far more to him than beautiful, and he approaches her not only as an admirer, but as a friend and devotee. She is not to be worshipped as a spirit, not to be looked at as though peopled with nymphs and goddesses. True, he very often personifies her and her manifestations (for she is always a real being), and the trick not only makes his descriptions more vivid and colorful, but it shows the strange fellowship that he felt for her. There is that which is friendly and companionable in his intercourse with trees and streams and wild things, as it were between neighbors. And with that, in his rare moments she speaks to him of God, and gives the final word of hope which echoes in all his pages. "He who hears the rippling of rivers in these degenerate days will not utterly despair." The song of the thrush exhilarates him. "It is a medicative draught to my soul, an elixir to my eyes, and a fountain of youth to all my senses." If a man would but drink at these springs, there is abundant reason why he should keep his life simple and healthful.

Thoreau was doubtless considered "queer" during his lifetime, and some of his poses strike us as radical and unusual; but for all that the best parts of his work have the clear, fresh, earthy touch which means health. It could not be otherwise. Any work which has its well-spring in the open, where the breezes play upon it, and with the blue of heaven and the green of earth reflected in its depths, must partake of the nature of these things and run pure.

It is a healthful thing, too, when he lifts his voice in favor of simplicity and shows himself so capable of celebrating the joys of small things. In the simplest occupation he finds some poetry which gives it dignity. Indeed, he made it his business at all times to chant the beauty of the common. Because a thing was with us every day, it was not therefore cheap; and a single red maple in the autumn time gave him as much pleasure as a glimpse of strange lands, and glorified all sublunary things for him. "Keep your eyes open and see the good about you," is his teaching, and "he found at home what other men went abroad to see."

It is a sign of health again that he hated all sham, and respected genuineness and sincerity wherever he saw it. Gossip and triviality had no place in his scheme, for he believed that they tainted the mind and crowded out better things and higher thoughts. In his ardor he sometimes condemns too widely; for many things which the world has thought necessary he treats with scant respect. Yet it will usually be found that it is not these things in themselves but undue attention to them which occasions his severity.

With all his sourness and sharpness, with all the pleasure he gets in pricking his fellows with a goad, one comes at times, and not rarely, upon reaches where the nature of the man flows sweet and delicate and romantic. Take his description of roses and lilies: "The red rose, with the intense color of many suns concentrated, spreads its tender petals perfectly fair, its flower not to be overlooked, modest, yet queenly, on the edges of shady copses and meadows, against its green leaves, surrounded by blushing buds, of perfect form, not only beautiful, but rightly commanding attention, unspoiled by the admiration of gazers. And the water-lily floats on the surface of slow waters, amid rounded shields of leaves, bucklers, red beneath, which simulate a green field, perfuming the air." And again he says: "I can go out in the morning and gather flowers with which to perfume my chamber where I read and write all day long."

One finds, moreover, a play of fancy which strikes you not so much by its whimsicality as by an airiness and grace which you had not expected. Delightful as he is, he is never, I should say, blithe. True, he says: "Not by constraint or severity shall you have access to true wisdom, but by abandonment to childlike mirthfulness." It was a truth which his intellect had grasped, but which he could not put to practice. Music enchants him because it speaks to him of higher things; an oak leaf delights him and sends him to telling himself stories about it. The laborer, singing, stirs his blood. The hand of romance has apparently touched him and left a mark.

There is, too, a sparkle of kindliness in his nature which makes you warm toward him. He appreciates the generosity of the farmer who feeds him, and is at pains to set down the incident. He seems to have been just on the verge of a full and warm sympathy with mankind, but continually sets it aside for what he believes are the more spiritual and higher virtues. So on the whole we are apt to count him cold.

Toward this higher life he is constantly striving. He lived on the border of a good land, where the wood thrush sang eternally and where the rarest flowers bloomed; a shadowy land on which he forever kept his eyes; and he had an abiding faith that some day he would be an inhabitant thereof. Something of its mystery reached out to him, and his allusions to it are constant. It was not the heaven of the Christian where the streets were more or less suggestive of a lapidary's shop, and where everybody was a musician. It was a place where a mortal should at last get hold of his ideals and make in the end a *man* of himself; a place where he should live up to the best that was in him and have fellowship with Nature and with God.

Thoreau is usually thought of as an advocate of Nature, and we do not remember that he drew from other sources. The mistake is natural, for Nature does seem everything. Looking a little closer one finds that he derived much from books. The sacred literature of many nations was familiar to him, while the Greek and Latin poets were his daily companions. The strength, freshness, and simplicity of the Greeks found in his heart a ready response. Homer got down "close to the bone" of life, and that made his election sure to Thoreau. No other literature does he praise so much as Greek, but he quotes widely—old French writers, and the English poets, Tennyson and Landor. Wordsworth he knew; and one's respect for Thoreau is a trifle increased because he makes record of his appreciation of *Peter Bell*. A list of the English writers he quotes would require pages, would begin before Chaucer, and be fullest, perhaps, at the seventeenth-century men. He knew, too, all the writings of old New England, the town histories, the chronicles of early travellers, and the like. If a writer had in any way touched Nature, Thoreau had the work at his tongue's end. Even obscure and dry treatises on agricultural or horticultural subjects seem to have been read with avidity and treasured against the day when he should have need of them. He loved to read those who, like the Greeks, wrote from the heart; who gave a true account of themselves and of their thoughts, who wrote sincerely and simply.

Sincere I always believe him, and it will perhaps be paradoxical to say that, after all, he is at times something of a *poseur*. But so it is, and the two things can and do exist together. He lays down the law in too dogmatic a fashion not to make one feel that he is straining a point for the effect. He takes pains to impress the fact that he is not a gentleman, but a common man; yet he wants to be different from many common men, and he is careful to make the most of these differences. There is a touch of vanity and affectation in the way he patronizes farmers. He lays a claim to knowing more of their farms than they do. If he dressed simply, he did so partly because it tickled his vanity. He was proud of a patch not because it was a patch, but because he liked to feel that he was above being ashamed of it. He was superior in some things, but we suspect a man who thrusts his superiority upon us. Like the boys on the links at night, he carried a lantern under his jacket. He liked to cast a big shadow, and he sometimes held the lantern so close that the shadow was distorted and not quite like the true man. It was doubtless this trick of posing, this habit of illogical exaggeration, which made Lowell say of him that he had no humor.

What he meant was, that Thoreau had not that faculty of turning an amused eye upon himself and of spying out his own faults. To have it saves one much of the worry of the world and sweetens the sour spots mightily. A man who can smile at himself will not be for long in any black humor. Thoreau could not do that. He could smile at his friends and neighbors, and he never loses occasion to. His wit is sharp, and he can be bitterly satirical; it is his delight to prick bubbles. But his smile is always at you, not with you; his humor is not genial and warm; he is a man with a twinkle in his gray eye, but with no laugh in his belly. Sometimes even his eyes do not show it—it is deeper than that. You feel, indeed, from his opinions, that he did not entirely grasp the meaning of humor, for in speaking of Carlyle he appears to think that a man is only at his best when he is too in earnest even to smile. As if a smile would taint the truth!

In talking about his style, one finds himself in the way to repeat many things that were said of his character; for the style, perhaps, is only the character shining through words. "I resolved," he says, in speaking of a certain lecture, "to give them a strong dose of myself." That is what one gets in reading him. First of all you put him down as unequal. At times he is careless in the structure of his sentences. You may have a lingering doubt as to the antecedent of a certain relative; or you come upon long, trailing clauses in which he has tangled himself and you may get him out at your leisure. But this is only occasional. For the greater part his meaning is cut clear.

Precise he always intends to be, and details delight him. He takes great care to tell exactly how everything was done, as in the building of his boat. It is like making a partner of the reader, who feels often that he was there himself and had a hand in the business. Thoreau must even measure the axe before a Maine settler's door that his description may be accurate. Long practice in trying to describe taught him the use of fit words. We find him searching for just the word that will suit his impression, and often in his journal he will put a question-mark after a word or phrase which does not entirely satisfy him.

Sometimes he has a paragraph of brilliant and charming description, overflowing with poetic feeling, full of delicate shading, and soft flower bloom. On the other hand, he will fill pages with paragraphs as hard as steel, full of sharp and pithy sayings, which glitter with satire and slip into the mind like proverbs. Of this oracular manner of delivery he is especially fond, and the serenity with which he lays down the laws of life gives one the sense of reading old philosophers. It is as though the writer had thousands of years at his back and spoke to you out of them. His whole compositions, like Emerson's, hang together rather by weight of the underlying idea rather than by any structural coherence.

The word whimsical fits certain of his turns. He gives unexpected twists to sentences, brings in puns and unlooked-for metaphors. The punning habit was one that he apparently chuckled over. His early works do not show any excess of it, but later it tickled him monstrously to make a bad pun. Then he has fancies which he dresses up for his own amusement, and we find him projecting a tea-party of sixty old women, from Eve to his mother. Lake Champlain looks "like the picture of Lake Lucerne on a music-box." This fancifulness made him speak often in metaphors, so that his sentences are at times riddles or half-riddles. He strove for a certain mystery of expression which should be tantalizing to a reader without completely misleading him. This habit of teasing you with phrases makes you like him all the better, for at least he counts somewhat on your intellect. One of his tricks was to speak of things spiritual and mental in terms of Nature, geography, and history. "Whenever a man fronts a fact there is an unsettled wilderness between him and it. Let him build himself a log-house with the bark on it, and wage an old French war."

The quality of mystery in his style is the mystery got from Nature. The landscape is vague, moving, and shadowy as the living atmosphere. Thoreau put it into his words. His quick feeling for Nature is that which gives his style charm,—that and the habit of tilting at things of which he disapproves. He says of Evelyn that "love of subject teaches him many impressive words." That could be said of his own writings with equal truth. The feel of the air, the color of a leaf, the smell of herbs, touched him, and he sought to put this on paper just as it came to him. It made him a poet. Where will you match for poetic sincerity that description of the old fisherman, his "old experienced coat hanging long and straight and brown as the yellow pine bark, glittering with so much smothered sunlight if you stood near enough." When he speaks thus you feel that he is akin to Ruskin in his great enthusiasm for Nature's wonders in small things.

There is something exhilarant and morning-like in his writing. It is crisp, and suggests the crackling of fire or the pungent odors of autumn. It is a product of outdoors, a thing which has escaped cultivation and grown up in the outlots. It is not so rich and rounded, perhaps, as indoor fruit, but it has a tang; it is like his own wild apples.

"I would have," he says, "my thoughts like wild apples, to be food for walkers, and will not warrant them to be palatable in the house." He had his wish; he can only be truly appreciated by outdoor men. His opinions are too audacious for the fireside. He shocks the steady by the way in which he girds at Christianity and sneers at churches. He is bitter in his denunciation of both priests and physicians. His criticism of Christ was that he taught imperfectly how to live. The sight of a church spire or a clergyman is to Thoreau as a red rag to a turkey cock. It sets him ruffling and crackling. But he is not so fierce as he looks. It was ordinary youthful affectation which made him talk of "his Buddha" as set over against "their Christ." But as you read farther you find that it was the cant and hypocrisy of some of its professors that set him railing at their religion. What he fought against was insincerity, not belief.

He did not wish a creed cut and measured for him, but must blaze his own way, have his own experience, and by favor of God find his own heaven. He wished to be free and open, ready to mind the least change in his spirit. On one side he was wise enough to know that all men cannot fit into the same hole, but on the other he was narrow enough not to credit men with a full measure of sincerity if they differed too widely from him. But perhaps such is the case with all reformers.

Society he claims to have found cheap and unsatisfying. The majority of people, he thought, led lives which stood for nothing; but gave their time over to the race for pleasure or pennies, all the while covering their better natures. He wanted men to work or play, or whatever they would be about, for love of it, and not for low ends. If he complained of his townsmen, it was because he thought they were not true to their best advices. And if he asked them to shun some things and embrace others, it was because he believed that life lay in the latter direction.

The usual criticism of Thoreau is that his ideas are unpractical. It will not do, so his critics say, if one is dissatisfied with one's fellows, to sulk in a corner and call names. I have tried in vain to prove from his writings that these persons are right in their point of view. It is easy to see how they have come to it by a superficial reading of the man, but it is not easy to see why one should persist in supposing that Thoreau ever wanted the world to live in a cottage on a pond's edge. If he chose to try an experiment or two, that was nobody's business,—or else it was everybody's,—and they should have thanked a pioneer. What Thoreau did proclaim from the housetops was, that the people he knew were chasing false ideals, laying up treasure on earth, intent on a fool's game indoors while all the time a parade was passing in the streets. It does not matter that the remedy he hit upon was a bit radical; it does not matter that there are some happy souls who can keep in the thick of the game and yet listen to the music out of their windows; he told the truth about the foolishness of the many as anybody who has spent a week in trade can testify. All he asked was that people be true to the call of their own genius. Always to keep clear-headed, fresh, and waiting, to be on tiptoe for the glorious facts of life,—that was the burden of his conjuration.

That he was forever calling his fellows to the front is one of the values of his writings. But his chief merit is the cheerful word that he has to say for life. Take it how you will, we are always in debate as to whether this life is, or is not, worth living. We can never come to a decision that we can call stable or that may not see change. But whether we decide one way or another, it is beyond dispute that the happiest way out of the matter is to believe that life is good. Otherwise we are soured at the start and at the last taste. There are too many men who pull long faces. When we find one who stands up and tells us that our little life is only the bud of some great flower, which with work we can make blossom gloriously, we may well hear him.

Thoreau is one of those men. "Every sound," says he, "is fraught with the mysterious assurance of health," and life is a good thing and will yield us something in proportion as we have courage and common-sense to face it. This is no sporadic idea which crops up unexpectedly in the intervals of gloom; it is a sense which pervades his whole work and makes you wonder how Stevenson could have called him a skulker. Passage after passage echoes with his shrill "chanticleer brag."

"It is very rare that you meet with an obstacle in this world which the humblest man has not the faculties to surmount."

"Love your life, poor as it is; meet it and live it; do not shun it and call it hard names."

"Mind your own business and endeavor to be what you were made."

He grumbles, we know, but he does not despair. He seeks to excite in us a "morning joy" which shall wake us to try with our might till the evening time, and the reward shall surely be with us. It is characteristic of him to end hopefully, and for us the thing is a gospel of hope and not of desperation. "The sun is but a morning star."

And so we look upon him as seldom smiling, never melancholy; severe with his neighbors, yet having in his heart the strands of sympathy, following his genius where it led him, and proclaiming his individuality in such strenuous terms that it sometimes becomes a pose; striving for simplicity of life because it gave him more time for living; an intimate of Nature, with an eye trained to catch the slightest nuance of her beauty, and a man's pen to set forth her glory and her sweetness and her strength; and, above everything, a heart to catch the meaning of it all, and a valiant word to say for life and living.

—Frederick M. Smith, "Thoreau,"
Critic, July 1900, pp. 60–67

EDWARD EMERSON "HENRY THOREAU AS REMEMBERED BY A YOUNG FRIEND" (1917)

Preface

I can remember Mr. Thoreau as early as I can remember anybody, excepting my parents, my sisters, and my nurse. He had the run of our house, and on two occasions was man of the house during my father's long absences. He was to us children the best kind of an older brother. He soon became the guide and companion of our early expeditions afield, and, later, the advisor of our first camping trips. I watched with him one of the last days of his life, when I was about seventeen years old.

Twenty-seven years ago I was moved to write a lecture, now taking form in this book, because I was troubled at the want of knowledge and understanding, both in Concord and among his readers at large, not only of his character, but of the events of his life,—which he did not tell to everybody,—and by the false impressions given by accredited writers who really knew him hardly at all. Mr. Lowell's essay on Thoreau is by no means worthy of the subject, and has unhappily prejudiced many persons against him.

When I undertook to defend my friend, I saw that I must at once improve my advantage of being acquainted, as a country doctor, with many persons who would never put pen to a line, but knew much about him— humble persons whom the literary men would never find out, like those who helped in the pencil mill, or in a survey, or families whom he came to know well and value in his walking over every square rod of Concord, or one of the brave and humane managers of the Underground Railroad, of which Thoreau was an operative. Also I had the good fortune to meet or correspond with six of the pupils of Thoreau and his brother John, all of whom bore witness to the very remarkable and interesting character of the teachers and their school.

Indeed, a half-century in advance of his time was Thoreau's attitude in many matters, as the change in thought and life in New England fifty years after his death shows. Of course, the people of that day went to temperance picnics, went fishing and huckleberrying and picked flowers, and enjoyed outdoors to that extent, and a very few took walks in the woods; but Thoreau, by the charm of his writings, led many young people to wood walks and river journeys, without gun or rod, but for the joy of out-of-doors in all the seasons in their splendor. A whole literature of this kind has sprung up since his day, unquestionably inspired by him. Nature study is in all the schools.

The interesting and original methods of teaching during the last thirty years recall those of the brothers; and where is corporal punishment?

As to the pencil business. I wish to show his dutiful and respectful attitude toward his family, and the important part he bore in improving their lead-pencil business and putting it for the time beyond competition in this country, giving them a good maintenance; although "his life was too valuable to him to put into lead-pencils." Suppose he had done so?

I wish to show that Thoreau, though brusque on occasions, was refined, courteous, kind and humane; that he had a religion and lived up to it.

"If you build castles in the air," he said, "that is where they should be. Now put the foundations under them."

An instinct, perhaps inherited, prompts me to introduce my subject with a text.

A Greek author, centuries ago, left these words behind, but not his name:

"You ask of the gods health and a beautiful old age; but your tables are opposed to it; they fetter the hands of Zeus."

I shall use yet another text; Wordsworth's lines:

"Yet was Rob Roy as wise as brave—
Forgive me if that phrase be strong—
A poet worthy of Rob Roy
Must scorn a timid song."

HENRY DAVID THOREAU

In childhood I had a friend,—not a house friend, domestic, stuffy in association; nor yet herdsman, or horseman, or farmer, or slave of bench, or shop, or office; nor of letters, nor art, nor society; but a free, friendly, youthful-seeming man, who wandered in from unknown woods or fields without knocking, —

"Between the night and day
When the fairy king has power,"—

as the ballad says, passed by the elders' doors, but straightway sought out the children, brightened up the wood-fire forthwith; and it seemed as if it were the effect of a wholesome brave north wind, more than of the armful of "cat-sticks" which he would bring in from the yard. His type was Northern,—

strong features, light brown hair, an open-air complexion with suggestion of a seafaring race; the mouth pleasant and flexible when he spoke, aquiline nose, deep-set but very wide-open eyes of clear blue grey, sincere, but capable of a twinkle, and again of austerity, but not of softness. Those eyes could not be made to rest on what was unworthy, saw much and keenly (but yet in certain worthy directions hardly at all), and did not fear the face of clay. A figure short and narrow, but thick; a carriage assuring of sturdy strength and endurance. When he walked to get over the ground one thought of a tireless machine, seeing his long, direct, uniform pace; but his body was active and well balanced, and his step could be light, as of one who could leap or dance or skate well at will.

His dress was strong and plain. He was not one of those little men who try to become great by exuvial methods of length of hair or beard, or broad collars, or conspicuous coat.

This youthful, cheery figure was a familiar one in our house, and when he, like the "Pied Piper of Hamelin," sounded his note in the hall, the children must needs come and hug his knees, and he struggled with them, nothing loath, to the fireplace, sat down and told stories, sometimes of the strange adventures of his childhood, or more often of squirrels, muskrats, hawks, he had seen that day, the Monitor-and-Merrimac duel of mud-turtles in the river, or the great Homeric battle of the red and black ants. Then he would make our pencils and knives disappear, and redeem them presently from our ears and noses; and last, would bring down the heavy copper warming-pan from the oblivion of the garret and unweariedly shake it over the blaze till reverberations arose within, and then opening it, let a white-blossoming explosion of popcorn fall over the little people on the rug.

Later, this magician appeared often in house or garden and always to charm.

Another tells of a picture that abides with her of this figure standing at the door of a friend, with one foot on the great stone step, surrounded by eager listeners, for he had just been seeing the doings, and hearing the songs, not of dull and busy workers,—great stupid humans,—but of those they above all desired to know about, the strange and shy dwellers in the deep woods and along the rivers.

Surely a True Thomas of Ercildoune returned from his stay in Faërie with its queen's gift of a "tongue that shall never lie."

And yet another tells how, though this being sometimes looked uncouth to her, like a "long-shore-man,"—she could never quite forgive the sin that his garments sat strangely on him,—when he told his tale to the ring of children it was, as it were, a defence, for he seemed abashed by them. Perhaps as the years came on him he began to feel with the sad Vaughan concerning childhood —

"I cannot reach it, and my striving eye
Dazzles at it, as at Eternity";

and his hope was with him to keep

"that innocence alive,
The white designs that children drive."

And it was this respect for unspoiled nature in the creatures of the wood that was his passport to go into their dwelling-places and report to the children that were like enough to them to care to hear.

This youth, who could pipe and sing himself, made for children pipes of all sorts, of grass, of leaf-stalk of squash and pumpkin, handsome but fragrant flageolets of onion tops, but chiefly of the golden willow-shoot, when the rising sap in spring loosens the bark. As the children grew older, he led them to choice huckleberry hills, swamps where the great high-bush blueberries grew, guided to the land of the chestnut and barberry, and more than all, opened that land of enchantment into which, among dark hemlocks, blood-red maples, and yellowing birches, we floated in his boat, and freighted it with leaves and blue gentians and fragrant grapes from the festooning vines.

A little later, he opened another romantic door to boys full of Robin Hood; made us know for ourselves that nothing was truer than

"'T is merry! 't is merry in the good green wood;
When mavis and merle are singing!" —

told us how to camp and cook, and especially how, at still midnight, in the middle of Walden, to strike the boat with an oar,—and, in another minute, the hills around awoke, cried out, one after another with incredible and startling *crash,* so that the Lincoln Hill and Fairhaven, and even Conantum, took up the tale of the outrage done to their quiet sleep. He taught us also the decorum and manners of the wood, which gives no treasures or knowledge to the boisterous and careless; the humanity not to kill a harmless snake because it was ugly, or in revenge for a start; and that the most zealous collector of eggs must always leave the mother-bird most of her eggs, and not go too often to watch the nest.

He showed boys with short purses, but legs stout, if short, how to reach the nearer mountains,—Wachusett, then Monadnoc,—and live there in a bough-house, on berries and meal and beans, happy as the gods on Olympus, and like them, in the clouds and among the thunders.

He always came, after an expedition afar, to tell his adventures and wonders, and all his speech was simple and clean and high. Yet he was associated with humble offices also, for, like the friendly Troll in the tale, he deftly came to the rescue when any lock or hinge or stove needed the hand of a master.

I saw this man ever gravely and simply courteous, quietly and effectively helpful, sincere, always spoken of with affection and respect by my parents and other near friends;—knew him strongly but not noisily interested on the side of Freedom in the great struggle that then stirred the country.

When the red morning began to dawn in Kansas and at Harper's Ferry, I saw him deeply moved, and though otherwise avoiding public meetings and organized civic action, come to the front and, moved to the core, speak among the foremost against oppression.

Fatal disease laid hold on him at this time and I saw him face his slow death with cheerful courage. Then I went away from home, and began to read his books; but in the light of the man I knew. I met persons who asked questions about him, had heard strange rumours and made severe criticisms; then I read essays and satires, even by one whose gifts render such obtuseness well-nigh unpardonable, in which he was held lightly or ridiculed—heard that he was pompous, rustic, conceited, that his thoughts were not original, that he strove to imitate another; that even his observations on natural history were of no value, and not even new.

Even in Concord among persons who had known him slightly at school or in the young society of his day, or had some acquaintance with him in village relations, I found that, while his manifest integrity commanded respect, he was regarded unsympathetically by many, and not only the purposes, but many of the events of his life were unknown. The indictments are numerous, but of varying importance:— When a school-teacher, he once flogged several pupils at school without just cause. Once some woodlots were burned through his carelessness. He carried a tree through the town while the folks came home from meeting. He, while living at Walden, actually often went out to tea, and carried pies home from his mother's larder. He let others pay his taxes. He was lazy. He was selfish. He did not make money, as he might have done for himself and family by attending to his business. He did not believe in Government and was unpatriotic. He was irreligious.

What, then, was Thoreau?

The man of whom I speak was the friend of my childhood and early youth, and living and dead has helped me, and in no common way. It is a natural duty, then, to acknowledge thankfully this help and render homage to his memory, because his name and fame, his life and lesson, have become part of America's property and are not merely the inheritance of the children who dwell by the Musketaquid.

Three of his friends have already written of him, yet I can add to their testimony, explain and illustrate some things more fully. Also I have gleaned in Concord homes and fields from others, now dead, who would never have written them, memories that might soon have faded away, and have done what I may to preserve them. To many persons he is but a name, or a character pictured by artists of varying skill, sometimes unsympathetic, if not unfriendly. Yet I will say alike to all, Let us fairly review the ground you perhaps deem well known, and see if with the light of the latter years, and the better perspective, you may not find values there, passed by as nought in earlier years.

David Henry Thoreau (his baptismal names were afterward transposed) was born in a farmhouse on the "Virginia Road," a mile and a half east of the village, July 12, 1817. Next year the family moved to Chelmsford, then to Boston, where his schooling began. They returned to Concord when he was six years old, and remained there.

Pleasant pictures remain of the children and the home. The father, John Thoreau, whose father came from the Isle of Jersey, was a kindly, quiet man, not without humour, who, though a canny and not especially ambitious mechanic, was intelligent and always tried to give good wares to his customers. He and his wife knew Concord woods thoroughly, and first led their children into them to study birds and flowers. The mother, Cynthia Dunbar, of Scotch ancestry, was spirited, capable, and witty, with an edge to her wit on occasion, but there is abundant and hearty testimony from many of her neighbours—to which I can add my own—to her great kindness, especially to young people, often shown with much delicacy; also to her thoughtfulness and her skill in making home pleasant, even on the smallest capital, by seasoning spare diet and humble furnishings by native good taste, and, more than all, by cheerfulness; for this good woman knew how to keep work and care in their proper places, and give life and love the precedence. A near neighbour and friend told me that for years the family had on ordinary days neither tea, coffee, sugar, nor other luxuries, that the girls might have the piano which their early musical taste showed they would want, and the education of all, especially the sending of the younger son to college, might be provided for; and yet her table was always attractive, and the food abundant and appetizing. There were two daughters and two sons, of whom Henry was the younger.

This little picture of Henry Thoreau's childhood survives, told by his mother to an old friend: John and Henry slept together in the trundlebed, that obsolete and delightful children's bed, telescoping on large castors under the parental four-poster. John would go to sleep at once, but Henry often lay long awake. His mother found the little boy lying so one night, long after he had gone upstairs, and said, "Why, Henry dear, why don't you go to sleep?" "Mother," said he, "I have been looking through the stars to see if I couldn't see God behind them."

Henry prepared himself for Harvard College in the Concord schools. Out of hours he attended the dame-school taught by Nature. She smoothed the way from the village by ice or glassy water, or baited the footpath to the woods with berries, and promised fabulous beasts and birds and fishes to the adventuring boy with box-trap, fish-hook, or flint-lock shotgun. With these Thoreau was very expert, though he early passed through that grade in this academy and left them behind. All of the family had out-of-door instincts, and the relation of the children to their parents and each other was unusually happy and harmonious.

He had such opportunities for formal spiritual training as were then afforded by the Unitarian and Orthodox churches in Concord, at both of which his family attended worship.

The comparatively small amount which it then cost to maintain a boy at Harvard (which, it must be remembered, strange as it may sound, was, and is, a charitable institution), was enough seriously to strain the resources of the family. The mother had saved for the emergency, as has been said, the older sister helped, the aunts reinforced, and Henry helped by winning and keeping a scholarship and (as was the wholesome custom of the day for a large proportion of the students) by teaching school for periods during the College course. But, thinking over the sacrifices, I was told, by a friend of his mother's, that he said that the result was not worth the outlay and the sacrifice it had called for.

Evidence of independence and character appear in his student life. Though an unusually good student of the classics and of mathematics, as his after use of these studies fully proves, he saw that the curriculum was narrow, and to make the sacrifice worth while he must not stick too closely to it, lured by College rank and honours and the chance of making a figure at Commencement. So believing, even although the loss of marks involved nearly cost the important relief of a scholarship and brought some disapproval of his teachers, he deliberately devoted much of his time to the College library—an opportunity and prize to a country boy who knew how to avail himself of it in those days, which now, when public and private libraries are common, it is hard to realize; and he acquired there a knowledge of good authors remarkable then or now. When I went to College he counselled me that the library was perhaps the best gift Harvard had to offer, and through life he constantly used it, braving the bull-dog official that foolish custom kept there to keep the books useless, and when he was surly, going at once to the College authorities and obtaining special privileges as a man not to be put aside when in the right.

He graduated in 1837 with fair rank and an excellent character and received the degree of Bachelor of Arts.

Highly interesting it is to find that Thoreau at twenty, in his "Part" at Commencement, pleaded for the life that, later, he carried out. An observer from the stars, he imagines, "of our planet and the restless animal for whose sake it was contrived, where he found one man to admire with him his fair dwelling-place, the ninety and nine would be scraping together a little of the gilded dust upon its surface. . . .

"Let men, true to their natures, cultivate the moral affections, lead manly and independent lives;. . . The sea will not stagnate, the earth will be as green as ever, and the air as pure. This curious world which we inhabit is more wonderful than it is convenient; more beautiful than it is useful; it is more to be admired and enjoyed than used. The order of things should be somewhat reversed; the seventh should be man's day of toil, wherein to earn his living by the sweat of his brow; and the other six his Sabbath of the affections and the soul,—in which to range this widespread garden, and drink in the soft influences and sublime revelations of Nature."

To teach was the work that usually offered itself to the hand of a country youth fresh from college. Failing to find at once a better opportunity afar, Thoreau took charge of the Town School in Concord, but, it is said, proving heretical as to Solomon's maxim concerning the rod, did not satisfy the Committeeman, who was a deacon. Deacon———sat through one session with increasing disapproval, waiting for corporal chastisement, the corner-stone of a sound education, and properly reproved the teacher. The story which one of Thoreau's friends told me was, that with a queer humour,—he was very young,—he, to avoid taking the town's money, without giving the expected equivalent, in the afternoon punished six children, and that evening resigned the place where such methods were required. One of the pupils, then a little boy, who is still living, all through life has cherished his grievance, not understanding the cause. But we may be sure his punishment would not have been cruel, for Henry Thoreau always liked and respected children. Later this pupil came to know and like him. He said "he seemed the sort of a man that wouldn't willingly hurt a fly," and, except on this occasion, had shown himself mild and kindly.

But next year began a different sort of teaching. John and Henry took the Concord Academy. John was the principal, perhaps twenty-three years old, of pleasant face, gay, bright, sympathetic, while the more original and serious younger brother was, I think, troubled with consciousness, and though very human, un-demonstrative. He mainly took charge of the classical department. Twenty-seven years ago I had the fortune to talk or correspond with six of their pupils and found that all remembered the school pleasantly, several with enthusiasm, and in their accounts of it, the influence of the character of the teachers and the breadth and quality of the instruction appear remarkable. One scholar said: "It was a peculiar school, there was never a boy flogged or threatened, yet I never saw so absolutely military discipline. How it was done I scarcely know. Even the incorrigible were brought into line."

This scholar, who, it should be remembered, was only John's pupil and one who craved affection, said to me: "Henry was not loved. He was a conscientious teacher, but rigid. He would not take a man's money for nothing: if a boy were sent to him, he could make him do all he could. No, he was not disagreeable. I learned to understand him later. I think that he was then in the green-apple stage."

Another scholar, who was more with Henry, told a different story, remembering both brothers with great affection and gratitude. He said that after morning prayers, one or other of the brothers often made a little address to their scholars, original and interesting, to put their minds in proper train for the day's work. Henry's talks especially remain with him: on the seasons, their cause, their advantages, their adaptation to needs of organic life; their beauty, which he brought actually into the school-room by his description; on design in the universe, strikingly illustrated for children's minds; on profanity, treated in a way, fresh, amusing, and sensible. At these times you could have heard a pin drop in the school-room. More than this, he won their respect. Such methods seem natural enough now, but were quite novel in those days.

Another says: "What impressed me, then and later, was Henry's knowledge of Natural History; a keen observer and great student of things, and a very pleasant talker. He reminded me more of Gilbert White of Selborne than any other character."

These brothers were just enough unlike to increase the interest and happiness of their relation. It was one of closest sympathy. It is believed that they were both charmed by one young girl: but she was denied them and passed out of their horizon. In reading what Thoreau says of Love and the two poems relating to his loss one sees that even his disappointment elevated his life.

The first of these is called "Sympathy," in which the lady is disguised as "a gentle boy." I give verses of the other below:

TO THE MAIDEN IN THE EAST

Low in the eastern sky
Is set thy glancing eye;
And though its gracious light
Ne'er riseth to my sight,
Yet every star that climbs
Above the gnarlèd limbs
 Of yonder hill
Conveys thy gentle will.
Believe I knew thy thought;
And that the zephyrs brought
Thy kindest wishes through,
As mine they bear to you;
That some attentive cloud
Did pause amid the crowd
 Over my head,
While gentle things were said.
Believe the thrushes sung,
And that the flower-bells rung,
That herbs exhaled their scent
And hearts knew what was meant,
The trees a welcome waved,
And lakes their margins laved,
 When thy free mind
To my retreat did wind
* * * * * *

Still will I strive to be
As if thou were with me;
Whatever path I take
It shall be, for thy sake,
Of gentle slope and wide
As thou were by my side
* * * * * *

During the summer vacation of their school the brothers made together that happy voyage, since famous, on the Rivers, but it was not in their dreams how soon Death, coming suddenly and in strange form, was to sunder their earthly lives. John, in full tide of happy life, died in a few days of lock-jaw following a most trifling cut. The shock, the loss, and the sight of his brother's terrible suffering at the end, for a time overthrew Henry so utterly that a friend told me he sat still in the house, could do nothing, and his sisters led him out passive to try to help him.

Near the same time died suddenly a beautiful child, with whom he had played and talked almost daily, in the house of near friends where he had a second home.

He had gone into a Valley of Sorrow, but when, first, the dream of helpmate and guiding presence passed away, and then his nearest companion was taken from him, who shall say but that the presence of these blessings would have prevented his accomplishing his strange destiny? For his genius was solitary, and though his need for friendly and social relation with his kind was great, it was occasional, and to his lonely happiness the world will owe the best gifts he has left. And even as these his most prized and his coveted ties were parting or becoming impossible, new ones, more helpful if less desired, were presenting.

It is hard to name another town in Middlesex where the prevailing influences would have given the same push to the growth of his strong and original character as did those which were then in Concord. For from various causes, there early came that awakening of thought and spirit soon to spread wide in New England, then lethargic in physical prosperity, formal and sleepy in religion, selfish in politics, and provincial in its literature. At this period the young Thoreau came into constant contact with many persons resident or visiting there, full of the courage, the happiness, and the hope given by thoughts of a freer, nobler relation to God, and simpler and more humane ones to man. But be it distinctly understood that Thoreau was not created by the Transcendental Epoch, so-called, though, without doubt, his growth was stimulated by kindred ideas. His thoughtfulness in childhood, his independent course in college themes and early journals, prove that Thoreau was Thoreau and not the copy of another. His close association, under the same roof, for months, with the maturer Emerson may, not unnaturally, have tinged his early writings, and some superficial trick of manner or of speech been unconsciously acquired, as often happens. But this is all that can be granted. Entire independence, strong individuality were Thoreau's distinguishing traits, and his foible was not subserviency, but combativeness in conversation, as his friends knew almost too well. Conscious imitation is not to be thought of as a possibility of this strong spirit.

Henry bravely recovered himself from the blow his brother's loss had been at first, when those who knew him said it seemed as if a part of himself had been torn away. Music seems to have been the first consoling voice that came to him, though great repairing Nature had silently begun to heal her son. He was thrown more upon himself than before, and then he went out to her. Yet he cherished his friends, as his fine letters at this time show. In the next few years he worked with his father in the pencil shop (where now the Concord Library stands), and wrote constantly, and the woods and river drew him to them in each spare hour. He wrote for the *Dial* as the organ of the new thought of the region and hour, though it paid nothing for articles, and he generously helped edit it. He relieved his friend Emerson from tasks hopeless to him by his skill in gardening and general household works, and went for a time to Staten Island as a private tutor to the son of Emerson's older brother, William. In this visit to New York he became acquainted with Horace Greeley, who appreciated his work and showed himself always generous and helpful in bringing it to publication in various magazines, and getting him paid for it.

Of Henry Thoreau as a mechanic this much is known: that he helped his father more or less in his business of making lead-pencils; was instrumental in getting a better pencil than had been made up to that time in this country, which received a prize at the Mechanics' Fair; and that, when this triumph had been achieved, he promptly dropped the business which promised a good maintenance to himself and family: which unusual proceeding was counted to him for righteousness by a very few, and for laziness by most.

This is the principal charge made against him in his own neighbourhood. Many solid practical citizens, whose love of wild Nature was about like Dr. Johnson's, asserted that he neglected a good business, which he might have worked with profit for his family and himself, to idle in the woods, and this cannot be forgiven.

From my relation to the Thoreau family I knew something of their black-lead business after Henry's death, while carried on by his sister, and later investigated the matter with some care and with results that are surprising. I will tell the story briefly.

John Thoreau, senior, went into the pencil business on his return to Concord in 1823. He made at first such bad pencils as were then made in America, greasy, gritty, brittle, inefficient, but tried to improve them, and did so. Henry found in the College library, in an encyclopædia published in Edinburgh, what the graphite ("black lead") was mixed with in the good German pencils, viz., a certain fine Bavarian clay; while here, glue, with a little spermaceti, or bayberry wax, was used. The Thoreaus procured that clay, stamped with a crown as a royal monopoly, and baked it with the lead, and thus got a harder, blacker pencil than any here, but gritty. Then it appears they invented a process, very simple, but which at once put their black lead for fineness at the head of all manufactured in America. This was simply to have the narrow churn-like chamber around the mill-stones prolonged some seven feet high, opening into a broad, close, flat box, a sort of shelf. Only lead-dust that was fine enough to rise to that height, carried by an upward draught of air, and lodge in the box was used, and the rest ground over. I talked with the mechanic who showed me this, and who worked with the Thoreaus from the first, was actively helpful in the improvements and at last bought out the business from Mrs. Thoreau and carried it on for years,—and with others who knew something of the matter. The evidence is strong that Henry's mind and hand were active in the rapid carrying of this humble business to the front. It seems to be probable that, whether the father thought out the plan alone or with Henry, it was the latter's mechanical skill that put it into working shape. Henry is said also to have made the machine used in making their last and best pencil, which drilled a round hole into a solid wood and cut lead to fit it, as an axle does a wheel-box, instead of the usual method of having the wood in two parts glued together after filling.

A friend who attended, in 1849, a fashionable school in Boston, kept by an English lady, tells me that the drawing-teacher used to direct the pupils to "ask at the art store for a *Thoreau pencil,* for they are the best"; for them they then had to pay a quarter of a dollar apiece. Henry Thoreau said of the best pencil when it was achieved, that it could not compete with the Fabers' because it cost more to make. They received, I am told, six dollars a gross for good pencils.

But there is another chapter to the black-lead story not so well known. About 1848-49 the process of electrotyping was invented, it is claimed, in Boston. It was a secret process, and a man engaged in it, knowing the Thoreau lead was the best, ordered it in quantity from Mr. John Thoreau, the latter guarding carefully the secret of his method, and the former concealing the purpose for which he used it. Mr. Thoreau, senior, therefore increased his business and received good prices, at first ten dollars a pound,—though later it gradually fell to two dollars,—and sometimes selling five hundred pounds a year. After a time the purpose for which their lead was bought was found out by the Thoreaus and they sold it to various firms until after the death of Mr. John Thoreau and his son Henry, when the business was sold by Mrs. Thoreau.

Now, when Henry Thoreau succeeded in making his best pencil and deliberately renounced his partnership, saying that he could not improve on that product, and that his life was too valuable to him to put what remained of it into pencils, the principal trade of the family was in lead to the electrotypers, and after 1852 few pencils were made, and then merely to cover up the more profitable business, for, if the secret were known, it might be destroyed.

As his father became feebler Henry had to look after the business to some degree for the family, and to give some help after his father's death, though Miss Sophia attended to the correspondence, accounts, and directing and shipping the lead (brought in bulk, after grinding, to the house, that its destination might not be known) to the customers in Boston and New York. Yet Henry had to oversee the mill, bring the lead down, and help at the heavier part of boxing and packing, and this I am assured by two friends he did until his fatal sickness. The work was done in an upstairs room, but the impalpable powder so pervaded the house, owing to the perfection of its reduction, that a friend tells me that, on opening Miss Sophia's piano, he found the keys coated with it. Thoreau's exposure to the elements and spare diet have been charged with shortening his life. He would probably much earlier have succumbed to a disease, hereditary in his family, had he held more closely to his trade with its irritant dust. The part he was obliged to bear in it certainly rendered him more susceptible to pulmonary disease, which his out-of-door life delayed.

Thus it appears that this ne'er-do-well worked at, and by his reading and thought and skill so helped on the improvements in the family's business, that they were far in advance of their competitors, and then, though he did not care to put his life into that trade, preferring trade with the Celestial City, yet found time quietly to oversee for the family the business which gave them a very good maintenance, and, when it was necessary, to work at it with his hands while health remained.

Yet he did not think fit to button-hole his neighbours on the street and say, "You mistake, Sir; I am not idle."

His own Spartan wants of plain food, strong clothing, and telescope, and a few books, with occasional travel in the cheapest way, were supplied in a variety of other ways. For he had what is called in New England, "faculty"; was a good gardener, mechanic, and emergency-man. He could do all sorts of jobbing and tinkering well at home and for other people. One or two fences were standing until lately, in town, which he built; he planted for his friend Emerson his barren pasture by Walden with pines. He especially loved to raise melons. I once went to a melon-party at his mother's with various people, young and old, where his work had furnished the handsome and fragrant pink or salmon fruit on which alone we were regaled; and he, the gardener, came in to help entertain the guests.

He wrote articles for magazines which brought him some money, and books, now classics, but hardly saleable in his day.

But his leading profession was that of a land-surveyor. In this, as in his mechanics, he did the best possible work. I remember his showing me some brass instrument which he had made or improved, with his own hands. Those who assisted him tell me that he was exceedingly particular, took more offsets than any other surveyor in these parts, often rectified bounds carelessly placed before. It amused him to call his friend Emerson from his study to ask him why he would steal his neighbour's meadow, showing him his hedge and ditch well inside the land that his good-natured neighbour, Sam Staples, had just bought and was entitled to by his deed, though the latter said, "No matter, let the ditch be the line," and would take no money.

Our leading surveyor, following Thoreau, told me that he soon learned by running over again Thoreau's lines that he was sure to find his plans minutely accurate if he made in them correction required by the variation of the compass, some degrees since Thoreau's day. Never but once did he find an error, and that was not in angular measurement and direction, but in distance, one chain, probably an error in count of his assistant. Thoreau did work in the spirit of George Herbert's prayer two hundred years before: —

"Teach me, my God, my King,
    In all things Thee to see,
And what I do in any thing
    To do it as for Thee.

"Not rudely as a beast
    To run into an action,
But still to make Thee prepossessed
    And give it its perfection."

He wrote: "I would not be one of those who will foolishly drive a nail into mere lath and plastering: such a deed would keep me awake nights. Give me a hammer and let me feel for the furring. Drive a nail home, and clinch it so faithfully, that you can wake up in the night and think of your work with satisfaction, a work at which you would not be ashamed to invoke the Muse.

So will help you God, and so only. Every nail driven should be as another rivet in the machine of the universe, you carrying on the work." Small things for him symbolized great.

Thoreau enjoyed his surveying, and the more if it led him into the wild lands *East of the Sun, West of the Moon*. But he construed his business largely, looking deeper than its surface. While searching for their bounds with his townsmen and neighbours in village, swamp, and woodlot, he found everywhere, marked far more distinctly than by blazed black-oak tree or stake and stones, lines, imaginary truly, but forming bounds to their lives more impassable than stone. Many he saw imprisoned for life, and he found these walls already beginning to hedge in his horizon, shut out the beautiful free life of his hope, and saw that, in the end, the converging walls might even shut out the blessed Heaven. What if the foundations of these walls were justice, natural right, human responsibility; and the first tier of blocks of experience, goodwill, and reverence, if the upper stories were fashion, conservatism, unenlightened public opinion, party politics, dishonest usage of trade, immoral law, and the arch and key-stones the dogmas still nominally accepted by Christian Congregational churches in the first half of the nineteenth century? Who would take a vault with the Last Judgment frescoed on it, even by Michael Angelo, in exchange for Heaven's blue cope, painted by the oldest Master with cloud and rainbow, and jewelled by night with his worlds and suns?

> "Heaven lies about us in our infancy,"

sang the poet, and Thoreau, mainly to save a view of those heavens, and, that the household clatter and village hum drowned not the music of the spheres, went into the woods for a time.

His lifelong friend, Mr. Harrison G.O. Blake, of Worcester, pointed out that Thoreau, feeling that the best institutions, home, school, public organization, were aimed to help the man or woman to lead a worthy life—"instead of giving himself to some profession or business, whereby he might earn those superfluities which men have agreed to call a living; instead of thus earning a position in society and so acting upon it; instead of trying to see how the town, the State, the Country might be better governed, so that future generations might come nearer to the ideal life, he proposed to lead that life at once himself, as far as possible." To this cause "he early turned with simplicity and directness."

When the spirit clearly shows a man of high purpose what his gift is, or may be, his neighbours must not insist on harnessing him into a team,—just one more to pull through their crude or experimental reform,—or require of him exact following of village ways or city fashion. We all know persons whose quiet light shining apart from public action has more illuminated and guided our lives.

As a man who once had some knowledge of the habits of our people, such as a country doctor acquires, I may say that I found that the root of much disease, disappointment, and blight was, that few persons stand off and look at the way their days pass, but live minute by minute, and as is customary, and therefore never find that the day, the year, and the lifetime pass in preparation to live, but the time to live never comes—here, at least. Thoreau couldn't do this, for he was a surveyor—one who oversees the ground, and takes account of direction and distance. Be sure his life at Walden was an experiment in keeping means and ends in their proper relative positions. He was not one who lived to eat. Speaking of what his solitary and distant wood-walks were worth to him, he writes in his journal: "I do not go there to get my dinner, but to get that sustenance which dinners only preserve me to enjoy, without which dinners were a vain repetition." "We dine," he said, "at the sign of the shrub-oak."

"If I should sell both my forenoons and afternoons to society," wrote Thoreau in his journal, "as most appear to do, I am sure that for me there would be nothing left worth living for. I trust that I shall never thus sell my birthright for a mess of pottage. I wish to suggest that a man may be very industrious, and yet not spend his time well. There is no more fatal blunderer than he who consumes the greater part of his life getting his living. All great enterprises are self-supporting. The poet, for instance, must sustain his body by his poetry, as a steam planing-mill feeds its boilers with the shavings it makes. You must get your living by loving."

Mr. Emerson noted in his journal, a few years before this Walden venture: "Henry made last night the fine remark that 'as long as a man stands in his own way, everything seems to be in his way,—governments, society, and even the sun and moon and stars, as astrology may testify.'" Now he put aside doubt and custom, and all went well.

In these changed days, when the shores of our beautiful pond have been devastated by fire and moths and rude and reckless visitors, when the white sand and whiter stony margin of the cove have been defiled by coke cinders, when even the clear waters have ebbed, it is pleasant to turn to the picture of what Thoreau looked out on seventy years ago: "When I first paddled a boat on Walden it was completely surrounded by thick and lofty pine and oak woods and in some of its coves grapevines had run over the trees next the water and formed bowers under which a boat could pass. The hills which form its shores were so steep, and the woods on them were then so high, that, as you looked down from the west end, it had the appearance of an amphitheatre for some kind of sylvan spectacle."

His sojourn in Walden woods, as seen by his townsmen, told by himself, and rumoured abroad, made a stronger impression, and more obvious, than any part of his strong and original life. He is more thought of as a hermit, preaching by life and word a breach with society, than in any other way; and this notion is so widespread that it seems to require a few words here.

And, first, it must be remembered that the part of his life lived in the Walden house was from July 4, 1845, to September 6, 1847, just two years and two months of his forty-four years of life. They were happy, wholesome years, helping his whole future by their teachings. He did not go there as a Jonah crying out on Nineveh, but simply for his own purposes, to get advantageous conditions to do his work, exactly as a lawyer or banker or any man whose work requires concentration is sure to leave his home to do it. He prepared there his first and perhaps best book, the "Week on the Concord and Merrimac Rivers," for publication; he tried his spiritual, intellectual, social and economic experiment, and recorded it; and incidentally made an interesting survey and history of one of the most beautiful and remarkable ponds in Massachusetts. Meantime he earned the few dollars that it took to keep him.

Unlike the prophet at Nineveh, he went to the woods to mind his own business in the strictest sense, and there found the freedom, joy, and blessed influences that came of so simple and harmless a life, nearer the flowers and stars, and the God that the child had looked for behind the stars, free from the millstones, even the carved and gilded ones, which customary town life hangs around the necks of most of us. Then, when he went down into the village, found the good people set at such elementary problems as they seem to us now, and then to him,—whether it was right for this country to uphold human slavery, or for man to withhold from woman her right in her property, or for persons to get somewhat drunk frequently, or for a citizen to violate a law requiring him to become a slave hunter, or whether an innocent, blameless person dying, not a church member, had any chance of escaping the terrible wrath, not of the Adversary, but of his Maker, which should be exercised on him for untold millions of years,—or perhaps found advanced philosophers spending their time discussing if more aspiration cannot come from eating upward-growing vegetables like wheat, instead of burrowing, darkling carrots or grovelling turnips; or the soul may not be polluted by eating "raised bread;" or again, when he found the people spending their rare holidays in the bar-room, or the old-time muster-field, strewn with fired ram-rods, and redolent of New England rum and bad language and worse discipline, or, having forced their farm-work that they might do so, spending days listening to the foul or degrading details of the Criminal Court session, or cheering blindly for Webster after his deliberate desertion of all that he had once stood for to best New England,—no wonder, then, I say, that he rejoiced that his neck was out of such yokes, and his eyes washed clearer by Walden water, and, as his generous instinct always bade him share the knowledge he won, he

"Chanted the bliss of his abode,
To men imprisoned in their own."

By village firesides on winter evenings his foolish whim was gossiped over with pity; but the wind harping gloriously in the pine boughs over his hut, as he sat at his Spartan feast below, sang to him like the Sea-King, whose

"hands that loved the oar,
Now dealt with the rippling harp-gold, and he sang of the shaping of
    earth,
And how the stars were lighted, and where the winds had birth;
And the gleam of the first of summers on the yet untrodden grass.
What though above the roof-tree they heard the thunder pass,
Yet had they tales for song-craft and the blossoming garth of rhyme,
Tales of the framing of all things, and the entering in of Time
From the halls of the outer heaven, so near they knew the door."

Hear his story of his high company:—
"I have occasional visits in the long winter evenings, when the snow falls fast and the wind howls in the woods, from an old settler and original proprietor, who is reported to have dug Walden Pond and stoned it around, and fringed it with pine woods; who tells me stories of old time and new eternity; and between us we manage to pass a cheerful evening with social mirth and pleasant views of things, even without apples and cider,—a most wise and humorous friend, whom I love much, who keeps himself more secret than ever did Goffe or Whalley; and though he is thought to be dead, none can show where he is buried. An elderly dame, too, dwells in my neighbourhood, invisible to most persons, in whose odorous herb-garden I love to stroll sometimes, gathering simples and listening to her fables; for she has a genius of unequalled fertility, and her memory runs back farther than mythology, and she can tell me the original of every fable, and on what fact every one is founded, for the incidents occurred when she was young. A ruddy and lusty

old dame, who delights in all weathers and seasons, and is likely to outlive all her children yet."

Again he wrote: "I silently smiled at my incessant good fortune."

They err entirely who suppose that he counselled every one to build hermitages in the woods, break with society and live on meal. This he distinctly disavows, but makes a plea for simple and brave living, not drowned in the details, not merely of cooking, sweeping, and dusting, but of politics, whether parish, town, state, or federal, and even of societies, religious, professional, charitable, or social, for, after all, these are but preparatory,—police regulations on a larger or smaller scale,—designed as means to make life possible, and not to be pursued as ends. Even by Walden, as he tells us, he wore a path, and he found that his life there was falling into it: evidently he saw it was incomplete, so, keeping its sweet kernel, he left the shell. In cheerful mood, years after, he discusses the matter: "Why did I change? Why did I leave the woods? I do not think that I can tell. I have often wished myself back. I do not know any better how I came to go there. Perhaps it is none of my business, even if it is yours. Perhaps I wanted change. There was a little stagnation, it may be, about 2 o'clock in the afternoon. Perhaps if I lived there much longer, I might live there forever. One would think twice before he accepted Heaven on such terms."

Taking a bird's-eye view of institutions and marking their provisional and makeshift and hence transitory character, he writes in his journal: "As for dispute about solitude and society, any comparison is impertinent. It is an idling down on a plain at the base of a mountain instead of climbing steadily to its top. Of course, you will be glad of all the society you can get to go up with. 'Will you go to Glory with me?' is the burden of the song. It is not that we love to be alone, but that we love to soar, and, when we do soar, the company grows thinner and thinner, till there is none at all. It is either the *Tribune* or the plain, a sermon on the Mount, or a very private ecstasy higher up. Use all the society that will abet you."

And now as to the belief that he was hard, stern, selfish, or misanthropic. Truly he was undemonstrative; a sisterly friend said of him, "As for taking his arm, I should as soon think of taking the arm of an elm-tree as Henry's"; and he, himself, said, "When I am dead you will find swamp-oak written on my heart"; but under this oak-bark was friendship and loyalty in the tough grain, through and through. He was a friend, "even to the altars," too sincere and true to stoop to weakness from his noble ideal. Hear his creed of sincere yet austere friendship as he states it in his journal: —

"It steads us to be as true to children and boors as to God himself. It is the only attitude which will suit all occasions, it only will make the Earth yield her increase, and by it do we effectually expostulate with the wind. If I run against a post, *that* is the remedy. I would meet the morning and evening on very sincere grounds. When the sun introduces me to a new day, I silently say to myself, 'Let us be faithful all round. We will do justice and receive it.' Something like this is the charm of Nature's demeanour towards us; strict conscientiousness and disregard of us when we have ceased to have regard to ourselves. So she can never offend us. How true she is, and never swerves. In her most genial moment her laws are as steadfastly and relentlessly fulfilled—though the Decalogue is rhymed and set to sweetest music—as in her sternest. Any exhibition of affection, as an inadvertent word, or act or look, seems premature, as if the time were not ripe for it, like the buds which the warm days near the end of winter cause to push out and unfold before the frosts are yet gone."

Again he writes that in the relation of friends: "There is no ambition except virtue, for why should we go round about who may go direct? All those contingencies which the philanthropist, statesman, and housekeeper write so many books to meet are simply and quietly settled in the intercourse of friends."

I can bring my own witness and that of many others to his quiet, dutiful, loyal attitude to his mother and father, how respectfully he listened to them, whether he agreed with them or not; how in his quiet way he rendered all sorts of useful and skillful help in domestic and household matters. After his father's death his mother said, "But for this I should never have seen the tender side of Henry," who had nursed him with loving care. His family were a little anxious and troubled when he went to Walden, fearing danger and hardship in this life, and they missed him; but they sympathized with his desire and wanted him to carry it out as pleased him. He came constantly home to see them and to help them in garden or house, and also dropped in at other friendly homes in the village, where he was always welcome at table or fireside.

The mighty indictment that he was not honest in his experiment, for he did not live exclusively on his own meal and rice, but often accepted one of his mother's pies, or chanced in at a friend's at supper-time, seems too frivolous to notice, but since it is so often made, I will say that Henry Thoreau, while he could have lived uncomplainingly where an Esquimau could, on *tripe de roche* lichen and blubber, if need were (for never was man less the slave of appetite and luxury), was not a prig, nor a man of so small pattern as to be tied to a rule-of-thumb in diet, and ungraciously thrust back on his loving mother her gift. Nor was there the slightest reason that he should forego his long-established habit of appearing from time to time at nightfall, a welcome guest at the fireside of friends. He came for friendship, not for food. "I was never so effectually deterred from frequenting a man's house by any kind of Cerberus whatever," he says, "as by the parade one made about dining me, which I took to be a very polite and roundabout hint never to trouble him so again." And, fully to satisfy cavil, it is certain that he overpaid his keep in mere handiwork, which he convinced all friends that it was a favour to him to allow him to do for them (such as burning out chimneys, setting stoves, door-knobs, or shutters to right), to make no mention of higher service.

He was not a professing philanthropist, though steadily friendly to his kind as he met them. His eminent, but unappreciative, critic, Lowell, said severely, among other charges, "Did his plan of life seem selfish—he condemned doing good as one of the weakest of superstitions." Here is Thoreau's word seventy-five years ago. Possibly it may commend itself to some good people who have large experience of the results of alms-giving: "There are a thousand hacking at the branches of evil to one who is striking at the root, and it may be that he who bestows the largest amount of time and money on the needy is doing the most by his mode of life to produce that misery which he strives in vain to relieve."

I cannot quite omit the discussion of his refusal to pay his poll-tax when the slave power had forced on the country a war of invasion of Mexico, and his consequent imprisonment in Concord jail. Ordinarily a good citizen, he held then that good government had sunk so low that his time to exercise the reserve right of revolution had come. He made no noise, but quietly said to the State, through its official, "No, I wash my hands of you, and won't contribute my mite to your wrong-doing." What if nine tenths of the money were well spent; he felt it was the only chance of protest a citizen had thus to show his disapproval of the low public measures of the day. It was the act of a poet rather than a logician—symbolic—but read his paper on "Civil Disobedience," and, whatever one thinks of the conclusion, one must respect the man. I must not fail to record the pleasant circumstance that the tax collector, good Sam Staples, also constable and jailor, before arresting him said, "I'll pay your tax, Henry, if you're hard up," not understanding, as he found by Henry's refusal, and, later, by Mr. Alcott's, that "'T was nothin' but principle." He always liked and respected Thoreau, but when he told me the story, he added, "I wouldn't have done it for old man Alcott." He knew a good fellow and surveyor, but did not prize a Platonist.

His short imprisonment was a slight enough matter to Thoreau. He mentions his night spent there in "Walden," in an entertaining line or two. An incident, not there told, I learned from a friend. He was kept awake by a man in the cell below ejaculating, "What is life?" and, "So this is life!" with a painful monotony. At last, willing to get whatever treasure of truth this sonorous earthen vessel might hold, Thoreau put his head to the iron window-bars and asked suddenly, "Well, what *is* life, then?" but got no other reward than the sleep of the just, which his fellow-martyr did not further molest.

After dark, some person, unrecognized by Staples's little daughter, who went to the door, left with the child some money "to pay Mr. Thoreau's tax." Her father came home too late to hear of it, but in the morning gladly sent Thoreau away.

To the criticism, Why did he allow his tax to be paid? the simple answer is, he couldn't help it, and did not know who did it. Why, then, did he go out of jail? Because they would not keep him there.

But in a few more years the Slavery question began to darken the day. Many good men woke in the morning to find themselves sick at heart because we were becoming a slave country. The aggressive tone of the South increased, and with it the subserviency of a large class of Northern business men and manufacturers of cotton cloth, who feared to offend the planters. John Randolph's hot words in the debate over the Missouri Compromise were recalled as too nearly true: "We do not govern the people of the North by our black slaves, but by their own white slaves. We know what we are doing. We have conquered you once, and we can and will conquer you again." The idolized Webster turned recreant and countenanced a law punishing with imprisonment and heavy fine any person who should shelter, hide, or help any alleged black fugitive. Of this law our honoured Judge Hoar said in Court from the bench, "If I were giving my private opinion I might say, that statute seems to me to evince a more deliberate and settled disregard of all principles of constitutional liberty than any other enactment that has ever come under my notice."

This question of Slavery came to Thoreau's cabin door. He did not seek it. He solved it as every true man must when the moment comes to choose whether he will obey the law, or do right. He sheltered the slave and helped and guided him, and others, later, on their way towards the North Star and the rights of a man.

After Stevenson had published in his "Men and Books" his views of Thoreau, whom, of course, he had never seen, saying, that in his whole works there is no trace of pity, Mr. Alexander H. Japp contributed this true story of the effective tenderness of the man. It was told by Moncure D. Conway, the brave young Virginian preacher, who had left his home and forgone his inheritance of slaves for conscience sake. He lived for a time in Concord, near the Thoreaus, when a hunted slave came to the village by night to the home of that family.

"When I went [there] next morning, I found them all in a state of excitement by reason of the arrival of a fugitive negro from the South, who had come fainting to their door about daybreak and thrown himself upon their mercy. Thoreau took me in to see the poor wretch, whom I found to be a man with whose face, as that of a slave from the South, I was familiar. The negro was much terrified at seeing me, supposing I was one of his pursuers. Having quieted his fears by the assurance that I, too, but in a different sense, was a refugee from the bondage he was escaping, and at the same time being able to attest the negro's genuineness, I sat and watched the singularly tender and lowly devotion of the scholar to the slave. He must be fed, his swollen feet bathed, and he must think of nothing but rest: again and again this coolest and calmest of men drew near to the trembling negro, and soothed him and bade him feel at home, and have no fear that any power should again wrong him. Thoreau could not walk with me that day, as had been agreed, but must mount guard over the fugitive, for slave-hunters were not extinct in those days, and so I went away, after a while, much impressed by many little traits that I had seen as they appeared in this emergency."

Thoreau by no means neglected all civic duties. The low moral tone of his country stirred him, so that again and again he left the quiet, consoling woods and meadows to speak in Concord and elsewhere for freedom of person, of thought, and of conscience. He gave the countenance of his presence and speech to the meetings for the relief and self-protection against murder and outrage of the Free State settlers in Kansas, and contributed money. He admired John Brown, the sturdy farmer with whom he had talked on his visits to Concord, as a liberator of men, and one who dared to defend the settlers' rights. But, later, when two successive administrations ignored the outrages, and steadily favoured the party which were committing them, Thoreau, hopeless of any good coming of the United States Government, thoroughly sympathized with a man who had courage to break its bonds in the cause of natural right. In the first days of the Harper's Ferry raid, when Brown's friends and backers, hitherto, were in doubt as to their attitude in this crisis, Thoreau, taking counsel of none, announced that he should speak in the church vestry, on John Brown, to whoever came. It was as if he spoke for his own brother, so deeply stirred was he, so searching and brave his speech. Agree or disagree,—all were moved. "Such a man as it takes ages to make, and ages to understand;. . . sent to be a redeemer of those in captivity;—and the only use to which you can put him is to hang him at the end of a rope!"

For Thoreau prized moral courage. He once wrote: "Nothing is so much to be feared as fear. The sin that God hates is fear: he thinks Atheism innocent in comparison."

Thoreau was a good talker, but a certain enjoyment in taking the other side for the joy of intellectual fencing, and a pleasure of startling his companions by a paradoxical statement of his highly original way of looking at things, sometimes, were baffling to his friends. His ancestry on his mother's side, the Dunbars, was Scotch, and he had the national instinct of disputation, pugnacity, love of paradoxical statement. This fatal tendency to parry and hit with the tongue, as his ancestors no doubt did with cudgel or broadsword, for no object but the fun of intellectual fence, as such, was a temperamental fault standing in the way of relations that would otherwise have been perfect with his friends. One could sometimes only think of his Uncle Charles Dunbar, once well known in the neighbourhood for his friendly desire to "burst" his acquaintances in wrestling. Thoreau held this trait in check with women and children, and with humble people who were no match for him. With them he was simple, gentle, friendly, and amusing; and all testify his desire to share all the pleasant things he learned in his excursions. But to a conceited gentleman from the city, or a dogmatic or patronizing clergyman or editor, he would, as Emerson said, appear as a "gendarme, good to knock down cockneys with and go on his way smiling." His friend Channing says: "Though nothing was less to his mind than chopped logic, he was ready to accommodate those who differed from him with his opinion and never too much convinced by opposition."

He could afford to be a philosopher, for he was first a good common man. It takes good iron to receive a fine polish. His simple, direct speech and look and bearing were such that no plain, common man would put him down in his books as a fool, or visionary, or helpless, as the scholar, writer, or reformer would often be regarded by him. Much of Alcibiades's description of Socrates in Plato's "Symposium" would apply to Thoreau. He loved to talk with all kinds and conditions of men if they had no hypocrisy or pretence about them, and though high in his standard of virtue, and most severe with himself, could be charitable to the failings of humble fellow-men. His interest in the Indian was partly one of natural history, and the human interest was because of the genuineness of the Indian's knowledge and his freedom from cant.

There was then a genus of man (now nearly extinct) well known along the Musketaquid, amphibious, weather-beaten, solitary, who though they had homes, and even kin in some remote little farmhouse, where at odd times they hoed corn and beans, yet spent the best of their lives floating in a flat skiff, which they mainly poled along the banks, and silent, consoled by Nature and by rum, passed their best days getting fish from the river, which in the end absorbed them, even as the beautiful Hylas was taken down, sleeping, by the nymphs to the dreamy ooze; and thus what was fitting happened, and the fishes had their turn. I cannot forego giving what some will recognize as a true picture of them by another hand:

"Among the blue-flowered pickerel-weed
In grey old skiff that nestles low
Half hid in shining arrow-leaves,
The fisher sits,—nor heeds the show.
His rounded back, all weather-stained,
Has caught the air of wave-worn rocks,
And sun and wind have bleached and tanned
To one dun hue, hat, face, and locks.
And Nature's calm so settled there
The fishes never know their danger
And playful take his careless bait—
Bait they would ne'er accept from stranger.
The blue eyes only are shrewd and living,
But of soft reflections and fair things seen
To you and me no hint they are giving—
Of Sunsets' splendor, or meadows green,
Never they prate of the cardinal's flame,
The lilies' freshness, and sunrise flush,
The solemn night, or the morning star,
The violets white and the wild rose flush.
Is it all a picture? Or does he ponder
The year's fair pageant he knows so well?
Or had it reached his heart, I wonder?
He and the rushes will never tell."

For these men Thoreau felt an especial attraction and, himself a good fisher, but in no cockney fashion, and able to startle them with secrets of their own craft, could win others from them. From the most ancient of these it appears that he got that description of Walden in the last century given in his book, exciting to read in these sad days of "Lake Walden," a miscellaneous picnic ground.

One of the young men who helped him survey had pleasant recollection of his wealth of entertainment by instruction given afield, opening the way to studies of his own; and also of his good humour and fun. One who made collections for Agassiz and the Smithsonian was thus fast led to natural history; but said that, were he in trouble and need of help, he thought he should as soon have turned to Henry Thoreau as any man in town. Another, born on a farm, who knew and had worked in the black-lead mill many years, said, when I asked what he thought of Thoreau: "Why, he was the best friend I ever had. He was always straight in his ways: and was very particular to make himself agreeable. Yes, he was always straight and true: you could depend upon him: all was satisfactory." Was he a kindly and helpful man? "Yes, he was all of that: what we call solid and true, but he couldn't bear any gouge-game and dishonesty. When I saw him crossing my field I always wanted to go and have a talk with him. He was more company for me than the general run of neighbours. I liked to hear his ideas and get information from him. He liked to talk as long as you did, and what he said was new; mostly about Nature. I think he went down to Walden to pry into the arts of Nature and get something that wasn't open to the public. He liked the creatures. He seemed to think their nature could be improved. Some people called him lazy: I didn't deem it so. I called him industrious, and he was a first-rate mechanic. He was a good neighbour and very entertaining. I found him a particular friend."

A lady in Indianapolis told me that President Jordan, of Leland Stanford University, California, told her that, when travelling in Wisconsin, some years since, he was driven by an Irish farmer, Barney Mullens, once of Concord. He asked him if he knew Thoreau. "Oh, yes," said Mullens. "He was a land surveyor. He had a way of his own, and didn't care naught about money, but if there was ever a gentleman alive he was one."

I had a pleasant talk with Mrs. Minot Pratt. She and her husband, who had been members of the Brook Farm Community, in the failure of which they had lost almost all their property, settled in Concord on its dispersal. They early became acquainted with the Thoreaus. Mr. Pratt was a high-minded, kindly farmer, and a botanist. So common tastes soon made him a friend of Thoreau.

Mrs. Pratt said that he used to come much to their house. He was sociable and kind, and always seemed at home. They liked his ways, like their own, and believed in them; no pretence, no show; let guests and friends come at any time, and take them as they find them. "Henry lived in a lofty way. I loved to hear him talk, but I did not like his books so well, though I often read them and took what I liked. They do not do him justice. I liked to see Thoreau rather in his life. Yes, he was religious; he was more like the ministers than others; that is, like what they would wish and try to be. I loved him, but . . . always felt a little in awe of him.

"He loved to talk, like all his family, but not to gossip: he kept the talk on a high plane. He was cheerful and pleasant."

Just before Thoreau built his Walden house the Fitchburg Railroad was being laid through Concord, and a small army of Irishmen had their rough shanties in the woods along the deep cuts, and some of them, later good Concord citizens, had their wives and little children in these rude abodes; the remains of excavation and banking can still be traced near Walden. These people seemed a greater innovation than Samoans would to-day. Thoreau talked with them in his walks and took some kindly interest. I well remember the unusual wrath and indignation he felt a few years later when one of these, a poor neighbour, industrious but ignorant, had his spading-match prize at Cattle Show taken by his employer, on the plea, "Well, as I pay for his time, what he gets in the time I pay for nat'rally comes to me," and I know that Thoreau raised the money to make good the poor man's loss, and, I think, made the farmer's ears burn.

Once or twice I knew of the kindling of that anger, and reproof bravely given, as when an acquaintance, who had a faithful dog, discarded and drove him away out of caprice; and again, when a buyer of hens set a dog to catch them. His remarks in his book about the man getting faithful work out of the horse day by day, but doing nothing whatever to help the horse's condition, is suggestive reading for any horse-owner. He felt real respect for the personality and character of animals, and could never have been guilty of asking with Paul, "Doth God care for oxen?" The humble little neighbours, in house or wood whose characters he thus respected, rewarded his regard by some measure of friendly confidence. He felt that until men showed higher behaviour, the less they said about the "lower animals" the better.

For all life he had reverence, and just where the limits of conscious life began and ended he was too wise, and too hopeful, to say.

Some naturalists of the Dry-as-dust School are critical of him because he was not, like them, a cataloguer, and mere student of dead plants and animals. I remember once hearing Virchow, the great authority on physiology and pathology in Berlin, laugh to scorn the study of dry bones, for he said they are

artificial, have no existence in Nature. The student of bones must study fresh
bones with the marrow in them, the ligaments and periosteum still attached,
the blood in their vessels and canals, if he would know anything of nature.
Thoreau considered that one living bird for study, in its proper haunts, was
worth more than a sackful of bird-skins and skeletons. A brown, brittle plant
in a portfolio gave him little comfort, but he knew the day in March when
it would show signs of life, the days in August when it would be in flower,
and what birds would come in January from far Labrador to winter on those
particular seeds that its capsule held stored for them above the snow.

His friend Emerson writing to another, whom he hoped to lure to Concord
said: "If old Pan were here, you would come: and we have young Pan here, under
another name, whom you shall see, and hear his reeds, if you tarry not."

Surely a better mortal to represent what the Greek typified in his sylvan
god we might search New England long to find. For years, a wanderer in the
outskirts of our village was like to meet this sturdy figure striding silently
through tangled wood or wild meadow at any hour of day or night; yet he
would vent his happiness in a wild and gay dance, or yet again lie motionless
in any weather in a lonely wood, waiting for his friends, the wild creatures,
and winning in the match with them of leisure and patience. When at length
the forest began to show its little heads, the utterance of a low, continuous
humming sound, like those of Nature, spoke to their instincts and drew them
to him. Like the wood-gods of all peoples, he guarded trees and flowers and
springs, showed a brusque hospitality to mortals wandering in the wood, *so
they violated not its sanctities;* and in him was the immortal quality of youth
and cheerfulness.

Thoreau had the humour which often goes with humanity. It crops out
slyly in all his writings, but sometimes is taken for dead earnest because the
reader did not know the man.

He would say with a certain gravity, "It does no harm whatever to mowing
to walk through it: but as it does harm to the owner's feelings, it is better
not to do it when he is by." Read his very human yet humorous remarks
upon his half-witted and his one-and-a-half-witted visitors at Walden, and
on the "spirit knockings" in Concord, and, in Mr. Channing's biography, his
charming description of the drunken young Dutch deck-hand on the boat.

While living at Walden he wrote: "One evening I overtook one of my
townsmen, who has accumulated what is called a handsome property,—
though I never got a fair view of it,—on the Walden road, driving a pair of
cattle to market, who inquired of me how I could bring my mind to give up
so many of the comforts of life. I answered that I was very sure that I liked it

passably well; I was not joking. And so I went home to my bed and left him to pick his way through the darkness and the mud to Brighton,—or Brighttown,—which place he would reach some time in the morning."

Thoreau said he once overheard one of his auditors at a country Lyceum after the lecture say to another, "What does he lecture for?"—a question which made him quake in his shoes.

I forget of what the following amusing utterance is apropos: "If you are chosen Town Clerk, forsooth, you cannot go to Terra del Fuego this summer: but you may go to the land of infernal fire nevertheless. The universe is wider than our views of it."

When, on occasion of some convention, some divines tarried at his mother's, one of these persons told the aunts that he wished Henry would go and hear him, saying, "I have a sermon on purpose for him." The aunts gave little hope, but presently Henry came in and was introduced. Immediately this clergyman slapped him on the shoulder with his fat hand, exclaiming familiarly, "So here's the chap who camped in the woods." Thoreau turned round and said promptly, "And here's the chap that camps in a pulpit." His assailant was discomfited and said no more.

In the reed-pipes of Pan slept the notes of enchantment for him to wake at will. Our Concord genius of the wood was a master of the flute. It was his companion in his life there and the echoes of Walden hills were his accompaniments.

Music was an early and life-long friend. His sisters made home pleasant with it. The sweet tunes of Mrs. Hawthorne's music-box were a comfort to him in the lonely days after John's death. "Row, Brothers, Row," which I have heard him sing, recalled the happy river-voyage; and no one who heard "Tom Bowling" from Thoreau could ask if he were capable of human feeling. To this day that song, heard long years ago, rings clear and moving to me.

He studied the songs of birds as eagerly as many a man how to make money. Milton calls Mammon, —

"The least erected spirit that fell
From Heaven, for even in Heaven his looks and thoughts
Were always downward bent, admiring more
The riches of Heaven's pavement, trodden gold,
Than aught divine or holy else enjoyed
In vision beatific."

Not so Henry Thoreau. As he walked the village street sometimes it happened that his towns-folk were hurt or annoyed that his eyes were far away and he did not stop "to pass the time of day." There was no affectation or unkindness here. The real man was then in the elm-arch high aloft, —

"The beautiful hanging gardens that rocked in the morning wind
And sheltered a dream of Faerie and a life so timid and kind,
The shady choir of the bluebird and the racecourse of squirrels gay."

He stopped once on the street and made me hear, clear, but far above, the red-eyed vireo's note and, rarely coming, that of his little white-eyed cousin. I had not known—I venture to say few persons know—that the little olive-brown bird whom we associate with her delicate nest hanging between two twigs in the woods, is one of the commonest singers on our main street in July, even as Thoreau wrote: —

"Upon the lofty elm-tree sprays,
The Vireo rings the changes meet,
During these trivial summer days,
Striving to lift our thoughts above the street."

Many a boy and girl owed to him the opening of the gate of this almost fairy knowledge, and thereafter pleasant voices, unnoted of others, spoke to him, like the sudden understanding of the eagle's voices to Sigurd in the Saga.

He was more than Naturalist. He said of Nature, "She must not be looked at directly, but askance, or by flashes: like the head of the Gorgon Medusa, she turns the men of Science to stone." But the walls of Troy are said to have builded themselves of stone obedient to immortal music, and though those walls be crumbled, they endure in the song of the blind harper.

In the ages called dark, and what we think of as rude times, one wanderer was sure of welcome,—wherever he went was free of market and inn, of camp and castle and palace; he who could tell in song or story of the gods and the darker powers; the saints, the helping heroes, and gracious beauty. These men by their magic made hard life seem sweet, and bloody death desirable, and raised in each the hope that even the short thread of life spun out to him by grudging Fate might yet gleam in the glorious tapestry of story.

And the men and maids for one moment knew
That the song was truer than what was true.

Our hero was a born story-teller, and of the Norseman type in many ways, a right Saga-man and Scald like them, telling of woods and waters and the dwarfkin that peopled them—and ever he knew what he saw for a symbol, and looked through it for a truth. "Even the facts of science," said he, "may dust the mind by their dryness, unless they are in a sense effaced by the dews of fresh and living truth."

When one asked Aristotle, why we like to spend much time with handsome people? "That is a blind man's question," was the wise man's answer; and Thoreau, looking at beautiful Mother Nature, might have given the same answer to a townsman anxious lest he stay in the fields too long for the good of pencil-making. How Thoreau felt when alone with Nature may be gathered from his words about her, "At once our Destiny and Abode, our Maker and our Life."

The humour, the raciness, and the flavour of the moor and the greenwood that is in the Robin Hood ballads he loved, was in his speech. In his books, particularly "Walden," the contentious tone may linger unpleasantly in the reader's ears and memory, but remember, Thoreau, in his day, was administering wholesome, if bitter, medicine.

Yet when he at last lays by his wholesome but fatiguing buffeting North-wind method, there comes winning sunshine; and the enchanting haze of a poet's thought brings out the true beauty in the commonest things.

Some of his verses are little better than doggerel, but others, hardly yet received, will, I think, remain when many who passed current as American poets, in his lifetime, are forgotten. Less artificial than much of the old classic English verse with which he became familiar in his youth, some of its best qualities are to be remarked in his poems. Those which remain—he destroyed many—were scattered in his writings, but have been brought together in a small volume by Mr. Sanborn. He did not often reach perfect rhythmical expression, but one cannot read far in his prose without coming on the thought and words of a true poet. Walden called out these by her colour, her purity, her reflections, her ice, her children.

One morning, when she had put on her white armour against the winter, he goes down for his morning draught, axe in hand. "I cut my way first through a foot of snow, and then a foot of ice, and open a window under my feet where, kneeling to drink, I look down into the quiet parlour of the fishes, pervaded by a softened light, as through a window of ground glass with its bright sanded floor the same as in summer; there a perennial waveless serenity reigns as in the amber twilight sky, corresponding to the cool and even temperament of the inhabitants. Heaven is under our feet as well as over our heads.

"Ah, the pickerel of Walden! when I see them lying on the ice, I am always surprised by their rare beauty, as if they were fabulous fishes, they are so foreign to the streets, even to the woods, foreign as Arabia to our Concord life. They possess a quite dazzling and transcendent beauty which separates them by a wide interval from the cadaverous cod and haddock whose fame is trumpeted in our streets. They are not green like the pines, nor gray like the stones, nor blue like the sky; but they have, to my eyes, if possible, yet rarer colours, like flowers and precious stones, as if they were the pearls, the animal nuclei or crystals of the Walden water. They, of course, are Walden all over and all through; are themselves small Waldens in the animal kingdom, Waldenses. It is surprising that they are caught here,—that in this deep and capacious spring, far beneath the rattling teams and chaises and tinkling sleighs that travel the Walden road, this great gold and emerald fish swims. I never chanced to see its kind in any market; it would be the cynosure of all eyes there. Easily, with a few convulsive quirks, they give up their watery ghosts, like a mortal translated before his time to the thin air of heaven.

Hear the message of beauty that the telegraph-wire sung for Thoreau's ears: —

"As I went under the new telegraph wire, I heard it vibrating like a harp high overhead. It was as the sound of a far-off, glorious life, a supernal life which came down to us and vibrated the latticework of this life of ours,—an Æolian harp. . . . It seemed to me as if every pore of the wood was filled with music. As I put my ear to one of the posts, it laboured with the strains, as if every fibre was affected, and being seasoned or timed, rearranged according to a new and more harmonious law. Every swell and change and inflection of tone pervaded it, and seemed to proceed from the wood, the divine tree or wood, as if its very substance was transmuted.

"What a recipe for preserving wood, to fill its pores with music! How this wild tree from the forest, stripped of its bark and set up here, rejoices to transmit this music. The resounding wood,—how much the ancients would have made of it! To have had a harp on so great a scale, girdling the very earth, and played on by the winds of every latitude and longitude, and that harp were (so to speak) the manifest blessing of Heaven on a work of man's."

It seems well here to introduce some passages shedding light on the relations of four men who, between the years 1835 and 1845, met as dwellers in our village,—though only Thoreau was born there,—all scholars in different ways, who, afterwards, won some fame by their lives and books.

Two newly married young men came to our quiet town to find homes. The shy Hawthorne went to the Manse, temporarily unoccupied by the Ripley family, and the interesting though perverse genius, William Ellery Channing, with his fair young wife (Margaret Fuller's sister), looking like a Madonna of Raphael's, took a little house on the broad meadow just beyond Emerson's.

Thoreau with friendly courtesy did the honours of the river and the wood to each man in turn, for he held with Emerson that Nature says "One to one, my dear." Though Channing remained in Concord most of his life, Hawthorne at that time stayed but two years. Thoreau, while a homesick tutor in Staten Island, in a letter to Emerson thus shows that friendship with the new-comers had begun: —

"DEAR FRIENDS:—I was very glad to hear your voices from so far. . . . My thoughts revert to those dear hills and that RIVER which so fills up the world to its brim,—worthy to be named with Mincius and Alpheus,—still drinking its meadows while I am far away. . . .

I am pleased to think of Channing as an inhabitant of the gray town. Seven cities contended for Homer dead. Tell him to remain at least long enough to establish Concord's right and interest in him. . . . And Hawthorne, too, I remember as one with whom I sauntered, in old heroic times, along the banks of the Scamander, amid the ruins of chariots and heroes. Tell him not to desert, even after the tenth year. Others may say, 'Are there not the cities of Asia?' But what are they? Staying at home is the heavenly way."

In these days when the classics are misprised, the old "humanities" so crowded out by the practical, it is good to observe how this sturdy villager's life and his writing were enriched by his love of Homer, Æschylus, Simonides and Pindar.

Thoreau and Alcott always had friendly relations, though they were not drawn one to the other. Thoreau, with his hardy independence, was impatient of Alcott's philosophic calm while failing to comfortably maintain his family. This invalidated his philosophy, of which Thoreau said he "hated a sum that did not prove." These lean periods occurred when this good man could find no hearing for the spiritual mission, especially to the young, to which he felt himself called.

Thoreau helped Alcott build the really beautiful summer-house of knotted oak and twisted pine for Mr. Emerson while he was in Europe in 1847-48. He sawed deftly, and drove the nails straight for the philosopher. He was at that time living at the house as kindly protector and friend of Mrs. Emerson and the three young children, and attending to his absent friend's affairs in house, garden, and wood-lot. He wrote to Emerson: "Alcott has heard that I laughed, and set the people laughing at his arbor, though I never laughed louder than when I was on the ridge-pole. But now I have not laughed for a long time, it is so serious. He is very grave to look at. But, not knowing all this, I strove innocently enough, the other day, to engage his attention to my mathematics. 'Did you ever study geometry, the relation of straight lines to

curves, the transition from the finite to the infinite? Fine things about it in
Newton and Leibnitz.' But he would hear none of it,—men of taste preferred
the natural curve. Ah, he is a crooked stick himself. He is getting on now so
many *knots* an hour."

Emerson was a good intermediate, and valued both his friends. Four years
later be wrote in his Journal: —

"I am my own man more than most men, yet the loss of a few persons
would be most impoverishing, a few persons who give flesh to what were else
mere thoughts, and which now I am not at liberty to slight, or in any manner
treat as fictions. It were too much to say that the Platonic world I might have
learned to treat as cloud-land, had I not known Alcott, who is a native of that
country; yet will I say that he makes it as solid as Massachusetts to me; and
Thoreau gives me, in flesh and blood and pertinacious Saxon belief, my own
ethics. He is far more real, and daily practically obeying them, than I, and
fortifies my memory at all times with an affirmative experience which refuses
to be set aside."

To go back a little to their first acquaintance. In 1837, the boy of twenty,
just graduated, and his writings, had been brought to Mrs. Emerson's notice
by Mr. Emerson's sister, Mrs. Brown, who boarded with the Thoreaus. In that
year, Mr. Emerson wrote: "My good Henry Thoreau made this else solitary
afternoon sunny with his simplicity and clear perception. How comic is
simplicity in this double-dealing, quacking world. Everything that boy says
makes merry with society, though nothing can be graver than his meaning."

Here is a pleasant record of friendship in a letter written to Carlyle in
1841: "One reader and friend of yours dwells now in my house, and, as I
hope, for a twelvemonth to come,—Henry Thoreau,—a poet whom you may
one day be proud of,—a noble, manly youth, full of melodies and inventions.
We work together day by day in my garden, and I grow well and strong." The
little garden which was being planted with fruit-trees and vegetables, with
Mrs. Emerson's tulips and roses from Plymouth at the upper end, needed
more care and much more skill to plant and cultivate than the owner had;
who, moreover, could only spare a few morning hours to the work. So
Thoreau took it in charge for his friend. He dealt also with the chickens,
defeating their raids on the garden by asking Mrs. Emerson to make some
shoes of thin morocco to stop their scratching.

This friendly alliance was a success. Emerson wrote: "Though we pine for
great men, we do not use them when they come. Here is a Damascus blade of
a man, such as you may search through nature in vain to parallel, laid up on
a shelf in our village to rust and ruin."

Mr. Emerson was chafing at the waste of this youth in the pencil mill, and impatient for his fruiting time, surely to come. And yet he did not quite see that Thoreau was steering a course true to his compass with happy result to his voyage, a course that would for him, Emerson, have been quite unfit. Thus, in 1848, he writes: "Henry Thoreau is like the wood-god who solicits the wandering poet, and draws him into 'antres vast and desarts idle,' and leaves him naked, plaiting vines and with twigs in his hand. Very seductive are the first steps from the town to the woods, but the end is want and madness." The result was not so, and it must be remembered that Emerson recorded one mood or aspect at a time.

On a luckier day he writes: "Henry is a good substantial childe, not encumbered with himself. He has no troublesome memory, no wake, but lives extempore, and brings today a new proposition as radical and revolutionary as that of yesterday, but different. The only man of leisure in the town. He is a good Abbot Samson; and carries counsel in his breast. If I cannot show his performance much more manifest than that of the other grand promises, at least I can see that with his practical faculty, he has declined all the kingdoms of this world. Satan has no bribe for him."

When Thoreau came, rather unwillingly, by invitation to dine with company, it often happened that he was in a captious mood, amusing himself by throwing paradoxes in the way of the smooth current of the conversation. It was like having Pan at a dinner party. Even when he "dropped in" to the study at the end of the afternoon, and had told the last news from the river or Fairhaven Hill, Mr. Emerson, at a later period, complained that Thoreau baulked his effort "to hold intercourse with his mind." With all their honour for one another, and their Spartan affection, satisfactory talks then seem to have been rare. But a long afternoon's ramble with Pan guiding to each sight, or sound, or fragrance, perhaps to be found only on that day, was dear privilege, and celebrated as such by Emerson in his journals.

But even Pan "took sides" when Liberty was in peril, the Greek tradition tells us, and so did his Concord followers. In the dark days of 1853 Mr. Emerson wrote: "I go for those who have received a retaining fee to this party of Freedom before they came into the world. I would trust Garrison, I would trust Henry Thoreau, that they would make no compromises."

It is good to know that it has been recorded of Alcott, the benign idealist, that when the Reverend Thomas Wentworth Higginson (later, a Colonel in the Northern Army), heading the rush on the United States Court House in Boston to rescue the fugitive slave, looked back for his following at the Court-room door, only the apostolic philosopher was there, cane in hand.

But Thoreau had qualities which the Platonist lacked. Emerson, writing of Mother-wit, says,—"Doctor Johnson, Milton, Chaucer and Burns had it. Aunt Mary Moody Emerson has it, and can write scrap letters. Who has it need never write anything but scraps. Henry Thoreau has it."

When "Walden" appeared Mr. Emerson seems to have felt as much pleasure as if his brother had written it. But when the Thoreau family, after Henry's death, submitted the journals to his friend's consideration, he, coming from his study, day by day, would tell his children his joyful surprise in the merit and the beauty which he found everywhere in those daily chronicles of Nature and of thought.

The virtue of Thoreau has always commanded respect; of his knowledge of Natural History, Lowell alone, as far as I know, has spoken slightingly. But his views of life,—when these are referred to, how often it is with a superior smile. True the fault lies partly with Thoreau, that his Scotch pugnacity sometimes betrayed him into rhetorical over-statement and he would not stoop to qualify: thought a maximum dose of bitter-tonic, in the condition of society in his day, would do it no harm. But let us also bethink ourselves before we give final judgment. Might not modesty whisper that some of us, the critics, live on a lower plane, and that the point of view made a difference? May not a man on a hill see that his friends below, though apparently on a clear ascending path, will soon come to thickets and ravines, while by taking what looks like a wildcat path to them they will soon reach the height. Have the conduct and words of most poets, prophets, even of the founders of the great religions, been considered sagacious "on 'Change"?

When one sees another, helpful and kindly in common relations, sincere and brave in speech, and ever trying to keep the conversation above gossip and triviality; easily earning a simple living by work, humble, but done as if for God's inspection, yet saving a share of each day for the life to which his instinct and genius lead him, yet, on occasion, leaving it readily to please and help others; able to rise above bitter bereavement; using disappointment in early love to purify life; fearless and in good heart in life and in death,—one may well ask, Is Folly behind all this?

Make allowance for strong statement due to any original, vigorous man, trying to arouse his neighbours from lethargy to freedom and happiness that he believed within their reach, and then, with the perspective of years to help us, look fairly at the main lines of his life and thought, which have been considered so strange and outré.

Consider the standards of education and religion in New England in Thoreau's youth,—the position of the churches, their distrust of the right of the individual to question the words of the Bible as interpreted by the Sects; the horror that Theodore Parker inspired, the shyness of the so-called Pagan Scriptures, the difficulty with which any one who spoke for the slave could get a hearing, the ridicule of the so-called Transcendentalists, the general practice of what is now called, "pauperizing Mediæval Charity," the indignant rejection of Evolution theories, the slight taste for Natural History, and the astonishment that a rich family "camping out" would have excited. Now we have long had intelligent system in schools, and vocational instruction too, and electives in the Universities; we blush to remember the rendition of Sims and Burns.

John Brown has been almost canonized by some people as the John Baptist of Freedom's Triumph; the "Dial" is spoken of with respect, the memory of Theodore Parker is honoured in the churches, the "light of Asia" read as a religious work, Mediæval alms-giving, we are told by the Associated Charities, is a sin; the so-called "lower animals" have their companions, yea, are practically owned as ancestors; and when a party is found under the greenwood tree no Orlando would say, now, —

> "Whatever you are
> That in this desert inaccessible
> Under the shade of melancholy boughs
> Lose and neglect the creeping hours of Time;
> If ever you have looked on better days,
> If ever been where bells have knolled to church," etc.

but, on the contrary, knows that they are trying to preserve or regain their sanity after a season of lecture, party, street-car, and telephone life. "Who laughs last, laughs best." Was society wrong in his day, or Thoreau?

This rare and happy venture of Thoreau's,—bringing his soul face to face with Nature as wondrous artist, as healer, teacher, as mediator between us and the Creator, has slowly spread its wide beneficence. Look at out-of-door life, and love of plant and tree, and sympathy with animals, now, as compared with these seventy years ago. Yet to-day the inestimable value of frequent solitude is much overlooked.

He devoutly listened. He writes in his Journal: "If I do not keep step with others, it is because I hear a different drummer. Let a man step to the music which he hears, however measured, and however far away."

Again: "If within the old man there is not a young man,—within the sophisticated one, an unsophisticated one,—then he is but one of the Devil's angels."

When we read the poems that have become great classics describing the man, pure, constant and upright; David's "Lord, who shall abide in Thy tabernacle?" the "Integer Vitæ" of Horace, Sir Henry Wotton's —

"How happy is he born and taught,
Who serveth not another's will"; —

or Herbert's "Constancie,"—to one who knew Henry Thoreau well, whose image would more quickly arise than his? Does one need to labor to prove that he had a religion? Read his acknowledgment of the sudden coming of spiritual help, —

"It comes in Summer's broadest noon,
By a grey wall, in some chance place,
Unseasoning time, insulting June,
And vexing day with its presuming face.

"I hearing get, who had but ears,
And sight, who had but eyes before;
I moments live, who lived but years,
And truth discern, who knew but learning's lore.

"I will not doubt the love untold,
Which not my worth or want hath bought,
Which woed me young, and woes me old,
And to this evening hath me brought."

Thoreau was but forty-four years old when he died. Even his health could not throw off a chill got by long stooping in a wet snow storm counting the growth-rings on the stumps of some old trees. The family infection became active. He lived a year and a half after this exposure and made a trip to Minnesota in vain for health. For the last months he was confined to the house, he was affectionate, and utterly brave, and worked on his manuscript until the last days. When his neighbour, Reverend Mr. Reynolds, came in he found him so employed, and he looked up cheerfully and, with a twinkle in his eye, whispered—his voice was gone—"you know it's respectable to leave an estate to one's friends." His old acquaintance Staples, once his jailor, coming out, meeting Mr. Emerson coming in, reported that he "never saw a man dying with so much pleasure and peace." To his Calvinistic Aunt who felt obliged to ask, "Henry, have you made your peace with God?"—"I did not know we had ever quarrelled, Aunt," was the pleasant answer.

His friend and companion, Edward Hoar, said to me, "With Thoreau's life something went out of Concord woods and fields and river that never will return. He so loved Nature, delighted in her every aspect and seemed to infuse himself into her." Yes, something went. But our woods and waters will always be different because of this man. Something of him abides and truly "for good" in his town. Here he was born, and within its borders he found a wealth of beauty and interest—all that he asked—and shared it with us all.

In his day, as now too, was much twilight, and men were slaves to their fears and to hobgoblins. Taking for his motto, —

"Make courage for life to be Capitaine Chief,"

he, with truth and Nature to help him, cut a way through to freedom.

"He looked up to a mountain tract
And saw that every morning, far withdrawn
Beyond the darkness and the cataract,
God made himself an awful rose of Dawn,
Unheeded; yes, for many a month and year
Unheeded ever."

But not by him. He learned this, he says, by his experiment of a life with Nature simply followed for his guide; that "if one advances confidently in the direction of his dreams, and endeavours to live the life that he has imagined, he will meet with a success unexpected in common hours. He will put some things behind, will pass an invisible boundary; new, universal, and more liberal laws will begin to establish themselves around and within him; or the old laws will be expanded and interpreted in his favour in a more liberal sense, and he will live with the license of a higher order of beings. In proportion as he simplifies his life, the laws of the universe will appear less complex, and solitude will not be solitude, nor poverty poverty, nor weakness weakness. If you have built castles in the air, your work need not be lost; that is where they should be. Now put the foundations under them."

This man, in his lifetime little known, except outwardly, even in his own town, whose books were returned to him as unsalable, is better known and prized more nearly at his worth each year, and today is giving freedom and joy in life to fellowmen in the far parts of this country, and beyond the ocean. Let us not misprize him, and regret that he did not make pencils and money. Something of his strange early prayer was granted. It was this:—

"Great God, I ask thee for no meaner pelf
Than that I may not disappoint myself;
That in my action I may soar as high
As I can now discern with this clear eye.
And, next in value which thy kindness lends,
That I may—greatly—disappoint my friends,
Howe'er they think or hope that it may be,
They may not dream how thou'st distinguished me.
That my weak hand may equal my firm faith,
And my life practise more than my tongue saith;
That my low conduct may not show,
Nor my relenting lines,
That I thy purpose did not know
Or overrated thy designs."

—Edward Emerson, "Henry Thoreau as
Remembered by a Young Friend," 1917

GENERAL

The excerpts in this section address a series of questions important to the development of Thoreau's critical reputation, including his credibility as a man of science, his relationship with Ralph Waldo Emerson, and his literary style.

Thoreau's writings on nature are inseparable from his views on science, as they are infused with scientific observations. This creates a dichotomy between objective reporting and subjective interpretation, a tension or duality reflected in William Ellery Channing's description of Thoreau as a "poet-naturalist." Yet not all the pieces collected in this section resolve this polarity so easily. As Alexander Hay Japp remarks, "the purely scientific men" rejected Thoreau for his search for an inner meaning in the processes he observed. Havelock Ellis faulted Thoreau for his lack of scientific sense. As Nina Baym wrote in her 1963 essay on Thoreau's view of science, "[n]aturalists continued to be appalled at the inaccuracy of the reporting, humanists to be exasperated at its inclusion at all." As a transcendentalist, Thoreau was part of a reaction against the scientism of the Enlightenment and was influenced by the theories of European romanticism. Thus, he never considers nature to be something that scientific reason should master and analyze. Thoreau considers natural phenomena as aspects of subjective experience that the individual's intuitive sense perceives. Facts are important to Thoreau, but they are means rather than ends in themselves. The facts of the natural world have a moral relevance to human lives, teaching people how to live.

Almost all the excerpts also address Thoreau's relationship with Ralph Waldo Emerson, a topic that has constituted a recurrent interest in the author's criticism. Early critics of Thoreau mainly considered him a minor Emerson, an accusation that was particularly voiced by American critics.

Alexander Hay Japp complained in 1878 that Thoreau was "treated as a mere disciple of Emerson," and Thomas Wentworth Higginson predicted a year later that "[t]he impression that Thoreau was but a minor Emerson will in time pass away." Emerson played an important part in the literary and intellectual development of Thoreau. The two met at Harvard in 1837 when Thoreau was twenty years old and Emerson, fourteen years Thoreau's senior, had just published his landmark essay *Nature*. The two immediately formed a friendship that lasted until Thoreau's death, despite periods of estrangement between the two. Emerson supported Thoreau materially as well as intellectually, allowing him to live with his family, providing him with work, and lending him money. Emerson also introduced Thoreau to the prestigious New England transcendentalist circles. Without Emerson's help, Thoreau probably would not have been able to focus on his writing as much as he did. At the same time, Emerson became an overshadowing presence in Thoreau's life. The author of *Walden* had to wait until the first decades of the twentieth century to be considered an important writer on his own terms rather than being unfavorably compared to his mentor.

A third concern informing many of the following critical excerpts is Thoreau's literary style. Much of the early criticism of Thoreau complained about the author's lack of artistic mastery and his unadorned style. Thoreau's biographer, social reformer Henry S. Salt, turned this criticism into praise when he explained that Thoreau was always "conscious of a fuller and higher calling than that of the literary man." Thoreau valued "nature before art" and "life before literature." Yet, more recent critics have dispelled this myth about Thoreau's simplicity. Critics such as Michael Warner have remarked that for Thoreau language is not simply an instrument of communication but a means to knowledge and experience. This makes Thoreau's language densely metaphoric and rich in linguistic puns.

THOMAS CARLYLE (1847)

This short piece in a letter to Emerson marks an important endorsement by Thomas Carlyle (1795–1881) of Thoreau. "I like Mr. Thoreau very well," Carlyle asserts. Although Carlyle points out the influence of Emerson on Thoreau, he is also one of the first to stress that the author of *Walden* has a distinctive personality. Thoreau was himself a great admirer of Carlyle and the author of an essay on him, "Thomas Carlyle and His Works" (1847).

Thomas Carlyle was one of the intellectuals to influence most profoundly American transcendentalism, particularly for his theory of correspondences between nature and spirit. His works were marketed in the United States through transcendentalist circles. Although Carlyle's family background prized hard, practical work over intellectual refinement, his parents were always supportive of their son's literary and academic ambitions. Carlyle attended Edinburgh University to become a minister in the Church of Scotland. Later, beset by doubts about dogmatic religion, he abandoned this plan. Carlyle turned to teaching math and translating German science books, which led to his reading of German idealist philosophers such as Schiller, Fichte, and Schelling. He also became an admirer of Goethe's works. The early 1820s were hard for Carlyle, who left teaching as he felt he was not suited to it and returned to the university to study law. In 1826, Carlyle married Jane Welsh who came from a wealthy family. He also began to write for the *Edinburgh Review* and to compose his philosophical novel *Sartor Resartus*. The novel had difficulty finding a publisher but eventually realized great success.

Carlyle's fame, however, was not to be derived entirely from the novel, but on his historical works, particularly his study of the French Revolution, which he completed after moving to London. The work had a difficult genesis, as a partially completed draft accidentally burned, leaving its author in poverty for months. When Carlyle finally completed *The French Revolution* in 1837, the work proved a commercial and critical success. Carlyle then launched a successful career as a lecturer bringing his financial problems to an end. *The French Revolution* was the first of a series of historical studies and social pamphlets that made Carlyle a revered figure on the British literary scene, an intellectual hero whose influence in the field of letters was comparable to that of the historical figures he wrote about in his studies. In April 1886, he accepted the rectorship of Edinburgh University but was soon grief stricken by his wife's death. Carlyle never recovered from that event and spent the last fifteen years of his life writing very little. His final years were also marked

by increasingly conservative positions such as his support for Governor
Eyre, who had violently crushed a rebellion of Jamaican slaves.

———⌐⌐/⌐⌐⌐——— ——⌐⌐/⌐⌐⌐—— ——⌐⌐/⌐⌐⌐⌐—

A vigorous Mr. Thoreau,—who has formed himself a good deal upon
one Emerson, but does not want abundant fire and stamina of his
own;—recognizes us, and various other things, in a most admiring great-
hearted manner; for which, as for *part* of the confused voice from the
jury-box (not yet summed into a verdict, nor likely to be summed till
Doomsday, nor needful to sum), the poor prisoner at the bar may justly
express himself thankful! In plain prose, I like Mr. Thoreau very well; and
hope yet to hear good and better news of him:—only let him not "turn to
foolishness"; which seems to me to be terribly easy, at present, both in New
England and Old!

—Thomas Carlyle, letter to
Ralph Waldo Emerson, May 18, 1847

James Russell Lowell "Thoreau" (1856)

Although his reputation declined in the twentieth century, James Russell
Lowell (1819–1891) was one of the most influential literary critics and
writers of the nineteenth century. Lowell came from a respected New
England family and, as tradition would have it, he attended Harvard
University and took a law degree in 1840, although he did not pursue a
career in that field. The poet Maria White, whom Lowell married in 1844,
was a source of inspiration for him and helped him discover his literary
vocation. It is generally argued that Lowell's best work dates back to the
early part of his literary career, when the writer was also deeply com-
mitted to the abolitionist cause. Lowell wrote a number of antislavery
articles for many periodicals and, in 1846, began to serialize the *Biglow
Papers*. These abolitionist pieces reached a vast audience and were published in book form two years later in 1848. In that same year, Lowell's
literary fame peaked with the publication of the two long poems, *The
Vision of Sir Launfal* and *A Fable for Critics*, which are generally considered
to be his masterpieces.

    In the 1850s, Lowell began to focus mainly on literary and social
criticism as well as on historical scholarship. Thanks to the fame acquired
through his literary lectures, he was appointed Smith Professor of Modern
Languages at Harvard, a position that he kept for the next twenty years.
In 1857, Lowell married Frances Dunlap (his first wife had died in 1853) and

also took on the editorship of the then newly established *Atlantic Monthly*. During the next four years, Lowell developed the journal, attracting many important New England authors as contributors. Although he was a staunch supporter of the Union during the Civil War and wrote political odes for its cause, he was deeply disillusioned with the corruption of the Grant administration. From 1864 to 1872, he acted as the editor of the *North American Review*. Lowell tried to counter what he perceived as the decline of American society with a series of essays on outstanding figures such as Dante, Chaucer, Wordsworth, and Keats who he believed could function as models for Americans. In the late 1870s, Lowell also began a diplomatic career and was first sent to Spain (1877–80) as minister and later as ambassador to Great Britain (1880–85). His second wife died in 1885. After her death, he retired from public life.

The following essay on Thoreau is highly critical of what Lowell considers to be a typically romantic trait that the author of *Walden* exhibits: "the modern sentimentalism about Nature." This is "a mark of disease" that Lowell finds in "unreal men" who willingly seclude themselves from their society and observe their fellow human beings with contempt. Among these unreal men, Lowell cites prominent figures in French romanticism such as Rousseau, Saint Pierre, and Chateaubriand who all privilege nature over humankind. Because of their haughty attitude toward their peers, Thoreau as well as these romantic writers did not benefit, in the end, from their communion with nature. To Lowell, Thoreau's later years were characterized by an increasing cynicism toward and disinterest in American society. Yet Lowell also finds a quest for an ideal truth in Thoreau's writings, which makes them noble and useful. It was through nature that Thoreau intended to get to this ideal world. To Lowell, the author's claim to independence from mankind was a contradiction in terms as it "presupposed all that complicated civilization which it theoretically abjured." Lowell is merciless in recording Thoreau's complete dependence on the benevolence of his friends in order to have the freedom to pursue his chosen lifestyle ("He squatted on another man's land"). He also goes as far as claiming that it was precisely "artificial civilization" that "rendered it possible that such a person as Henry D. Thoreau should exist at all." Yet, Lowell finds that Thoreau's life, though plagued by this inconsistency, should be appreciated as a criticism of the aimless materialism that was increasingly becoming a part of American society. In addition, Lowell praises Thoreau for his ability to adopt a literary style "in keeping with the simplicity and purity of his life."

I have just been renewing my recollection of Mr. Thoreau's writings, and have read through his six volumes in the order of their production. I shall try to give an adequate report of their impression upon me both as critic and as mere reader. He seems to me to have been a man with so high a conceit of himself that he accepted without questioning, and insisted on our accepting, his defects and weaknesses of character as virtues and powers peculiar to himself. Was he indolent, he finds none of the activities which attract or employ the rest of mankind worthy of him. Was he wanting in the qualities that make success, it is success that is contemptible, and not himself that lacks persistency and purpose. Was he poor, money was an unmixed evil. Did his life seem a selfish one, he condemns doing good as one of the weakest of superstitions. To be of use was with him the most killing bait of the wily tempter Uselessness. He had no faculty of generalization from outside of himself, or at least no experience which would supply the material of such, and he makes his own whim the law, his own range the horizon of the universe. He condemns a world, the hollowness of whose satisfactions he had never had the means of testing, and we recognize Apemantus behind the mask of Timon. He had little active imagination; of the receptive he had much. His appreciation is of the highest quality; his critical power, from want of continuity of mind, very limited and inadequate. He somewhere cites a simile from Ossian, as an example of the superiority of the old poetry to the new, though, even were the historic evidence less convincing, the sentimental melancholy of those poems should be conclusive of their modernness. He had none of the artistic mastery which controls a great work to the serene balance of completeness, but exquisite mechanical skill in the shaping of sentences and paragraphs, or (more rarely) short bits of verse for the expression of a detached thought, sentiment, or image. His works give one the feeling of a sky full of stars,—something impressive and exhilarating certainly, something high overhead and freckled thickly with spots of isolated brightness; but whether these have any mutual relation with each other, or have any concern with our mundane matters, is for the most part matter of conjecture,—astrology as yet, and not astronomy.

It is curious, considering what Thoreau afterwards became, that he was not by nature an observer. He only saw the things he looked for, and was less poet than naturalist. Till he built his Walden shanty, he did not know that the hickory grew in Concord. Till he went to Maine, he had never seen phosphorescent wood, a phenomenon early familiar to most country boys. At forty he speaks of the seeding of the pine as a new discovery, though one should have thought that its gold-dust of blowing pollen might have earlier drawn his eye. Neither his attention nor his genius was of the spontaneous kind. He discovered nothing. He thought everything a discovery of his own, from moonlight to the planting of acorns and nuts by squirrels. This is a defect in his character, but one of his chief charms as a writer. Everything grows fresh under his hand. He delved in his mind and nature; he planted them with all manner of native and foreign seeds, and reaped assiduously. He was not merely solitary, he would be isolated, and succeeded at last in almost persuading himself that he was autochtonous. He valued everything in proportion as he fancied it to be exclusively his own. He complains in *Walden* that there is no one in Concord with whom he could talk of Oriental literature, though the man was living within two miles of his hut who had introduced him to it. This intellectual selfishness becomes sometimes almost painful in reading him. He lacked that generosity of "communication" which Johnson admired in Burke. De Quincey tells us that Wordsworth was impatient when any one else spoke of mountains, as if he had a peculiar property in them. And we can readily understand why it should be so: no one is satisfied with another's appreciation of his mistress. But Thoreau seems to have prized a lofty way of thinking (often we should be inclined to call it a remote one) not so much because it was good in itself as because he wished few to share it with him. It seems now and then as if he did not seek to lure others up "above our lower region of turmoil," but to leave his own name cut on the mountain peak as the first climber. This itch of originality infects his thought and style. To be misty is not to be mystic. He turns commonplaces end for end, and fancies it makes something new of them. As we walk down Park Street, our eye is caught by Dr. Winship's dumb-bells, one of which bears an inscription testifying that it is the heaviest ever put up at arm's length by any athlete; and in reading Mr. Thoreau's books we cannot help feeling as if he sometimes invited our attention to a particular sophism or parodox as the biggest yet maintained by any single writer. He seeks, at all risks, for perversity of thought, and revives the age of *concetti* while he fancies himself going back to a pre-classical nature. "A day," he says, "passed in the society of those Greek sages, such as described in the Banquet of Xenophon, would not be comparable with the dry wit of decayed cranberry-vines and the fresh Attic salt of the moss-beds." It is not so much the True that he loves as the Out-of-the-Way. As the Brazen Age shows itself in other men by exaggeration of phrase, so in him by extravagance of statement. He wishes always to trump your suit and to *ruff* when you least expect it. Do you love Nature because she is beautiful? He will find a better argument in her ugliness. Are you tired of the artificial man? He instantly dresses you up an ideal in a Penobscot Indian, and attributes to this creature of his otherwise-mindedness as peculiarities things that are common to all woodsmen, white or red, and this simply because he has not studied the pale-faced variety.

This notion of an absolute originality, as if one could have a patent-right in it, is an absurdity. A man cannot escape in thought, any more than he can in language, from the past and the present. As no one ever invents a word, and yet language somehow grows by general contribution and necessity, so it is with thought. Mr. Thoreau seems to me to insist in public on going back to flint and steel, when there is a match-box in his pocket which he knows very well how to use at a pinch. Originality consists in power of digesting and assimilating thought, so that they become part of our life and substance. Montaigne, for example, is one of the most original of authors, though he helped himself to ideas in every direction. But they turn to blood and coloring in his style, and give a freshness of complexion that is forever charming. In Thoreau much seems yet to be foreign and unassimilated, showing itself in symptoms of indigestion. A preacher-up of Nature, we now and then detect under the surly and stoic garb something of the sophist and the sentimentalizer. I am far from implying that this was conscious on his part. But it is much easier for a man to impose on himself when he measures only with himself. A greater familiarity with ordinary men would have done Thoreau good, by showing him how many fine qualities are common to the race. The radical vice of his theory of life was that he confounded physical with spiritual remoteness from men. A man is far enough withdrawn from his fellows if he keep himself clear of their weaknesses. He is not so truly withdrawn as exiled, if he refuse to share in their strength. "Solitude," says Cowley, "can be well fitted and set right but upon a very few persons. They must have enough knowledge of the world to see the vanity of it, and enough virtue to despise all vanity." It is a morbid self-consciousness that pronounces the world of men empty and worthless before trying it, the instinctive evasion of one who is sensible of some innate weakness, and retorts the accusation of it before any has made it but himself. To a healthy mind, the world is a constant challenge of opportunity. Mr. Thoreau had not a healthy mind, or he would not have been so fond of prescribing. His whole life was a search for the doctor. The old mystics had a wiser sense of what the world was worth. They ordained a severe apprenticeship to law, and even ceremonial, in order to the gaining of freedom and mastery over these. Seven years of service for Rachel were to be rewarded at last with Leah. Seven other years of faithfulness with her were to win them at last the true bride of their souls. Active Life was with them the only path to the Contemplative.

Thoreau had no humor, and this implies that he was a sorry logician. Himself an artist in rhetoric, he confounds thought with style when he undertakes to speak of the latter. He was forever talking of getting away from the world, but he must be always near enough to it, nay, to the Concord corner of it, to feel the impression he makes there. He verifies the shrewd remark of Sainte-Beuve, «On touche encore a son temps et tres-fort, meme quand on le repousse.» This egotism of his is a Stylites pillar after all, a seclusion which keeps him in the public eye. The dignity of man is an excellent thing, but therefore to hold one's self too sacred and precious is the reverse of excellent. There is something delightfully absurd in six volumes addressed to a world of such "vulgar fellows" as Thoreau affirmed his fellowmen to be. I once had a glimpse of a genuine solitary who spent his winters one hundred and fifty miles beyond all human communication, and there dwelt with his rifle as his only confidant. Compared with this, the shanty on Walden Pond has something the air, it must be confessed, of the Hermitage of La Chevrette. I do not believe that the way to a true cosmopolitanism carries one into the woods or the society of musquashes. Perhaps the narrowest provincialism is that of Self; that of Kleinwinkel is nothing to it. The natural man, like the singing birds, comes out of the forest as inevitably as the natural bear and the wildcat stick there. To seek to be natural implies a consciousness that forbids all naturalness forever. It is as easy—and no easier—to be natural in a *salon* as in a swamp, if one do not aim at it, for what we call unnaturalness always has its spring in a man's thinking too much about himself. "It is impossible," said Turgot, "for a vulgar man to be simple."

I look upon a great deal of the modern sentimentalism about Nature as a mark of disease. It is one more symptom of the general liver-complaint. To a man of wholesome constitution the wilderness is well enough for a mood or a vacation, but not for a habit of life. Those who have most loudly advertised their passion for seclusion and their intimacy with nature, from Petrarch down, have been mostly sentimentalists, unreal men, misanthropes on the spindle side, solacing an uneasy suspicion of themselves by professing contempt for their kind. They make demands on the world in advance proportioned to their inward measure of their own merit, and are angry that the world pays only by the visible measure of performance. It is true of Rousseau, the modern founder of the sect, true of Saint Pierre, his intellectual child, and of Chateaubriand, his grandchild, the inventor, we might almost say, of the primitive forest, and who first was touched by the solemn falling of a tree from natural decay in the windless silence of the woods. It is a very shallow view that affirms trees and rocks to be healthy, and cannot see that men in communities are just as true to the laws of their organization and destiny; that can tolerate the puffin and the fox, but not the fool and the knave; that would shun politics because of its demagogues, and snuff up the stench of the obscene fungus. The divine life of Nature is more wonderful, more various, more sublime in man than in any other of her works, and the wisdom that is gained by commerce with men, as Montaigne and Shakespeare gained it, or with one's own soul among men, as Dante, is the most delightful, as it is the most precious, of all. In outward nature it is still man that interests us, and we care far less for the things seen than the way in which they are seen by poetic eyes like Wordsworth's or Thoreau's, and the reflections they cast there. To hear the to-do that is often made over the simple fact that a man sees the image of himself in the outward world, one is reminded of a savage when he for the first time catches a glimpse of himself in a looking-glass. "Venerable child of Nature," we are tempted to say, "to whose science in the invention of the tobacco-pipe, to whose art in the tattooing of thine undegenerate hide not yet enslaved by tailors, we are slowly striving to climb back, the miracle thou beholdest is sold in my unhappy country for a shilling!" If matters go on as they have done, and everybody must needs blab of all the favors that have been done him by roadside and river-brink and woodland walk, as if to kiss and tell were no longer treachery, it will be a positive refreshment to meet a man who is as superbly indifferent to Nature as she is to him. By and by we shall have John Smith, of No. –12 –12th Street, advertising that he is not the J. S. who saw a cowlily on Thursday last, as he never saw one in his life, would not see one if he could, and is prepared to prove an alibi on the day in question.

Solitary communion with Nature does not seem to have been sanitary or sweetening in its influence on Thoreau's character. On the contrary, his letters show him more cynical as he grew older. While he studied with respectful attention the minks and woodchucks, his neighbors, he looked with utter contempt on the august drama of destiny of which his country was the scene, and on which the curtain had already risen. He was converting us back to a state of nature "so eloquently," as Voltaire said of Rousseau, "that he almost persuaded us to go on all fours," while the wiser fates were making it possible for us to walk erect for the first time. Had he conversed more with his fellows, his sympathies would have widened with the assurance that his peculiar genius had more appreciation, and his writings a larger circle of readers, or at least a warmer one, than he dreamed of. We have the highest testimony[1] to the natural sweetness, sincerity, and nobleness of his temper, and in his books an equally irrefragable one to the rare quality of his mind.

He was not a strong thinker, but a sensitive feeler. Yet his mind strikes us as cold and wintry in its purity. A light snow has fallen everywhere in which he seems to come on the track of the shier sensations that would elsewhere leave no trace. We think greater compression would have done more for his fame. A feeling of sameness comes over us as we read so much. Trifles are recorded with an over-minute punctuality and conscientiousness of detail. He registers the state of his personal thermometer thirteen times a day. We cannot help thinking sometimes of the man who

> Watches, starves, freezes, and sweats
> To learn but catechisms and alphabets
> Of unconcerning things, matters of fact,

and sometimes of the saying of the Persian poet, that "when the owl would boast, he boasts of catching mice at the edge of a hole." We could readily part with some of his affectations. It was well enough for Pythagoras to say, once for all, "When I was Euphorbus at the siege of Troy"; not so well for Thoreau to travesty it into "When I was a shepherd on the plains of Assyria." A naive thing said over again is anything but naive. But with every exception, there is no writing comparable with Thoreau's in kind, that is comparable with it in degree where it is best; where it disengages itself, that is, from the tangled roots and dead leaves of a second-hand Orientalism, and runs limpid and smooth and broadening as it runs, a mirror for whatever is grand and lovely in both worlds.

George Sand says neatly, that "Art is not a study of positive reality," (*actuality* were the fitter word,) "but a seeking after ideal truth." It would be doing very inadequate justice to Thoreau if we left it to be inferred that this ideal element did not exist in him, and that too in larger proportion, if less obtrusive, than his nature-worship. He took nature as the mountain-path to an ideal world. If the path wind a good deal, if he record too faithfully every trip over a root, if he botanize somewhat wearisomely, he gives us now and then superb outlooks from some jutting crag, and brings us out at last into an illimitable ether, where the breathing is not difficult for those who have any true touch of the climbing spirit. His shanty-life was a mere impossibility, so far as his own conception of it goes, as an entire independency of mankind. The tub of Diogenes had a sounder bottom. Thoreau's experiment actually presupposed all that complicated civilization which it theoretically abjured. He squatted on another man's land; he borrows an axe; his boards, his nails, his bricks, his mortar, his books, his lamp, his fish-hooks, his plough, his hoe, all turn state's evidence against him as an accomplice in the sin of that artificial civilization which rendered it possible that such a person as Henry D. Thoreau should exist at all. *Magnis tamen excidit ausis.* His aim was a noble and a useful one, in the direction of "plain living and high thinking." It was a practical sermon on Emerson's text that "things are in the saddle and ride mankind," an attempt to solve Carlyle's problem (condensed from Johnson) of "lessening your denominator." His whole life was a rebuke of the waste and aimlessness of our American luxury, which is an abject enslavement to tawdry upholstery. He had "fine translunary things" in him. His better style as a writer is in keeping with the simplicity and purity of his life. We have said that his range was narrow, but to be a master is to be a master. He had caught his English at its living source, among the poets and prose-writers of its best days; his literature was extensive and recondite; his quotations are always nuggets of the purest ore: there are sentences of his as perfect as anything in the language, and thoughts as clearly crystallized; his metaphors and images are always fresh from the soil; he had watched Nature like a detective who is to go upon the stand; as we read him, it seems as if all-out-of-doors had kept a diary and become its own Montaigne; we look at the landscape as in a Claude Lorraine glass; compared with his, all other books of similar aim, even White's "Selborne," seem dry as a country clergyman's meteorological journal in an old almanac. He belongs with Donne and Browne and Novalis; if not with the originally creative men, with the scarcely smaller class who are peculiar, and whose leaves shed their invisible thought-seed like ferns.

Notes

1. Mr. Emerson, in the Biographical Sketch prefixed to the Excursions

—James Russell Lowell, from "Thoreau,"
1865, *Works*, Riverside ed., 1890, vol. 1,
pp. 368–381

A. Bronson Alcott "Thoreau" (1869)

American philosopher, teacher, and reformer Amos Bronson Alcott (1799–1888) was an important member of the transcendentalist group and the father of writer Louisa May Alcott. Although Bronson Alcott does not prominently feature in historical accounts of American literature, he was involved in all the major reform debates of his century, particularly those concerning education, abolition, and women's rights.

Alcott was the son of a flax farmer and, because of the family's limited means, he did not receive a formal education. Largely self-educated,

Alcott soon became interested in ways of innovating teaching methods. This interest led him to establish a series of schools for children, including Boston's Temple School, whose innovative methods were not readily accepted by everyone. Bronson believed that children are naturally good and that the development of their morality and expression depends on a motivating and caring educational environment. In the 1830s, however, Alcott fell into debt and was forced to close his schools, including the main one in Boston. In 1843, he founded Fruitlands, a utopian community in Massachusetts, based on asceticism and vegetarianism, which lasted less than a year. After this failed experiment, Alcott secured a place as Concord school superintendent from 1859 to 1864. However, the family's financial security was not established until the late 1860s when his daughter Louisa May Alcott enjoyed nationwide success with the publication of her novel *Little Women* (1868).

As other transcendentalist critics, Alcott too points out that Thoreau was a "lover of the wild" and "a son of nature." He compares Thoreau's inspiration in his descriptions of nature to those of classic Greek and Latin authors such as Theocritus and Virgil. An important part of their literary production consisted of pastoral elegies, where a shepherd-poet sings his love lament. The genre was characterized by homoerotic desire and a nostalgia for simpler times. Alcott places Thoreau in this classic tradition, as he shared with these authors a sense of communion with natural elements. This classical referencing, however, is not the only tradition into which Alcott places Thoreau. At the same time, the critic describes the author of *Walden* as a proud and typical New Englander. As with many other transcendentalists, Alcott downplayed Thoreau's social concerns, a surprising move as both of them shared a common adversity to slavery. To Alcott, Thoreau's preferred themes were "nature, poetry, life,—not politics, not strict science, not society as it is." As has been mentioned in the introductions to other critical pieces collected in this volume, such an assessment has been revised by later criticism of Thoreau taking into account his contacts with other transcendentalists and his life-long battle for abolitionism.

Although Alcott admits that Thoreau's writings did not reach a vast audience during the author's lifetime, he prophesizes that such large readership will be granted to them in the future. Literary history has proved him right.

My friend and neighbor united these qualities of sylvan and human in a more remarkable manner than any whom it has been my happiness to know.

Lover of the wild, he lived a borderer on the confines of civilization, jealous of the least encroachment upon his possessions.

> Society were all but rude
> In his umbrageous solitude.

I had never thought of knowing a man so thoroughly of the country, and so purely a son of nature. I think he had the profoundest passion for it of any one of his time; and had the human sentiment been as tender and pervading, would have given us pastorals of which Virgil and Theocritus might have envied him the authorship had they chanced to be his contemporaries. As it was, he came nearer the antique spirit than any of our native poets, and touched the fields and groves and streams of his native town with a classic interest that shall not fade. Some of his verses are suffused with an elegiac tenderness, as if the woods and brooks bewailed the absence of their Lycidas, and murmured their griefs meanwhile to one another,—responsive like idyls. Living in close companionship with nature, his muse breathed the spirit and voice of poetry. For when the heart is once divorced from the senses and all sympathy with common things, then poetry has fled and the love that sings.

The most welcome of companions was this plain countryman. One seldom meets with thoughts like his, coming so scented of mountain and field breezes and rippling springs, so like a luxuriant clod from under forest leaves, moist and mossy with earth-spirits. His presence was tonic, like ice-water in dog-days to the parched citizen pent in chambers and under brazen ceilings. Welcome as the gurgle of brooks and dipping of pitchers,—then drink and be cool! He seemed one with things, of nature's essence and core, knit of strong timbers,—like a wood and its inhabitants. There was in him sod and shade, wilds and waters manifold,—the mould and mist of earth and sky. Self-poised and sagacious as any denizen of the elements, he had the key to every animal's brain, every plant; and were an Indian to flower forth and reveal the scents hidden in his cranium, it would not be more surprising than the speech of our Sylvanus. He belonged to the Homeric age,—was older than pastures and gardens, as if he were of the race of heroes and one with the elements. He of all men seemed to be the native New-Englander, as much so as the oak, the granite ledge; our best sample of an indigenous American, untouched by the old country, unless he came down rather from Thor, the Northman, whose name he bore.

A peripatetic philosopher, and out-of-doors for the best part of his days and nights, he had manifold weather and seasons in him; the manners of an animal of probity and virtue unstained. Of all our moralists, he seemed the wholesomest, the busiest, and the best republican citizen in the world; always at home minding his own affairs. A little over-confident by genius, and stiffly individual, dropping society clean out of his theories, while standing friendly in his strict sense of friendship, there was in him an integrity and love of justice that made possible and actual the virtues of Sparta and the Stoics,—all the more welcome in his time of shuffling and pusillanimity. Plutarch would have made him immortal in his pages had he lived before his day. Nor have we any so modern withal, so entirely his own and ours: too purely so to be appreciated at once. A scholar by birthright, and an author, his fame had not, at his decease, travelled far from the banks of the rivers he described in his books; but one hazards only the truth in affirming of his prose, that in substance and pith, it surpasses that of any naturalist of his time; and he is sure of large reading in the future. There are fairer fishes in his pages than any swimming in our streams; some sleep of his on the banks of the Merrimack by moonlight that Egypt never rivalled; a morning of which Memnon might have envied the music, and a greyhound he once had, meant for Adonis; frogs, better than any of Aristophanes; apples wilder than Adam's. His senses seemed double, giving him access to secrets not easily read by others; in sagacity resembling that of the beaver, the bee, the dog, the deer; an instinct for seeing and judging, as by some other, or seventh sense; dealing with objects as if they were shooting forth from his mind mythologically, thus completing the world all round to his senses; a creation of his at the moment. I am sure he knew the animals one by one, as most else knowable in his town; the plants, the geography, as Adam did in his Paradise, if, indeed, he were not that ancestor himself. His works are pieces of exquisite sense, celebrations of Nature's virginity exemplified by rare learning, delicate art, replete with observations as accurate as original; contributions of the unique to the natural history of his country, and without which it were incomplete. Seldom has a head circumscribed so much of the sense and core of Cosmos as this footed intelligence.

If one would learn the wealth of wit there was in this plain man, the information, the poetry, the piety, he should have accompanied him on an afternoon walk to Walden, or elsewhere about the skirts of his village residence. Pagan as he might outwardly appear, yet he was the hearty worshipper of whatsoever is sound and wholesome in nature,—a piece of russet probity and strong sense, that nature delighted to own and honor. His talk was suggestive, subtle, sincere, under as many masks and mimicries as the shows he might pass; as significant, substantial,—nature choosing to speak through his mouth-piece,—cynically, perhaps, and searching into the marrows of men and times he spoke of, to his discomfort mostly and avoidance.

Nature, poetry, life,—not politics, not strict science, not society as it is,—were his preferred themes. The world was holy, the things seen symbolizing the things unseen, and thus worthy of worship, calling men out-of-doors and under the firmament for health and wholesomeness to be insinuated into their souls, not as idolators, but as idealists. His religion was of the most primitive type, inclusive of all natural creatures and things, even to "the sparrow that falls to the ground," though never by shot of his, and for whatsoever was manly in men, his worship was comparable to that of the priests and heroes of all time. I should say he inspired the sentiment of love, if, indeed, the sentiment did not seem to partake of something purer, were that possible, but nameless from its excellency. Certainly he was better poised and more nearly self-reliant than other men.

> The happy man who lived content
> With his own town, his continent,
> Whose chiding streams its banks did curb
> As ocean circumscribes its orb,
> Round which, when he his walk did take,
> Thought he performed far more than Drake;
> For other lands he took less thought
> Than this his muse and mother brought.

More primitive and Homeric than any American, his style of thinking was robust, racy, as if Nature herself had built his sentences and seasoned the sense of his paragraphs with her own vigor and salubrity. Nothing can be spared from them; there is nothing superfluous; all is compact, concrete, as nature is.

—A. Bronson Alcott, "Thoreau,"
April 5, 1869, *Concord Days*, 1872,
pp. 11–16

WILLIAM ELLERY CHANNING (1873)

William Ellery Channing (1780–1842) was the author of the first biography of Thoreau, *Thoreau: The Poet-Naturalist* (1873). Channing is usually described as the father of Unitarianism, a new denomination that emerged in the 1820s from splits within New England Calvinism. Unitarians criticized Calvinism for its belief in the innate depravity of man and the predestination to God's grace. Against these somber doctrines, Unitarians described spiritual life as a process of strengthening the spiritual potentialities of the self. Unitarians did not take for granted salvation and sainthood, on the contrary, they stressed the importance of pursuing spiritual perfection. Such perfection was, however, attainable, because of the inherent likeness of the human soul with God. Channing was the most prominent leader of Unitarianism and was, for almost forty years, the minister of the Federal Street Church in Boston, the most prominent Unitarian congregation in America.

Channing was also well known in New England transcendentalist circles. Although the relationship between transcendentalism and Unitarianism was a complex one and transcendentalists at times criticized the new religious denomination, they both shared a fundamental faith in the potentialities of the self.

Channing studied theology in Newport and Harvard and became an inspirational preacher in and around Boston. Because of his unorthodox Calvinism, he was attacked as a "Unitarian," a negative label that he adopted for his new denomination. At first Channing did not wish to found a new church, claiming that he did not want to replace Calvinism with another orthodoxy and, in 1820, he simply formed a conference of liberal congregational ministers. Five years later, this was reorganized as the American Unitarian Association. During his life, Channing also took part in the many reform movements of his age, and, with the treatise *Negro Slavery* (1835), he took a firm stance against slavery. This position was rooted in his religious beliefs that individuals should have the opportunity to develop to their fullest capability. Slavery obviously thwarted such possibility.

Channing was the first to address explicitly the dichotomy in Thoreau's writings between objective reporting and subjective interpretation. He describes the author of *Walden* as a "poet-naturalist," a definition that tries to bridge the two poles usually detected in Thoreau's writings. Channing finds that Thoreau's style combines detailed observations of nature with a deep awareness of literary heritage. For example, commenting on *A Week on the Concord and Merrimack Rivers*, Channing writes that the book is "a faithful record of the scenery" observed by the author and that, at the same time, the volume is also of great literary merit with its "treasury of citations from other authors."

One of the objects of our poet-naturalist was to acquire the art of writing a good English style. So Goethe, that slow and artful formalist, spent himself in acquiring a good German style. And what Thoreau thought of this matter of writing may be learned from many passages in this sketch, and from this among the rest: "It is the fault of some excellent writers, and De Quincey's first impressions on seeing London suggest it to me, that they express themselves with too great fulness and detail. They give the most faithful, natural, and lifelike account of their sensations, mental and physical, but they lack moderation and sententiousness. They do not affect us as an ineffectual earnest, and a reserve of meaning, like a stutterer: they say all they mean. Their sentences are not concentrated and nutty,—sentences which suggest far more than they say, which have an atmosphere about them, which do not report an old, but make a new impression; sentences which suggest on many things, and are as durable as a Roman aqueduct: to frame these,—that is the *art* of writing. Sentences which are expressive, towards which so many volumes, so much life, went; which lie like boulders on the page up and down, or across; which contain the seed of other sentences, not mere repetition, but creation; and which a man might sell his ground or cattle to build. De Quincey's style is nowhere kinked or knotted up into something hard and significant, which you could swallow like a diamond, without digesting."

As in the story, "And that's Peg Woffington's notion of an actress! Better it, Cibber and Bracegirdle, if you can!" This moderation does, *for the most part,* characterize his works, both of prose and verse. They have their stoical merits, their uncomfortableness! It is one result to be lean and sacrificial; yet a balance of comfort and a house of freestone on the sunny side of Beacon Street can be endured, in a manner, by weak nerves. But the fact that our author lived for a while alone in a shanty near a pond or *stagnum,* and named one of his books after the place where it stood, has led some to say he was a barbarian or a misanthrope. It was a writing-case:—

This, as an amber drop enwraps a bee,
Covering discovers your quick soul, that we
May in your through-shine front your heart's thoughts see.
                              (Donne)

Here, in this wooden inkstand, he wrote a good part of his famous *Walden;* and this solitary woodland pool was more to his muse than all oceans of the planet, by the force of that faculty on which he was never weary of descanting,—Imagination. Without this, he says, human life, dressed in its Jewish or other gaberdine, would be a kind of lunatic's hospital,—insane with the prose of it, mad with the drouth of society's remainder-biscuits; but add the phantasy, that glorious, that divine gift, and then—

The earth, the air, and seas I know, and all
The joys and horrors of their peace and wars;
And now will view the gods' state and the stars.
(Chapman)

Out of this faculty was his written experience chiefly constructed,—upon this he lived; not upon the cracked wheats and bread-fruits of an outward platter. His essays, those masterful creations, taking up the commonest topics; a sour apple, an autumn leaf, are features of this wondrous imagination of his; and, as it was his very life-blood, he, least of all, sets it forth in labored description. He did not bring forward his means, or unlock the closet of his Maelzel's automaton chess-player. The reader cares not that the writer of a novel, with two lovers in hand, should walk out in the fool's-cap, and begin balancing some peacock's feather on his nose.

Begin, murderer,—leave thy damnable faces, and begin!

He loved antithesis in verse. It could pass for paradox,—something subtractive and unsatisfactory, as the four herrings provided by Caleb Balderstone for Ravenswood's dinner: come, he says, let us see how miserably uncomfortable we can feel. Hawthorne, too, enjoyed a grave, and a pocket full of miseries to nibble upon.

There was a lurking humor in almost all that he said,—a dry wit, often expressed. He used to laugh heartily and many times in all the interviews I had, when anything in that direction was needed. Certainly he has left some exquisitely humorous pieces, showing his nice discernment; and he has narrated an encounter truly curious and wonderful,—the story of a snapping-turtle swallowing a horn-pout. In the latest pieces on which he worked he showed an anxiety to correct them by leaving out the few innuendoes, sallies, or puns, that formerly luxuriated amid the serious pages. No one more quickly entertained the apprehension of a jest; and his replies often came with a startling promptness, as well as perfection,—as if premeditated. This offhand talent lay in his habit of deep thought and mature reflection; in the great treasury of his wit he had weapons ready furnished for nearly all occasions.

Of his own works, the *Week* was at his death for the most part still in the sheets, unbound; a small edition of *Walden* was sold in some seven years after its publishing. His dealings with publishers (who dealt with him in the most mean and niggardly style) affected him with a shyness of that class. It was with the utmost difficulty he was paid for what he wrote by the persons who bought his wares; for one of his printed articles the note of the publishers was put by him in the bank for collection. Of the non-sale of the *Week* he said, "I believe that this result is more inspiring and better for me than if a thousand had bought my wares. It affects my privacy less, and leaves me freer." Some cultivated minds place *Walden* in the front rank; but both his books are so good they will stand on their own merits. His latest-written work (the *Excursions*—a collection of lectures, mainly) is a great favorite with his friends. His works are household words to those who have long known them; and the larger circle he is sure, with time, to address will follow in our footsteps. Such a treasure as the *Week*,—so filled with images from nature,—such a faithful record of the scenery and the people on the banks,—could not fail to make a deep impression. Its literary merit is also great; as a treasury of citations from other authors, it gives a favorable view of his widely extended reading. Few books in this respect can be found to surpass it.

In his discourse of Friendship, Thoreau starts with the idea of *"underpropping* his love by such pure hate, that it would *end* in sympathy," like sweet butter from sour cream. And in this:—

> Two solitary stars,—
> Unmeasured systems far
> Between us roll;

getting off into the agonies of space, where everything freezes, yet he adds as inducement,—

> But by our conscious light we are
> Determined to one pole.

In other words, there was a pole apiece. He continues the antithesis, and says there is "no more use in friendship than in the tints of flowers" (the chief use in them); "pathless the gulf of feeling yawns," and the reader yawns, too, at the idea of tumbling into it. And so he packs up in his mind "all the clothes which outward nature wears," like a young lady's trunk going to Mount Desert.

We must not expect literature, in such case, to run its hands round the dial-plate of style with cuckoo repetition: the snarls he criticises De Quincey for *not* getting into are the places where *his* bundles of sweetmeats untie. As in the Vendidad, "Hail to thee, O man! who art come from the transitory place to the imperishable":—

In Nature's nothing, be not nature's toy.

This feature in his style is by no means so much bestowed upon his prose as his poetry. In his verse he more than once attained to beauty, more often to quaintness. He did not court admiration, though he admired fame; and he might have said to his reader,—

Whoe'er thou beest who read'st this sullen writ,
Which just so much courts thee as thou dost it.

—William Ellery Channing, *Thoreau:
The Poet-Naturalist*, 1873, ed.
F.B. Sanborn, 1902, pp. 229–234

ALEXANDER HAY JAPP (1878)

The Scottish writer, publisher, and editor Alexander Hay Japp (1837–1895) was the author, after Channing's, of a second biography of Thoreau, *Thoreau: His Life and Aims* (1877). An expert on the Victorian literary scene, he played a crucial role in securing the serialized publication of Robert Louis Stevenson's *The Sea Cook*, which went on to become an international best-seller under the title *Treasure Island*.

In the excerpt that follows, Japp complains that Thoreau has been treated so far as a mere disciple of Emerson. He also points out the fact that Thoreau's reputation as a transcendentalist has earned him many enemies in the scientific community. Japp here refers to the reaction against science and the Enlightenment of which transcendentalism, like European romanticism, was an important part. The Scottish writer confronts the dichotomy in Thoreau's writings between humanism and science, two polarities that much subsequent criticism on the author of *Walden* has addressed. Far from being a handicap, the fact that Thoreau was also a poet and not only a man of science enriches his scientific dimension. According to Japp, because Thoreau was also a poet, he was able to uplift science and avoid its separation from humanity. Contrary to the majority of the early critical pieces on Thoreau, Japp's characterization of the New England writer emphasizes his philanthropic and Christian vision. Japp's portrayal of Thoreau is thus in stark contrast to those that depict Thoreau as a hermit aloof from society.

Thoreau has been too absolutely claimed by the transcendentalists and treated as a mere disciple of Emerson. This has led in large measure to his being rejected all too decisively by the purely scientific men, for whom, nevertheless, he has many hints that are equally original and valuable. It must be admitted, however, that if he had been less of a poet, he would have recommended himself better to the scientific class, precisely as he would have been a better Emersonian, if his eye for concrete facts had been less keen. He is impatient of certain forms of analysis—more concerned to gain insight into the inner nature than to anatomize and win knowledge of the mere details of structure.

Both these circumstances have tended to deprive Thoreau of the credit that belongs to him. After you deduct in the most exacting manner all that is due to Emerson and Transcendentalism, and allow that in some points he failed under the most rigid reckonings of science, much remains to establish his claims on our sympathy and deference. His instincts were true; his patience was unbounded; he never flinched from pain or labour when it lay in the way of his object; and complaint he was never known to utter on his own account.

No hard logical line ought to be laid to his utterances in the sphere of personal opinion or liking. He confessedly wrote without regard to abstract consistency. His whole life was determined by sympathy, though he sometimes seemed cynical. We are fain to think, indeed, that under his brusqueness, there lay a suppressed humorous questioning of his reader's capacity and consequent right to understand him and to offer sympathy. If, on this account, he may be said to have sacrificed popularity, he paid the penalty, which people often pay in actual life for too consciously hiding their true feelings under a veil of indifference; and it is much if we find that the cynical manner seldom intruded on the real nature.

The story of Thoreau's life has a value too, inasmuch as we see in him how the tendency of culture, and of theoretic speculation, towards rationalistic indifference, and a general unconcern in the fate of others, may be checked by a genuine love of nature, and by the self-denials she can prompt in the regard that she conveys and enforces for the individual life and for freedom. The practical lesson of a true Transcendentalism, faithfully applied, must issue thus—and it is the same whether we see it in St. Francis, in the saintly Eckhart, in William Law, or in the naturalist Thoreau. All life is sanctified by the relation in which it is seen to the source of life—an idea which lies close to the Christian spirit, however much a fixed and rationalized dogmatic relation to it may tend to dessicate and render bare and arid those spaces of the individual nature, which can bloom and blossom only through sympathy and emotions that ally themselves with what is strictly mystical.

It was through nature, to which he retreated, that Thoreau recovered his philanthropic interests—his love of mankind, which he might have come near to losing through the spirit of culture which can only encourage cynicism and weariness in view of artificial conventions and pretexts. Thoreau would have shrunk with loathing horror from the touch of that savant, who, as Agassiz seriously assures us, said to him that the age of real civilization would have begun when you could go out and shoot a man for scientific purposes. This seems very awful when put baldly on paper: it is but the necessary expression of the last result of culture coldly rationalistic, of science determinately materialistic, since both alike must operate towards loosening the bonds of natural sympathy. Thoreau was saved from the "modern curse of culture" by his innocent delights, and his reverence for all forms of life, so stimulated. His strong faith in the higher destiny of humanity through the triumph of clearer moral aims, and the apprehension of a good beyond the individual or even the national interest, would have linked him practically with the Christian philanthropist rather than with the cultured indifferentist or worshipper of artistic beauty or knowledge for their own sakes.

In this view Thoreau, in spite of his transcendentalism, or, as some would say, professed pantheism, was a missionary. His testimony bears in the direction of showing that the study of nature, when pursued in such a way as to keep alive individual affection and the sentiments of reverence, is one that practically must work in alliance with enlightened Christian conceptions, and that in a moment of real peril, when cruelty and wrong and disorder else would triumph, the true votary of nature will be on the side of the Christian hero, who suffers wrong to redeem the weak. Thoreau thus exhibits to us one way of uplifting science, in relieving her from the false associations which would disconnect her from common humanity, and set her in opposition to its strongest instincts—the science falsely so called, which by baseless asumptions would demoralize, materialize, and brutify, and refuse scope to the exercise of the more ideal and beneficient part of man because it fails to comprehend it or to cover it adequately by its exacting definitions.

It would be ungrateful in us, who are so deeply indebted to Emerson for many benefits, to analyze at length the deteriorating effect which his teachings had, in certain directions, on Thoreau. But they are too outstanding to be wholly passed over without notice. It is patent that Thoreau's peculiar gifts led him to deal with outward things. He was an observer, a quick-eyed and sympathetic recorder of the inner life of nature. Emerson's teaching developed a certain self-conscious and theorising tendency far from natural to Thoreau. He is often too concerned to seek justification for certain facts in purely ideal conceptions which nevertheless have not been reduced to coherency with a general scheme. He is too indifferent to the ordinary scientific order, too much intent on giving us a cosmology in fragments, in which paradox shall startle, if it does not enlighten. Whenever Thoreau proceeds to air abstract statements he is treading on insecure ground; his love of Emersonian philosphy leads him some strange dances. Above all, this foreign element is seen in the effusive egotism which constantly appears when he leaves the ground of facts for general disquisition. He would fain attract us by forced freshness and by the effort to utter paradoxical and startling statements. No man could be more clear, simple, direct, incisive than he is when he has a real nature-object before his eye or his mind; for memory never fails him. But when he is abstract and oracular, he is oftentimes more puzzling than his master. When Thoreau is telling his own story—what he saw, what he heard, what he did,—he is simply delightful. His pantheism, so far as it was a conscious thing with him, is not inviting; and would often be very hard and unattractive, were it not that his instincts were far truer than his mind was exact on the logical side, and saved him from the natural effects of such vagary and paradoxical assertions. But we can dissociate Thoreau's merits from these adhesions. His Emersonian pantheism did not destroy his finer sensibilities and sympathies, which made him, as he certainly was, one of nature's diviners and reconcilers—a pantheist as all true poets have been, as Christ Himself was. Like many others, he brought a double gift; but that which is truest and most available is that of which he made but little account. So it is that we believe we can detach from his writings what will serve to illustrate the better side of his genius. Fitly and fully done, this cannot but prove a service; for we can ill afford wholly to miss the benefit of the record of such a peculiar experience—a discerning and divining instinct, on the whole wisely directed to its true purpose, and revealing rare possibilities in human life, new relationships and sources of deep joy.

—Alexander Hay Japp, as "H.A. Page",
Thoreau: His Life and Aims, 1878, pp. 257–264

THOMAS WENTWORTH HIGGINSON
"THOREAU" (1879)

Thomas Wentworth Higginson (1823–1911) shared with Thoreau abolitionist sympathies. A graduate of Harvard Divinity School, Higginson became a Unitarian pastor at the First Religious Society of Newburyport,

Massachusetts. Yet, his progressive and liberal views on topics such as slavery and women's and workers' rights caused him to be dismissed by his congregation. He actively campaigned against the Fugitive Slave Act (1850) and supported John Brown's raid on Harpers Ferry. During the Civil War, Higginson led the first black regiment in the U.S. armed forces. After the end of the war, he became the author of popular novels and biographies.

Given their common abolitionist background, it is surprising that Higginson's description of Thoreau is based on the usual opposition between the author and the larger society. Higginson regrets that Thoreau's lack of contacts with society deprived him of meaningful influences that might have "liberalized some of his judgments, and softened some of his verdicts." Despite this regret, Higginson disagrees with the common critical assessment of his times that saw in Thoreau only a minor Emerson. In particular, like Channing, Higginson appreciates Thoreau's combination of natural observations and literary learning in his writing style.

It will always be an interesting question, how far Thoreau's peculiar genius might have been modified or enriched by society or travel. In his diary he expresses gratitude to Providence, or, as he quaintly puts it, "to those who have had the handling of me," that his life has been so restricted in these directions, and that he has thus been compelled to extract its utmost nutriment from the soil where he was born. Yet in examining these diaries, even more than in reading his books, one is led to doubt, after all, whether this mental asceticism was best for him, just as one suspects that the vegetable diet in which he exulted may possibly have shortened his life. A larger experience might have liberalized some of his judgments, and softened some of his verdicts. He was not as just to men as to woodchucks; and his "simplify, I say, simplify," might well have been relaxed a little for mankind, in view of the boundless affluence of external nature. The world of art might also have deeply influenced him, had the way been opened for its closer study. Emerson speaks of "the raptures of a citizen arrived at his first meadow;" but a deep, ascetic soul like Thoreau's could hardly have failed to be touched to a far profounder emotion by the first sight of a cathedral.

The impression that Thoreau was but a minor Emerson will in time pass away, like the early classification of Emerson as a second-hand Carlyle. All three were the children of their time, and had its family likeness; but Thoreau had the *lumen siccum*, or "dry light," beyond either of the others; indeed, beyond all men of his day. His temperament was like his native air in winter,—clear, frosty, inexpressibly pure and bracing. His power of literary appreciation was something marvellous, and his books might well be read for their quotations, like the sermons of Jeremy Taylor. His daring imagination ventured on the delineation of just those objects in nature which seem most defiant of description, as smoke, mist, haze; and his three poems on these themes have an exquisite felicity of structure such as nothing this side of the Greek anthology can equal. Indeed, the value of the classic languages was never better exemplified than in their influence on his training. They were real "humanities" to him; linking him with the great memories of the race, and with high intellectual standards, so that he could never, like some of his imitators, treat literary art as a thing unmanly and trivial. His selection of points in praising his favorite books shows this discrimination. He loves to speak of "the elaborate beauty and finish, and the lifelong literary labors of the ancients . . . works as refined, as solidly done, and as beautiful almost, as the morning itself." I remember how that fine old classical scholar, the late John Glen King, of Salem, used to delight in Thoreau as being "the only man who thoroughly loved both nature and Greek."

—Thomas Wentworth Higginson,
"Thoreau," 1879, *Short Studies of
American Authors,* 1888, pp. 27–30

HENRY JAMES (1880)

Henry James (1843–1916) was a central literary figure on the American and transatlantic scene. The major theme of his novels is the contrast between the innocence of the New World with the corruption and complex hierarchies of European society. James was also a prolific essayist. In the following piece on Hawthorne, James praises Thoreau's genius. Although the cosmopolitan James cannot avoid finding Thoreau "parochial," he values his originality and his spiritual observations of nature.

I said, a little way back, that the New England Transcendental movement had suffered, in the estimation of the world at large, from not having (putting Emerson aside) produced any superior talents. But any reference to it would be ungenerous which should omit to pay a tribute, in passing, to the author of *Walden.* Whatever question there may be of his talent, there can be none, I think, of his genius. It was a slim and crooked one, but it was eminently personal. He was imperfect, unfinished, inartistic; he was worse than provincial—he was parochial; it is only at his best that he is readable. But at his best he has an extreme natural charm, and he must always be mentioned after those Americans—Emerson, Hawthorne, Longfellow, Lowell, Motley—who have written originally. He was Emerson's independent moral man made flesh—living for the ages, and not for Saturday and Sunday; for the Universe, and not for Concord. In fact, however, Thoreau lived for Concord very effectually; and by his remarkable genius for the observation of the phenomena of woods and streams, of plants and trees, and beasts and fishes, and for flinging a kind of spiritual interest over these things, he did more than he perhaps intended towards consolidating the fame of his accidental human sojourn. He was as shy and ungregarious as Hawthorne; but he and the latter appear to have been sociably disposed towards each other, and there are some charming touches in the preface to the *Mosses* in regard to the hours they spent in boating together on the large, quiet Concord river. Thoreau was a great voyager, in a canoe which he had constructed himself, and which he eventually made over to Hawthorne, and as expert in the use of the paddle as the Red men who had once haunted the same silent stream.

—Henry James, *Hawthorne*, 1880, pp. 93–94

F.B. SANBORN (1882)

American journalist and reformer Franklin Benjamin Sanborn (1831–1917) became one of the chief biographers of transcendentalist intellectuals. In addition to Thoreau, he wrote on Emerson, Hawthorne, and Bronson Alcott. Sanborn descended from an old New England family and lived in the region's intellectual center of Concord. Like many of the transcendentalists he wrote about, Sanborn was an abolitionist, and, in the later part of his life, he was involved in various charitable and welfare causes, such as the prison reform movement.

As Sanborn was John Brown's New England agent, he particularly appreciated Thoreau's vigorous defense of Brown. According to Sanborn, Thoreau was so stirred by Brown's capture that he wrote his defense directly from the pages of his journal making few changes. This was unusual for Thoreau. While he used the observations in his diaries as the basis for his writings, he always elaborated on them and subjected them to constant change. Sanborn's characterization of Thoreau is that of a romantic writer constantly writing by night and by day and whose mind "tended naturally to the ideal side."

Emerson is primarily and chiefly a poet, and only a philosopher in his second intention; and thus also Thoreau, though a naturalist by habit, and a moralist by constitution, was inwardly a poet by force of that shaping and controlling imagination, which was his strongest faculty. His mind tended naturally to the ideal side. He would have been an idealist in any circumstances; a fluent and glowing poet, had he been born among a people to whom poesy is native, like the Greeks, the Italians, the Irish. As it was, his poetic light illumined every wide prospect and every narrow cranny in which his active, patient spirit pursued its task. It was this inward illumination as well as the star-like beam of Emerson's genius in "Nature," which caused Thoreau to write in his senior year at college, "This curious world which we inhabit is more wonderful than it is convenient; more beautiful than it is useful," and he cherished this belief through life. In youth, too, he said, "The other world is all my art, my pencils will draw no other, my jackknife will cut nothing else; I do not use it as a means." . . .

It seems to have been the habit of Thoreau, in writing verse, to compose a couplet, a quatrain, or other short metrical expression, copy it in his journal, and afterward, when these verses had grown to a considerable number, to arrange them in the form of a single piece. This gives to his poems the epigrammatic air which most of them have. After he was thirty years old, he wrote scarcely any verse, and he even destroyed much that he had previously written, following in this the judgment of Mr. Emerson, rather than his own, as he told me one day during his last illness. He had read all that was best in English and in Greek poetry, but was more familiar with the English poets of Milton's time and earlier, than with those more recent, except his own townsmen and companions. He valued Milton above Shakespeare, and had a special love for Eschylus, two of whose tragedies he translated. He had read Pindar, Simonides, and the Greek Anthology, and wrote, at his best, as well as the finest of the Greek lyric poets. Even Emerson, who was a severe critic of his verses, says, "His classic poem on 'Smoke' suggests Simonides, but is better than any poem of Simonides." . . .

His method in writing was peculiarly his own, though it bore some external resemblance to that of his friends, Emerson and Alcott. Like them he early began to keep a journal, which became both diary and commonplace book. But while they noted down the thoughts which occurred to them, without premeditation or consecutive arrangement, Thoreau made studies and observations for his journal as carefully and habitually as he noted the angles and distances in surveying a Concord farm. In all his daily walks and distant journeys, he took notes on the spot of what occurred to him, and these, often very brief and symbolic, he carefully wrote out, as soon as he could get time, in his diary, not classified by topics, but just as they had come to him. To these he added his daily meditations, sometimes expressed in verse, especially in the years between 1837 and 1850, but generally in close and pertinent prose. Many details are found in his diaries, but not such as are common in the diaries of other men,—not trivial but significant details. From these daily entries he made up his essays, his lectures, and his volumes; all being slowly, and with much deliberation and revision, brought into the form in which he gave them to the public. After that he scarcely changed them at all; they had received the last imprint of his mind, and he allowed them to stand and speak for themselves. But before printing, they underwent constant change, by addition, erasure, transposition, correction, and combination. A given lecture might be two years, or twenty years in preparation; or it might be, like his defense of John Brown, copied with little change from the pages of his diary for the fortnight previous. But that was an exceptional case; and Thoreau was stirred and quickened by the campaign and capture of Brown, as perhaps he had never been before.

The fact that Thoreau noted down his thoughts by night as well as by day, appears also from an entry in one of his journals, where he is describing the coming on of day, as witnessed by him at the close of a September night in Concord. "Some bird flies over," he writes, "making a noise like the barking of a puppy (it was a cuckoo). It is yet so dark that I have dropped my pencil and cannot find it." No writer of modern times, in fact, was so much awake and abroad at night, or has described better the phenomena of darkness and of moonlight.

—F.B. Sanborn, *Henry D. Thoreau,*
1882, pp. 284–287, 301–304

ALFRED H. WELSH (1883)

His English, we might judge, was acquired from the poets and prose-writers of its best days. His metaphors and images have the freshness of the soil. His range was narrow, but within his limits he was a master. He needed only a tender and pervading sentiment to have been a Homer. Pure and guileless, and fond of sympathy, he yet was cold and wintry. 'I love Henry,' said one of his friends, 'but I cannot like him; and as for taking his arm, I should as soon think of taking the arm of an elm-tree.' His works are replete with fine observations, finely expressed. One cannot fail to see the resemblance of his style to Emerson's and Alcott's. Nothing that he wrote can be spared.

—Alfred H. Welsh, *Development of English Literature and Language,* 1883, vol. 2, p. 413

Edwin P. Whipple
"American Literature" (1886)

American essayist and critic Edwin Percy Whipple (1819–1886) puts Thoreau in the tradition of American nature writers such as John James Audubon and Wilson Flagg. Thoreau is favorably compared to these two authors and is described as the American writer who managed to get closer "to the physical heart of Nature."

There are certain writers in American literature who charm by their eccentricity as well as by their genius, who are both original and originals. The most eminent, perhaps, of these was Henry D. Thoreau—a man who may be said to have penetrated nearer to the physical heart of Nature than any other American author. Indeed, he "experienced" nature as others are said to experience religion. Lowell says that in reading him it seems as "if all out-doors had kept a diary, and become its own Montaigne." He was so completely a naturalist that the inhabitants of the woods in which he sojourned forgot their well-founded distrust of man, and voted him the freedom of their city. His descriptions excel even those of Wilson, Audubon, and Wilson Flagg, admirable as these are, for he was in closer relations with the birds than they, and carried no gun in his hand. In respect to human society, he pushed his individuality to individualism; he was never happier than when absent from the abodes of civilization, and the toleration he would not extend to a Webster or a Calhoun he extended freely to a robin or a woodchuck. With all this peculiarity, he was a poet, a scholar, a humorist,—also, in his way, a philosopher and philanthropist; and those who knew him best, and entered most thoroughly into the spirit of his character and writings, are the warmest of all the admirers of his genius.

—Edwin P. Whipple, "American Literature," 1886, *American Literature and Other Papers,* 1887, pp. 111–12

CHARLES F. RICHARDSON (1887)

As a rule, . . . Thoreau is a remarkably even writer; his chapters were like his days, merely separate parts of a serene and little-diversified life, free from the restraints and pleasures of a real home, remote from burning human hopes and struggles, and, while caring much for the slave, caring little for country. No one would have thought of turning to this isolated life for personal sympathy, but Thoreau, in his turn, stood in small need of eliciting human help beyond his family, between whose members and himself there was a mild but genuine affection. He seemed to add something to the Emersonian courageous individuality, but in fact he let go from it the strongest part, its helpful humanity. It would not be a pleasant task to cull from Thoreau's writings proofs of an individualism which, to speak plainly, was terribly unlike the individualism of Jesus. After all, we read and praise Thoreau for what he tells us of the things he saw, and not for his records of himself.

—Charles F. Richardson, *American Literature, 1607–1885*, 1887, vol. 1, pp. 388–389

HAVELOCK ELLIS "WHITMAN" (1890)

Havelock Ellis (1858–1939) was an English essayist and physician who was among the first to challenge Victorian sexual taboos. His professional interest in medicine and sexual behavior was always paralleled by a keen fascination with literature. Ellis began his medical studies in 1881 at St. Thomas' Hospital, London. His meetings with dramatist George Bernard Shaw and critic Arthur Symons led to his appointment as editor of the *Mermaid Series of Old Dramatists*, publications that aimed to make drama a more popular genre with the general public. Ellis's major work is the seven-volume *Studies in the Psychology of Sex* (1897–1928), which caused a public and legal furor for its explicit treatment of forbidden topics such as homosexuality and masturbation. Throughout his life, Ellis continued to write on literary topics, publishing works on authors such as Whitman, Casanova, Ibsen, and Tolstoy.

Several pages in Ellis's study of Whitman are devoted to Thoreau. While other critics such as Channing had tried to reconcile the dichotomy between science and literature in Thoreau's writings, Ellis describes the author of *Walden* as lacking scientific sense. Ellis praises Thoreau for his peculiar powers of observation, which make him "an almost ideal naturalist." Yet, to Ellis, Thoreau's observation are, in the end, "dull and unprofitable reading" for the scientist as Thoreau has no perception of "the vital and organic relationships of facts." This is because he was essentially a literary author and his primary concern was to create a suggestive literary style. Ellis agrees with other critics of Thoreau on the topic of his remoteness from other people. Because he was fundamentally a cynic, Thoreau could not fully understand his peers, who, Ellis provocatively points out, represent more than half of nature's treasure.

It has been claimed for Thoreau by some of his admirers, never by himself, that he was a man of science, a naturalist. Certainly, in some respects, he had in him the material for an almost ideal naturalist. His peculiar powers of observation, and habits of noting and recording natural facts, his patience, his taste for spending his days and nights in the open air, seem to furnish everything that is required. Nor would his morbid dislike of dissection have been any serious bar, for the least worked but by no means the least important portion of natural history is the study of living forms, and for this Thoreau seems to have been peculiarly adapted; he had acquired one of the rarest of arts, that of approaching birds, beasts and fishes, and exciting no fear. There are all sorts of profoundly interesting investigations which only such a man can profitably undertake. But that right question which is at least the half of knowledge was hidden from Thoreau; he seems to have been absolutely deficient in scientific sense. His bare, impersonal records of observations are always dull and unprofitable reading; occasionally he stumbles on a good observation, but, not realizing its significance, he never verifies it or follows it up. His science is that of a fairly intelligent schoolboy—a counting of birds' eggs and a running after squirrels. Of the vital and organic relationships of facts, or even of the existence of such relationships, he seems to have no perception. Compare any of his books with, for instance, Belt's *Naturalist in Nicaragua,* or any of Wallace's books: for the men of science, in their spirit of illuminating inquisitiveness, all facts are instructive; in Thoreau's hands they are all dead. He was not a naturalist: he was an artist and a moralist.

He was born into an atmosphere of literary culture, and the great art he cultivated was that of framing sentences. He desired to make sentences which would "suggest far more than they say," which would "lie like boulders on the page, up and down or across, not mere repetition, but creation, and which a man might sell his ground or cattle to build," sentences "as durable as a Roman aqueduct." Undoubtedly he succeeded; his sentences frequently have all the massive and elemental qualities that he desired. They have more; if he knew little of the architectonic qualities of style, there is a keen exhilarating breeze blowing about these boulders, and when we look at them they have the grace and audacity, the happy, natural extravagance of fragments of the finest Decorated Gothic on the site of a fourteenth century abbey. He was in love with the things that are wildest and most untamable in Nature, and of these his sentences often seem to be a solid artistic embodiment, the mountain side, "its sublime gray mass, that antique, brownish-gray, Ararat colour," or the "ancient, familiar, immortal cricket sound," the thrush's song, his *ranz des vâches,* or the song that of all seemed to rejoice him most, the clear, exhilarating, braggart, clarion-crow of the cock. Thoreau's favourite reading was among the Greeks, Pindar, Simonides, the Greek Anthology, especially Eschylus, and a later ancient, Milton. There is something of his paganism in all this, his cult of the aboriginal health-bearing forces of Nature. His paganism, however unobtrusive, was radical and genuine. It was a paganism much earlier than Plato, and which had never heard of Christ.

Thoreau was of a piece; he was at harmony with himself, though it may be that the elements that went to make up the harmony were few. The austerity and exhilaration and simple paganism of his art were at one with his morality. He was, at the very core, a preacher; the morality that he preached, interesting in itself, is, for us, the most significant thing about him. Thoreau was, in the noblest sense of the word, a Cynic. The school of Antisthenes is not the least interesting of the Socratic schools, and Thoreau is perhaps the finest flower that that school has ever yielded. He may not have been aware of his affinities, but it will help us if we bear them in mind. The charm that Diogenes exercised over men seems to have consisted in his peculiarly fresh and original intellect, his extravagant independence and self-control, his coarse and effective wit. Thoreau sat in his jar at Walden with the same originality, independence, and sublime contentment; but his wisdom was suave and his wit was never coarse—exalted, rather, into a perennial humour, flashing now and then into divine epigram. A life in harmony with Nature, the culture of joyous simplicity, the subordination of science to ethics—these were the principles of Cynicism, and to these Thoreau was always true. . . .

Every true Cynic is, above all, a moralist and a preacher. Thoreau could never be anything else; that was, in the end, his greatest weakness. This unfailing ethereality, this perpetual challenge of the acridity and simplicity of Nature, becomes at last hypernatural. Thoreau breakfasts on the dawn: it is well; but he dines on the rainbow and sups on the Aurora borealis. Of Nature's treasure more than half is man. Thoreau, with his noble Cynicism, had, as he thought, driven life into a corner, but he had to confess that of all phenomena his own race was to him the most mysterious and undiscoverable. . . .

Thoreau has heightened for us the wildness of Nature, and his work—all written, as we need not be told, in the open air—is full of this tonicity; it is a sort of moral quinine, and, like quinine under certain circumstances, it leaves a sweet taste behind.

—Havelock Ellis, "Whitman,"
The New Spirit, 1890, pp. 93–99

Henry S. Salt (1890)

Henry Salt (1851–1939) was an English literary critic and a social reformer. He was particularly active in the fields of prison and educational reform, and he was also a pioneer supporter of animal rights. Salt was born in India, the son of an English army officer, and was educated in England. After completing his education, he became a schoolmaster at Eaton. As the founder of the Humanitarian League, he actively campaigned for the banning of hunting as a sport. He was also a vegetarian and, in 1886, he published *A Plea for Vegetarianism*. His 1890 biography of Thoreau was an influential turning point in the criticism of the New England author. Salt was instrumental in introducing Mahatma Gandhi to Thoreau's ideas of nonviolent protest. He was also acquainted with many socialist and leftist personalities of his day, including the founders of the Fabian Society Hubert Bland and Annie Besant.

Salt downplays the importance of Thoreau's outer literary form in comparison to his ideas and his value as a philosopher. According to Salt, Thoreau's originality lies in his reaction against the division of labor that rigidly separates between literary and manual work. Salt reads in Thoreau's writings a plea for a combination of the two so that the student is not deprived of "healthy out-door work" and the laborer is not deprived of "opportunity for self-culture." Thoreau is interested in demonstrating the unity of nature, and he is always careful in pointing out its perfection. Even when he treats common subjects such as "the cottage of the poor and humble," he idealizes them to such an extent as to give them a new status. An important literary tool that Thoreau uses to present this fundamental harmony between the different components of reality is his metaphoric language that gives his writing an almost mystic quality. This emphasis on metaphor is all the more valuable as it does not lead to a single "superfluous word or syllable" nor to "artificial tropes and embellishments." To Salt, Thoreau's distinguishing trait is "concentration."

The lack of system which is noticeable in Thoreau's character may be traced in the style of his writings as plainly as in his philosophical views. He was not careful as to the outer form and finish of his works, for he believed that the mere literary contour is of quite secondary importance in comparison with the inner animating spirit; let the worthiness of the latter once be assured, and the former will fall naturally into its proper shape. Furthermore, although, as we have seen, writing was more and more recognised by him as his profession in his later years, he was at all times conscious of a fuller and higher calling than that of the literary man—as he valued nature before art, so he valued life before literature. He both preached and practised a combination of literary work and manual; of the pen and of the spade; of the study and of the open sky. He protested against that tendency in our civilisation which carries division of labour to such an extent that the student is deprived of healthy out-door work, while the labourer is deprived of opportunity for self-culture. He imagines the case of some literary professor, who sits in his library writing a treatise on the huckleberry, while hired huckleberry-pickers and cooks are engaged in the task of preparing him a pudding of the berries. A book written under such conditions will be worthless. "There will be none of the spirit of the huckleberry in it. I believe in a different kind of division of labour, and that the professor should divide himself between the library and the huckleberry field." His opinions on the subject of literary style are clearly stated in *The Week,* and are no doubt in great measure a record of his own practice:

> Can there be any greater reproach than an idle learning? Learn to split wood at least. The necessity of labour and conversation with many men and things to the scholar is rarely well remembered; steady labour with the hands, which engrosses the attention also, is unquestionably the best method of removing palaver and sentimentality out of one's style, both of speaking and writing. If he has worked hard from morning till night, though he may have grieved that he could not be watching the train of his thoughts during that time, yet the few hasty lines which at evening record his day's experience will be more musical and true than his freest but idle fancy could have furnished. Surely the writer is to address a world of labourers, and such therefore must be his own

discipline. He will not idly dance at his work who has wood to cut and cord before nightfall in the short days of winter, but every stroke will be husbanded, and ring soberly through the wood; and so will the strokes of that scholar's pen, which at evening record the story of the day, ring soberly, yet cheerily, on the ear of the reader, long after the echoes of his axe have died away.

Such were, in fact, the conditions under which Thoreau wrote many of the pages of the journal from which his own essays were constructed; and, whatever may be thought of the force of his general principle, there can be no doubt that in his particular case the result was very felicitous. It was his pleasure and his determination that his writing should be redolent of the open-air scenery by which it was primarily inspired. "I trust," he says of *The Week* (and the same may be said of all his volumes), "it does not smell so much of the study and library, even of the poet's attic, as of the fields and woods; that it is a hypaethral or unroofed book, lying open under the ether, and permeated by it, open to all weathers, not easy to be kept on a shelf." In this way Thoreau added a new flavour to literature by the unstudied freshness and wildness of his tone, and succeeded best where he made least effort to be successful. "It is only out of the fulness of thinking," says Mr. R. L. Stevenson, "that expression drops perfect like a ripe fruit; and when Thoreau wrote so nonchalantly at his desk, it was because he had been vigorously active during his walk." Even Mr. Lowell, a far less friendly critic, is compelled, on this point, to express his admiration "With every exception, there is no writing comparable with Thoreau's in kind that is comparable with it in degree, where it is best. His range was narrow, but to be a master is to be a master. There are sentences of his as perfect as anything in the language, and thoughts as clearly crystallised; his metaphors and images are always fresh from the soil."

This success, although naturally and unconsciously attained, had of course been rendered possible in the first instance by an honest course of study; for Thoreau, like every other master of literary expression, had passed through his strict apprenticeship of intellectual labour. Though comparatively indifferent to modern languages, he was familiar with the best classical writers of Greece and Rome, and his style was partly formed on models drawn from one of the great eras in English literature, the post-Elizabethan period. It is a noticeable fact that "mother-tongue" was a word which he loved to use even in his college days; and the homely native vigour of his own writings was largely due to the sympathetic industry with which he had laboured in these quiet but fertile fields. Nor must it be supposed, because he did not elaborate his work according to the usual canons, that he was a careless or indolent writer—on the contrary, it was his habit to correct his manuscripts with unfailing diligence. He deliberately examined and re-examined each sentence of his journal before admitting it into the essays which he sent to the printer, finding that a certain lapse of time was necessary before he could arrive at a satisfactory decision. His absolute sincerity showed itself as clearly in the style of his writing as in the manner of his life. "The one great rule of composition—and if I were a professor of rhetoric I should insist on this—is to *speak the truth*. This first, this second, this third."

In his choice of subjects it was the common that most often enlisted his sympathy and attention. "The theme," he says, "is nothing; the life is everything. Give me simple, cheap, and homely themes. I omit the unusual—the hurricanes and earthquakes, and describe the common. This has the greatest charm, and is the true theme of poetry. Give me the obscure life, the cottage of the poor and humble, the work-days of the world, the barren fields." But while he took these as the subjects for his pen, he so idealised and transformed them by the power of his imagination as to present them in aspects altogether novel and unsuspected; it being his delight to bring to view the latent harmony and beauty of all existent things, and thus indirectly to demonstrate the unity and perfection of nature.

Numerous passages might be quoted from Thoreau's works which exhibit these picturesque and suggestive qualities. He had a poet's eye for all forms of beauty, moral and material alike, and for the subtle analogies that exist between the one class and the other—in a word, he was possessed of a most vivid and quickening imagination. His images and metaphors are bold, novel, and impressive—as when, to take but a couple of instances, he alludes to the lost anchors of vessels wrecked off the coast of Cape Cod as "the sunken faith and hope of mariners, to which they trusted in vain;" or describes the autumnal warmth on the sheltered side of Walden as "the still glowing embers which the summer, like a departing hunter, had left." And, with all his simplicity and directness of speech, he has an unconscious, almost mystic, eloquence which stamps him unmistakably as an inspired writer, a man of true and rare genius; so that it has been well said of him that "he lived and died to transfuse external nature into human words." In this respect his position among prose-writers is unique; no one, unless it be Richard Jefferies, can be placed in the same category with him.

In so far as he studied the external form of his writings, the aim and object which Thoreau set before him may be summed up in one word—

concentration. He avows his delight in sentences which are "concentrated and nutty." The distinctive feature of his own literary style could not have been more accurately described. The brief, barbed, epigrammatic sentences which bristle throughout his writings, pungent with shrewd wisdom and humour, are the appropriate expression of his keen thrifty nature; there is not a superfluous word or syllable, but each passage goes straight to the mark, and tells its tale, as the work of a man who has some more urgent duty to perform than to adorn his pages with artificial tropes and embellishments. He is fond of surprising and challenging his readers by the piquancy and strangeness of his sayings, and his use of paradox is partly due to the same desire to stimulate and awaken curiosity, partly to his wayward and contradictory nature. The dangers and demerits of a paradoxical style are sufficiently obvious; and no writer has ever been less careful than Thoreau to safeguard himself against misunderstandings on this score. He has consequently been much misunderstood, and will always be so, save where the reader brings to his task a certain amount of sympathy and kindred sense of humour.

To those who are not gifted with the same sense of the inner identity which links together many things that are externally unlike, some of Thoreau's thoughts and sayings must necessarily appear to be a fair subject for ridicule. Yet that he should have been charged with possessing no "humour" would be inexplicable, save for the fact that the definitions of that quality are so various and so vague. Broad wit and mirthful genial humour he certainly had not, and he confessedly disliked writings in which there is a conscious and deliberate attempt to be amusing. He found Rabelais, for instance, intolerable; "it may be sport to him," he says, "but it is death to us; a mere humorist, indeed, is a most unhappy man, and his readers are most unhappy also." But though he would not or could not recognise humour as a distinct and independent quality, and even attempted, as we are told, to eliminate what he considered "levity" from some of his essays, he none the less enjoyed keenly—and himself unmistakably exhibited—the quiet, latent, unobstrusive humour which is one of the wholesome and saving principles of human life. Among Thoreau's own writings, *Walden* is especially pervaded by this subtle sense of humour, grave, dry, pithy, sententious, almost saturnine in its tone, yet perhaps for that very reason the more racy and suggestive to those readers who have the faculty for appreciating it.

—Henry S. Salt, from *Life of Henry David Thoreau*, 1890, pp. 170–176

P. Anderson Graham
"The Philosophy of Idleness" (1891)

He never was out of America, and with the exception of one or two short periods, the whole of his life was spent in and about Concord, yet his reflections might have come from Fleet Street. His railings against the world, his protests against luxury and competition, his fierce condemnation of the aims and labour of his fellow-men are more suggestive of a disappointed cit than of an ingenuous wild man of the woods. At college and at the feet of Emerson he had imbibed a second-hand and discoloured Carlylean philosophy, the effect of which was to spoil him for his obvious life-work. Without it he might have developed into a great naturalist, one to inform that science with new life, and from that pursuit he would assuredly have sucked more pleasure than from hoeing beans and surveying wood lots. The world is not after all so stupid as to refuse a livelihood for a service that his journals prove Thoreau to have been eminently capable of rendering. There was an element of weakness in his character, however, that led him to curb and hamper his inclinations in small things and in great.

Just as he was a born hunter who forswore the gun, scrupled at the angle, and refused to eat flesh, so also he was a most companionable man who chose an artificial solitude. If he made an excursion, he was as careful to look out for a fellow-traveller, as is the ordinary pedestrian tourist. He was 'a man of good fellowship' who loved a 'dish of gossip,' and one who never could stay long away from his fellows; and it was not long before he wearied of the Walden loneliness. Though love of out-of-door life was the predominant feature of his character, he must needs sandwich his descriptions with preaching and moralisation about a world of which he was ignorant. When the editors of the future approach their inevitable duty of separating the dead from the living in the swiftly accumulating literature of our time, the works of Thoreau will be the easiest to deal with; all they require is for every passage with a precept, a teaching or a doctrine to be ruthlessly excised, and the remainder will be his lasting and valuable contribution.

Students of extraordinary phenomena, those who have described the avalanche, the earthquake, and the volcano, great battles by sea and land, plague, famine, and tempest, untrodden mountain tops, unfurrowed seas, and lands virgin to the explorer, may well ask in wonder the secret of that charm by which Thoreau pins the interest of his hearer to things the most trivial and homely—a warfare of emmets, the helve of a lost axe waving at the bottom of a pond, the musical thrum of telegraph wires, an owl's hooting, or a cockerel's cry.

When a Pasteur deals with bacteria infinitely smaller, or a Darwin examines the infinitesimal grains of sand borne hither on a migrant's feet, a further interest of science is reflected on the description. It is not so with Thoreau; he aims neither at an exhaustive and orderly examination nor at discovery. He was a correspondent and helper of Agassiz, but not himself a toiler in the field of formal natural history, and he declined to write for the Boston Society, because he could not properly detach the mere external record of observation from the inner associations with which such facts were connected in his mind. To have laboured for the increase of positive knowledge would have been heresy to his doctrine of idleness. No one reads *Walden* for information.

—P. Anderson Graham,
"The Philosophy of Idleness,"
Nature in Books, 1891, pp. 85–87

Brander Matthews (1896)

He was always more poet than naturalist, for his observation, interesting as it ever is, is rarely novel. It is his way of putting what he has seen that takes us rather than any freshness in the observation itself. His sentences have sometimes a Greek perfection; they have the freshness, the sharpness, and the truth which we find so often in the writings of the Greeks who came early into literature, before everything had been seen and said. Thoreau had a Yankee skill with his fingers, and he could whittle the English language in like manner; so he had also a Greek faculty of packing an old truth into an unexpected sentence. He was not afraid of exaggeration and paradox, so long as he could surprise the reader into a startled reception of his thought. He was above all an artist in words, a ruler of the vocabulary, a master phrasemaker. But his phrases were all sincere; he never said what he did not think; he was true to himself always.

—Brander Matthews, *An Introduction to
the Study of American Literature,* 1896,
pp. 192–193

Thomas Wentworth Higginson
"Henry David Thoreau" (1898)

His scholarship, like his observation of nature, was secondary to his function as poet and writer. Into both he carried the element of whim;

but his version of the *Prometheus Bound* shows accuracy, and his study of birds and plants shows care. It must be remembered that he antedated the modern school, classed plants by the Linnaean system, and had necessarily Nuttall for his elementary manual of birds. Like all observers he left whole realms uncultivated; thus he puzzles in his journal over the great brown paper cocoon of the *Attacus Cecropia,* which every village boy brings home from the winter meadows. If he has not the specialized habit of the naturalist of to-day, neither has he the polemic habit; firm beyond yielding, as to the local facts of his own Concord, he never quarrels with those who have made other observations elsewhere; he is involved in none of those contests in which palaeontologists, biologists, astronomers, have wasted so much of their lives.

His especial greatness is that he gives us standing ground below the surface, a basis not to be washed away. A hundred sentences might be quoted from him which make common observers seem superficial and professed philosophers trivial, but which, if accepted, place the realities of life beyond the reach of danger. He was a spiritual ascetic to whom the simplicity of nature was luxury enough; and this, in an age of growing expenditure, gave him an unspeakable value. To him life itself was a source of joy so great that it was only weakened by diluting it with meaner joys. This was the standard to which he constantly held his contemporaries. "There is nowhere recorded," he complains, "a simple and irrepressible satisfaction with the gift of life, any memorable praise of God. If the day and the night are such that you greet them with joy, and life emits a fragrance, like flowers and sweet-scented herbs,—is more elastic, starry, and immortal,—that is your success."

—Thomas Wentworth Higginson,
"Henry David Thoreau," *American Prose,* ed.
George Rice Carpenter, 1898, pp. 341–342

DONALD G. MITCHELL (1899)

Unlike many book-making folk, this swart, bumptious man has grown in literary stature since his death; his drawers have been searched, and cast-away papers brought to day. Why this renewed popularity and access of fame? Not by reason of newly detected graces of style; not for weight of his *dicta* about morals, manners, letters; there are safer guides in all these. But there is a new-kindled welcome for the independence, the tender particularity, and the outspokenness of this journal-maker.

If asked for a first-rate essayist, nobody would name Thoreau; if a poet, not Thoreau; if a scientist, not Thoreau; if a political sage, not Thoreau; if a historian of small socialities and of town affairs, again not Thoreau. Yet we read him—with zest, though he is sometimes prosy, sometimes overlong and tedious; but always—Thoreau.

—Donald G. Mitchell, *American Lands and Letters (Leather-Stocking to Poe's "Raven")*, 1899, pp. 278–280

WALTER C. BRONSON (1900)

His writings cleave so closely to the man that they can hardly be studied wholly apart, nor is it necessary so to consider them at length here. What is most remarkable in them is their wild "tang," the subtlety and the penetrative quality of their imaginative sympathy with the things of field, forest, and stream. The minuteness, accuracy, and delicacy of the observation and feeling are remarkable; while mysticism, fancy, poetic beauty, and a vein of shrewd humor often combine with the other qualities to make a whole whose effect is unique. Thoreau's verse is much like Emerson's on a smaller scale and a lower plane, having the same technical faults and occasionally the same piercing felicity of phrase. On the whole, Thoreau must be classed with the minor American authors; but there is no one just like him, and the flavor of his best work is exceedingly fine.

—Walter C. Bronson, *A Short History of American Literature,* 1900, p. 213

BARRETT WENDELL (1900)

Barrett Wendell (1855–1921) was a leading American academic and educator. He graduated from Harvard in 1877 and three years later was appointed instructor of English at that institution. He became professor in 1898, a position he held until 1917. He was the first academic to offer a complete course in American literature and in 1900 he published *A Literary History of America.*

In this groundbreaking work, Wendell gave Thoreau an important position for his "sympathetic observation of Nature." Such observation may seem at first simply an imitation of the English romantic movement. Yet, to Wendell, what distinguished Thoreau from English romantic poets such as Wordsworth was that the nature he chose as his topic was "characteristically American." His writings are therefore a proud affirmation of American landscape and scenery. Although Wendell gives Thoreau an important position in American literature, he still largely agrees with earlier critics who had ranked Thoreau as inferior to Emerson. This is motivated by the fact that Thoreau's philosophical speculations are constantly filtered through "his own distinctive individuality."

Of course Thoreau was eccentric, but his eccentricity was not misanthropic. Inclined by temperament and philosophy alike to this life of protestant solitude, he seems to have regarded his course as an experimental example. He was not disposed to quarrel with people who disagreed with him. All he asked was to be let alone. If his life turned out well, others would ultimately imitate him; if it turned out ill, nobody else would be the worse. Though his philosophising often seems unpractically individual, then, it never exhales such unwholesomeness as underlay Alcott's self-esteem. What is more, there can be no question that his speculations have appealed to some very sensible minds. All the same, if he had confined himself to ruminating on the eternities and human nature, with which his sympathy was at best limited, his position in literary history would hardly be important. What gave him lasting power was his unusually sympathetic observation of Nature. A natural vein of indolence, to be sure, prevented him from observing either precociously or systematically; but when, as was more and more the case, he found himself alone with woods and fields and waters, he had true delight in the little sights which met his eyes, in the little sounds which came to his ears, in all the constant, inconspicuous beauties which the prosaic toil-someness of Yankee life had hitherto failed to perceive.

Nature, as every one knows, had been a favourite theme of that romantic revival in England whose leader was Wordsworth. In one aspect, then, Thoreau's writing often seems little more than an American evidence of a temper which had declared itself in the old world a generation before. Nothing, however, can alter the fact that the Nature he delighted in was characteristically American. First of all men, Thoreau brought that revolutionary temper which recoils from the artificialities of civilisation face to face with the rugged fields, the pine woods and the apple orchards, the lonely ponds and the crystalline skies of eastern New England. His travels occasionally ranged so far as the Merrimac River, Cape Cod, or even beyond Maine into Canada; but pleasant as the books are in which he recorded these wanderings, as exceptional as were Cotton Mather's infrequent excursions through the bear-haunted wilds to Andover, we could spare them far better than *Walden*, or than the journals in which for years he set down his daily observations in the single town of Concord. Thoreau's individuality is often so assertive as to repel a sympathy which it happens not instantly to attract; but that sympathy must be unwholesomely sluggish which would willingly resist the appeal of his communion with Nature. If your lot be ever cast in some remote region of our simple country, he can do you, when you will, a rare service, stimulating your eye to see, and your ear to hear, in all the little commonplaces about you, those endlessly changing details which make life everywhere so unfathomably, immeasurably wondrous. For Nature is truly a miracle; and he who will regard her lovingly shall never lack that inspiration which miracles breathe into the spirit of mankind.

Nor is Thoreau's vitality in literature a matter only of his observation. Open his works almost anywhere,—there are ten volumes of them now,—and even in the philosophic passages you will find loving precision of touch. He was no immortal maker of phrases. Amid bewildering obscurities, Emerson now and again flashed out utterances which may last as long as our language. Thoreau had no such power; but he did possess in higher degree than Emerson himself the power of making sentences and paragraphs artistically beautiful. Read him aloud, and you will find in his work a trait like that which we remarked in the cadences of Brockden Brown and of Poe; the emphasis of your voice is bound to fall where meaning demands. An effect like this is attainable only through delicate sensitiveness to rhythm. So when you come to Thoreau's pictures of Nature you have an almost inexhaustible series of verbal sketches in which every touch has the grace of precision. On a large scale, to be sure, his composition falls to pieces; he never troubled himself about a systematically made book, or even a systematic chapter. In mere choice of words, too, he is generally so simple as to seem almost commonplace. But his sentences and paragraphs are often models of art so fine as to seem artless. Take, for example, this well-known passage from *Walden:*

> Early in May, the oaks, hickories, maples, and other trees, just
> putting out amidst the pine woods around the pond, imparted
> a brightness like sunshine to the landscape, especially in cloudy
> days, as if the sun were breaking through mists and shining faintly
> on the hillsides here and there. On the third or fourth of May I
> saw a loon in the pond, and during the first week of the month

I heard the whippoorwill, the brown thrasher, the veery, the wood-pewee, the chewink, and other birds. I had heard the wood-thrush long before. The phebe had already come once more and looked in at my door and window, to see if my house were cavern-like enough for her, sustaining herself on humming wings with clinched talons, as if she held by the air, while she surveyed the premises. The sulphur-like pollen of the pitch-pine soon covered the pond and the stones and the rotten wood along the shore, so that you could have collected a barrelful. This is the "sulphur showers" we hear of. Even in Calidas' drama of Sacontala, we read of "rills dyed yellow with the golden dust of the lotus." And so the seasons went rolling on into summer, as one rambles into higher and higher grass.

The more you read work like that, the more admirable you will find its artistic form.

With Thoreau's philosophising the case is different. Among Emerson's chief traits was the fact that when he scrutinised the eternities in search of ideal truth, his whole energy was devoted to the act of scrutiny. Vague, then, and bewildering as his phrases may often seem, we are sensible of a feeling that this Emerson is actually contemplating the immensities; and these are so unspeakably vaster than all mankind—not to speak of the single human being who for the moment is striving to point our eyes toward them—that our thoughts again and again concern themselves rather with the truths thus dimly seen than with anything concerning the seer. The glass through which Emerson contemplated the mysteries is achromatic. Now, Thoreau's philosophic speculations so surely appeal to powerful minds who find them sympathetic that we may well admit them to involve more than they instantly reveal to minds not disposed to sympathise. Even their admirers, however, must admit them to be coloured throughout by the unflagging self-consciousness involved in Thoreau's eccentric, harmless life. Perhaps, like Emerson, Thoreau had the true gift of vision; but surely he could never report his visions in terms which may suffer us to forget himself. The glass which he offers to our eyes is always tinctured with his own disturbing individuality. In spite, then, of the fact that Thoreau was a more conscientious artist than Emerson, this constant obstrusion of his personality ranges him in a lower rank, just as surely as his loving sense of nature ranges him far above the half-foolish egotism of Bronson Alcott. More and more the emergence of Emerson from his surroundings grows distinct. Like truly great men, whether he was truly great or not, he possessed the gift of such common-sense as saves men from the perversities of eccentricity.

—Barrett Wendell, *A Literary History of America*, 1900, pp. 333–337

PAUL ELMER MORE
"A HERMIT'S NOTES ON THOREAU" (1901)

A leading conservative intellectual of the New Humanist movement, Paul Elmer More (1864–1937) was educated at Washington University, St. Louis, and Harvard. It was during his years at Harvard that More met Irving Babbit, the founder of New Humanism. The movement was based on the theories of English social critic Matthew Arnold and was a reaction against the increasingly materialistic tendencies of American society at the turn of the century. Because of this approach to social reality, Thoreau, with his apparent rejection of social conventions and any money-oriented ethos, was clearly appealing to the group.

More started his career as the literary editor of *The Independent* and the *New York Evening Post*. From 1909 to 1914, he served as the editor of *The Nation*. From these influential positions, More fought against the literary conventions and social concerns adopted by such naturalist writers as Theodore Dreiser and Sinclair Lewis. More wrote the following essay on Thoreau before becoming an influential literary critic. "A Hermit's Notes on Thoreau" is one of the earliest *Shelburne Essays*, which More eventually collected in eleven volumes. The essay on Thoreau was written after More's graduation, during a period of retirement to a rundown farmhouse near Shelburne, New Hampshire. Thus, More's condition was similar to Thoreau's during the writing of *Walden,* and it is significant that the New Humanist intellectual is led to write on Thoreau through his reading of exactly that book. "*Walden* studied in the closet, and *Walden* mused over under the trees, by running water," More concludes, "are two quite different books."

To More, Thoreau represents by far the greatest American nature writer as he created a new way of writing about the topic. What distinguishes Thoreau's style from that of his predecessors and his imitators is, according to More, the ability to capture "the qualities of awe and wonder" that nature stimulates in the beholder. Because of his literary background and his reaction against scientifically oriented philosophies, More appreciates precisely those literary qualities that for some critics of

Thoreau represented his major limitation to becoming a man of science. Objective descriptions of nature are simply cheap forms of literature, while the best parts of Thoreau's writings are those in which he shows himself to be a contemplative philosopher. In addition, because New Humanists looked at the past for models that could inform the present, More particularly appreciated the historical awareness of New England heritage that Thoreau's writings communicate to the reader. Although the English romantics may be superior poets, Thoreau is to be appreciated as distinctively American. More's critical piece also challenges the gender assumptions made by earlier critics of Thoreau such as Robert Louis Stevenson. While Stevenson found that Thoreau's writings smacked of effeminacy, More argues that the author's confrontation with the "rude forces of the forest" saved him from the "taint of effeminacy" that can be detected in the British romantics. Through his acquaintance with Nature, Thoreau was able to develop "manly virtues."

In a secluded spot in the peaceful valley of the Androscoggin I took upon myself to life two years as a hermit, after a mild Epicurean fashion of my own. Three maiden aunts wagged their heads ominously; my nearest friend inquired cautiously whether there was any taint of insanity in the family; an old gray-haired lady, a veritable saint, who had not been soured by her many deeds of charity, admonished me on the utter selfishness and godlessness of such a proceeding. But I clung heroically to my resolution. Summer tourists in that pleasant valley may still see the little red house among the pines,—empty now, I believe; and I dare say gaudy coaches still draw up at the door, as they used to do, when the gaudier bonnets and hats exchanged wondering remarks on the cabalistic inscription over the lintel, or spoke condescendingly to the great dog lying on the steps. As for the hermit within, having found it impossible to educe any meaning from the tangled habits of mankind while he himself was whirled about in the imbroglio, he had determined to try the efficacy of undisturbed meditation at a distance. So deficient had been his education that he was actually better acquainted with the aspirations and emotions of the old dwellers on the Ganges than with those of the modern toilers by the Hudson or the Potomac. He had been deafened by the "indistinguishable roar" of the streets, and could make no sense of the noisy jargon of the market place. But—shall it be confessed?—although he learned many things during his contemplative sojourn in the wilderness, he returned to civilization, alas, as ignorant of its meaning as when he left it.

However, it is not my intention to justify the saintly old lady's charge of egotism by telling the story of my exodus to the desert; that, perhaps, may come later and at a more suitable time. I wish now only to record the memories of one perfect day in June, when woods and mountains were as yet a new delight.

The fresh odors of morning were still swaying in the air when I set out on this particular day; and my steps turned instinctively to the great pine forest, called the Cathedral Woods, that filled the valley and climbed the hill slopes behind my house. There, many long roads, that are laid down in no map, wind hither and thither among the trees, whose leafless trunks tower into the sky, and then meet in evergreen arches overhead. There

The tumult of the times disconsolate

never enters, and no noise of the world is heard save now and then, in winter, the ringing strokes of the woodchopper at his cruel task. How many times I have walked those quiet cathedral aisles, while my great dog paced faithfully on before! Underfoot the dry, purple-hued moss was stretched like a royal carpet; and at intervals a glimpse of the deep sky, caught through an aperture in the groined roof, reminded me of the other world, and carried my thoughts still farther from the desolating memories of this life. Nothing but pure odors were there, sweeter than cloistral incense; and murmurous voices of the pines, more harmonious than the chanting of trained choristers; and in the heart of the wanderer nothing but tranquillity and passionless peace. Often now the recollection of those scenes comes floating back upon his senses when, in the wakeful seasons of a summer night, he hears the wind at work among the trees; even in barren city streets some sound or spectacle can act upon him as a spell, banishing for a moment the hideous contention of commerce, and placing him beneath the restful shadows of the pines. May his understanding cease its function, and his heart forget to feel, when the memory of those days has utterly left him, and he walks in the world without this consolation of remembered peace.

Nor can I recollect that my mind, in these walks, was much called away from contemplation by the petty curiosities of the herbalist or bird-lorist, for I am not one zealously addicted to scrutinizing closely into the secrets of Nature. It never seemed to me that a flower was made sweeter by knowing the construction of its ovaries, or assumed a new importance when I learned its trivial or scientific name. The wood thrush and the veery sing as melodiously to the uninformed as to the subtly curious. Indeed, I sometimes think a little ignorance is wholesome in our communion with Nature, until we are ready to part with her altogether. She is feminine in this as in other respects, and loves to shroud herself in illusions, as the Hindus taught in their books. For they called her Maya, the very person and power of deception, whose sway over the beholder must end as soon as her mystery is penetrated.

Like as a dancing girl to sound of lyres
Delights the king and wakens sweet desires
    For one brief hour, and having shown her art
With lingering bow behind the scene retires:

So o'er the Soul alluring Nature vaunts
Her lyric spell, and all her beauty flaunts;
    And she, too, in her time withdrawing, leaves
The Watcher to his peace—'t is all she wants.

"Now have I seen it all!" the Watcher saith,
And wonders that the pageant lingereth:
    And, "He hath seen me!" then the other cries,
And wends her way: and this they call the Death.

Dear as the sound of the wood thrush's note still is to my ears, something of charm and allurement has gone from it since I have become intimate with the name and habits of the bird. As a child born and reared in the city, that wild, ringing call was perfectly new and strange to me when, one early dawn, I first heard it, during a visit to the Delaware Water Gap. To me, whose ears had grown familiar only with the rumble of paved streets, the sound was like a reiterated unearthly summons inviting me from my narrow prison existence out into a wide and unexplored world of impulse and adventure. Long afterwards I learned the name of the songster whose note had made so strong an impression on my childish senses, but still I associate the song with the grandiose scenery, with the sheer forests and streams and the rapid river of the Water Gap. I was indeed almost a man—though the confession may sound incredible in these days—before I again heard the wood thrush's note, and my second adventure impressed me almost as profoundly as the first. In the outer suburbs of the city where my home had always been, I was walking one day with a brother, when suddenly out of a grove of laurel oaks sounded, clear and triumphant, the note which I remembered so well, but which had come to have to my imagination the unreality and mystery of a dream of long ago. Instantly my heart leapt within me. "It is the fateful summons once more!" I cried; and, with my companion, who was equally ignorant of bird-lore, I ran into the grove to discover the wild trumpeter. That was a strange chase in the fading twilight, while the unknown songster led us on from tree to tree, ever deeper into the woods. Many times we saw him on one of the lower boughs, but could not for a long while bring ourselves to believe that so wondrous a melody should proceed from so plain a minstrel. And at last, when we had satisfied ourselves of his identity, and the night had fallen, we came out into the road with a strange solemnity hanging over us. Our ears had been opened to the unceasing harmonies of creation, and our eyes had been made aware of the endless drama of natural life. We had been initiated into the lesser mysteries; and if the sacred pageantry was not then, and never was to be, perfectly clear to our understanding, the imagination was nevertheless awed and purified.

If the knowledge and experience of years have made me a little more callous to these deeper influences, at least I have not deliberately closed the door to them by incautious prying. Perhaps a long course of wayward reading has taught me to look upon the world with eyes quite different from those of the modern exquisite searchers into Nature. I remember the story of Prometheus, and think his punishment is typical of the penalty that falls upon those who grasp at powers and knowledge not intended for mankind,—some nemesis of a more material loneliness and a more barren pride torturing them because they have turned from human knowledge to an alien and forbidden sphere. Like Prometheus, they shall in the end cry out in vain:—

> O air divine, and O swift-winged winds!
> Ye river fountains, and thou myriad-twinkling
> Laughter of ocean waves! O mother earth!
> And thou, O all-discerning orb o' the sun!—
> To you, I cry to you; behold what I,
> A god, endure of evil from the gods.

Nor is the tale of Prometheus alone in teaching this lesson of prudence, nor was Greece the only land of antiquity where reverence was deemed more salutary than curiosity. The myth of the veiled Isis passed, in those days, from people to people, and was everywhere received as a symbol of the veil of illusion about Nature, which no man might lift with impunity. And the same idea was, if anything, intensified in the Middle Ages. The common people, and the Church as well, looked with horror on such scholars as Pope Gerbert, who was thought, for his knowledge of Nature, to have sold himself to the devil; and on such discoverers as Roger Bacon, whose wicked searching into forbidden things cost him fourteen years in prison. And even in modern times did not the poet Blake say: "I fear Wordsworth loves nature, and nature is the work of the Devil. The Devil is in us as far as we are nature"? It has remained for an age of skepticism to substitute science for awe. After all, can any course of study or open-air pedagogics bring us into real communion with the world about us? I fear much of the talk about companionship with Nature that pervades our summer life is little better than cant and self-deception, and he best understands the veiled goddess who most frankly admits her impenetrable secrecy. The peace that comes to us from contemplating the vast panorama spread out before us is due rather to the sense of a great passionless power entirely out of our domain than to any real intimacy with the hidden deity. It was John Woolman, the famous New Jersey Quaker, who wrote, during a journey through the wilderness of Pennsylvania: "In my traveling on the road, I often felt a cry rise from the centre of my mind, thus, 'O Lord, I am a stranger on the earth, hide not thy face from me.'"

But I forget that I am myself traveling on the road; and all this long disquisition is only a chapter of reminiscences, due to the multitudinous singing of the thrushes on this side and that, as we—I and my great dog— trod the high cathedral aisles. After a while the sound of running water came to us above the deeper diapason of the pines, and, turning aside, we clambered down to a brook which we had already learned to make the terminus of our walks. Along this stream we had discovered a dozen secret nooks where man and dog might lie or sit at ease, and to-day I stretched myself on a cool, hollow rock, with my eyes looking up the long, leafy chasm of the brook. Just above my couch the current was dammed by a row of mossy boulders, over which the water poured with a continual murmur and plash. My head was only a little higher than the pool beyond the boulders, and, lying motionless, I watched the flies weaving a pattern over the surface of the quiet water, and now and then was rewarded by seeing a greedy trout leap into the sunlight to capture one of the winged weavers. Surely, if there is any such thing as real intimacy with Nature, it is in just such quiet spots as this; the grander scenes require of us a moral enthusiasm which can come to the soul only at rare intervals and for brief moments.

But at last I turned from dreaming and moralizing on the little life about me, and began to read. The volume chosen was the most appropriate to the time and place that could be imagined,—Thoreau's *Walden;* and having entered upon an experiment not altogether unlike his, I now set myself to reading the record of his two years of solitude. I learned many things from that morning's perusal. Several times I had read the *Odyssey* within sight of the sea, and the murmur of the waves on the beach beating through the rhythm of the poem had taught me how vital a thing a book might be, and how it could acquire a peculiar validity from harmonious surroundings; but now the reading of Thoreau in this charmed and lonely spot emphasized this commonplace truth in a peculiar manner. *Walden* studied in the closet, and *Walden* mused over under the trees, by running water, are two quite different books. And then, from Thoreau, the greatest by far of our writers on Nature, and the creator of a new sentiment in literature, my mind turned to the long list of Americans who have left, or are still composing, a worthy record of their love and appreciation of the natural world. Our land of multiform activities had produced so little that is really creative in literature or art! Hawthorne and Poe, and possibly one or two others, were masters in their own field; yet even they chose not quite the highest realm for their genius to work in. But in one subject our writers have led the way, and are still preeminent: Thoreau was the creator of a new manner of writing about Nature. In its deeper essence his work is inimitable, as it is the voice of a unique personality; but in its superficial aspects it has been taken up by a host of living writers, who have caught something of his method, even if they lack his genius and singleness of heart. From these it was an easy transition to compare Thoreau's attitude of mind with that of Wordsworth and the other great poets of the century who have gone to Nature for their inspiration, and have made Nature-writing the characteristic note of modern verse. What is it in Thoreau that is not to be found in Byron and Shelley and Wordsworth, not to mention old Izaak Walton, Gilbert White of Selborne, and a host of others? It was a rare treat, as I lay in that leafy covert, to go over in memory the famous descriptive passages from these authors, and to contrast their spirit with that of the book in my hand.

As I considered these matters, it seemed to me that Thoreau's work was distinguished from that of his American predecessors and imitators by just these qualities of awe and wonder which we, in our communings with Nature, so often cast away. Mere description, though it may at times have a scientific value, is after all a very cheap form of literature; and, as I have already intimated, too much curiosity of detail is likely to exert a deadening influence on the philosophic and poetic contemplation of Nature. Such an influence is, as I believe, specially noticeable at the present time, and even Thoreau was not entirely free from its baneful effect. Much of his writing, perhaps the greater part, is the mere record of observation and classification, and has not the slightest claim on our remembrance,—unless, indeed, it possesses some scientific value, which I doubt. Certainly the parts of his work having permanent interest are just those chapters where he is less the minute observer, and more the contemplative philosopher. Despite the width and exactness of his information, he was far from having the truly scientific spirit; the acquisition of knowledge, with him, was in the end quite subordinate to his interest in the moral significance of Nature, and the words he read in her obscure scroll were a language of strange mysteries, oftentimes of awe. It is a constant reproach to the prying, self-satisfied habits of small minds to see the reverence of this great-hearted observer before the supreme goddess he so loved and studied.

Much of this contemplative spirit of Thoreau is due to the soul of the man himself, to that personal force which no analysis of character can explain. But, besides this, it has always seemed to me that, more than any other descriptive writer of the country, his mind is the natural outgrowth, and his essays the natural expression, of a feeling deep-rooted in the historical beginnings of New England; and this foundation in the past gives a strength and convincing force to his words that lesser writers utterly lack. Consider the new life of the Puritan colonists in the strange surroundings of their desert home. Consider the case of the adventurous Pilgrims sailing from the comfortable city of Leyden to the unknown wilderness over the sea. As Governor Bradford wrote, "the place they had thoughts on was some of those vast & unpeopled countries of America, which are frutfull & fitt for habitation, being devoyd of all civill inhabitants, wher ther are only salvage & brutish men, which range up and downe, little otherwise than ye wild beasts of the same." In these vast and unpeopled countries, where beast and bird were strange to the eye, and where "salvage" men abounded,—men who did not always make the land so "fitt" for new inhabitants as Bradford might have desired,—it was inevitable that the mind should be turned to explore and report on natural phenomena and on savage life. It is a fact that some of the descriptions of sea and land made by wanderers to Virginia and Massachusetts have a directness and graphic power, touched occasionally with an element of wildness, that render them even to-day agreeable reading. This was before the time of Rousseau, and before Gray had discovered the beauty of wild mountain scenery; inevitably the early American writers were chiefly interested in Nature as the home of future colonists, and their books are for the most part semi-scientific accounts of what they studied from a utilitarian point of view.

But the dryness of detailed description in the New World was from the first modified and lighted up by the wondering awe of men set down in the midst of the strange and often threatening forces of an untried wilderness; and this sense of awful aloofness, which to a certain extent lay dormant in the earlier writers, did nevertheless sink deep into the heart of New England, and when, in the lapse of time, the country entered into its intellectual renaissance, and the genius came who was destined to give full expression to the thoughts of his people before the face of Nature, it was inevitable that his works should be dominated by just this sense of poetic mystery.

It is this New World inheritance, moreover,—joined, of course, with his own inexplicable personality, which must not be left out of account,—that makes Thoreau's attitude toward Nature something quite distinct from that of the great poets who just preceded him. There was in him none of the fiery spirit of the revolution which caused Byron to mingle hatred of men with enthusiasm for the Alpine solitudes. There was none of the passion for beauty and voluptuous self-abandonment of Keats; these were not in the atmosphere he breathed at Concord. He was not touched with Shelley's unearthly mysticism, nor had he ever fed

> on the aerial kisses
> Of shapes that haunt thought's wildernesses;

his moral sinews were too stark and strong for that form of mental dissipation. Least of all did he, after the manner of Wordsworth, hear in the voice of Nature any compassionate plea for the weakness and sorrow of the downtrodden. Philanthropy and humanitarian sympathies were to him a desolation and a woe. "Philanthropy is almost the only virtue which is sufficiently appreciated by mankind. Nay, it is greatly overrated; and it is our selfishness which overrates it," he writes. And again: "The philanthropist too often surrounds mankind with the remembrance of his own cast-off griefs as an atmosphere, and calls it sympathy." Similarly his reliance on the human will was too sturdy to be much perturbed by the inequalities and sufferings of mankind, and his faith in the individual was too unshaken to be led into humanitarian interest in the masses. "Alas! this is the crying sin of the age," he declares, "this want of faith in the prevalence of a man." But the deepest and most essential difference is the lack of pantheistic reverie in Thoreau. It is this brooding over the universal spirit embodied in the material world which almost always marks the return of sympathy with Nature, and which is particularly noticeable in the poets of the present century. So Lord Byron, wracked and broken by his social catastrophes, turns for relief to the fair scenes of Lake Leman, and finds in the high mountains and placid waters a consoling spirit akin to his own.

> Are not the mountains, waves, and skies, a part
> Of me and of my soul, as I of them?

he asks; and in the bitterness of his human disappointment he would "be alone, and love Earth only for its earthly sake." Shelley, too, "mixed awful talk" with the "Great Parent," and heard in her voice an answer to all his vague dreams of the soul of universal love. No one, so far as I know, has yet studied the relation between Wordsworth's pantheism and his humanitarian sympathies, but we need only glance at his "Lines on Tintern Abbey" to see how closely the two feelings were interknit in his mind. It was because he felt this

> sense sublime
> Of something far more deeply interfused,
> Whose dwelling is the light of setting suns,
> And the round ocean, and the living air,
> And the blue sky, and in the mind of man;

it was because the distinctions of the human will and the consequent perception of individual responsibility were largely absorbed in this dream of the universal spirit, that he heard in Nature "the still, sad music of humanity," and reproduced it so sympathetically in his own song. Of all this pantheism, whether attended with revolt from responsibility or languid reverie or humanitarian dreams, there is hardly a trace in Thoreau. The memory of man's struggle with the primeval woods and fields was not so lost in antiquity that Nature had grown into an indistinguishable part of human life. Governor Bradford wrote his story of the Pilgrims, "that their children may see with what difficulties their fathers wrastled in going through these things in their first beginnings," and the lesson had not been lost. If Nature smiled upon Thoreau at times, she was still an alien creature who only succumbed to his force and tenderness, as she had before given her bounty, though reluctantly, to the Pilgrim Fathers. A certain companionship he had with the plants and wild beasts of the field, a certain intimacy with the dumb earth; but he did not seek to merge his personality in their impersonal life, or look to them for a response to his own inner moods; he associated with them as the soul associates with the body.

More characteristic is his sense of awe, even of dread, toward the great unsubdued forces of the world. The loneliness of the mountains such as they appeared to the early adventurers in a strange, unexplored country; the repellent loneliness of the barren heights frowning down inhospitably upon the pioneer who scratched the soil at their base; the loneliness and terror of the dark, untrodden forests, where the wanderer might stray away and be lost forever, where savage men were more feared than the wild animals, and where superstition saw the haunt of the Black Man and of all uncleanness,—

all this tradition of sombre solitude made Nature to Thoreau something very different from the hills and valleys of Old England. "We have not seen pure Nature," he says, "unless we have seen her thus vast and drear and inhuman. . . Man was not to be associated with it. It was Matter, vast, terrific,—not his Mother Earth that we have heard of, not for him to tread on, or be buried in,—no, it were being too familiar even to let his bones lie there,—the home, this, of Necessity and Fate." After reading Byron's invocation to the Alps as the palaces of Nature; or the ethereal mountain scenes in Shelley's Alastor, where all the sternness of the everlasting hills is dissolved into rainbow hues of shifting light as dainty as the poet's own soul; or Wordsworth's familiar musings in the vale of Grasmere,—if, after these, we turn to Thoreau's account of the ascent of Mount Katahdin, we seem at once to be in the home of another tradition. I am tempted to quote a few sentences of that account to emphasize the point. On the mountain heights, he says of the beholder: "He is more lone than you can imagine. There is less of substantial thought and fair understanding in him than in the plains where men inhabit. His reason is dispersed and shadowy, more thin and subtile, like the air. Vast, Titanic, inhuman Nature has got him at disadvantage, caught him alone, and pilfers him of some of his divine faculty. She does not smile on him as in the plains. She seems to say sternly, Why came ye here before your time? This ground is not prepared for you. Is it not enough that I smile in the valleys? I have never made this soil for thy feet, this air for thy breathing, these rocks for thy neighbors. I cannot pity nor fondle thee here, but forever relentlessly drive thee hence to where I *am* kind."

I do not mean to present the work of Thoreau as equal in value to the achievement of the great poets with whom I have compared him, but wish merely in this way to bring out more definitely his characteristic traits. Yet if his creative genius is less than theirs, I cannot but think his attitude toward Nature is in many respects truer and more wholesome. Pantheism, whether on the banks of the Ganges or of the Thames, seems to bring with it a spreading taint of effeminacy; and from this the mental attitude of our Concord naturalist was eminently free. There is something tonic and bracing in his intercourse with the rude forces of the forest; he went to Walden Pond because he had "private business to transact," not for relaxation and mystical reverie. "To be a philosopher," he said, "is not merely to have subtle thoughts, not even to found a school, but so to love wisdom as to live according to its dictates, a life of simplicity, independence, magnanimity, and trust;" and by recurring to the solitudes of Nature he thought he could best develop in himself just these manly virtues. Nature was to him a discipline of the will as much as a stimulant to the imagination. He would, if it were possible, "combine the hardiness of the savages with the intellectualness of the civilized man;" and in this method of working out the philosophical life we see again the influence of long and deep-rooted tradition. To the first settlers, the red man was as much an object of curiosity and demanded as much study as the earth they came to cultivate; their books are full of graphic pictures of savage life, and it would seem as if now in Thoreau this inherited interest had received at last its ripest expression. When he traveled in the wilderness of Maine, he was as much absorbed in learning the habits of his Indian guides as in exploring the woods. He had some innate sympathy or perception which taught him to find relics of old Indian life where others would pass them by, and there is a well-known story of his answer to one who asked him where such relics could be discovered: he merely stooped down and picked an arrowhead from the ground.

And withal his stoic virtues never dulled his sense of awe, and his long years of observation never lessened his feeling of strangeness in the presence of solitary Nature. If at times his writing descends into the cataloguing style of the ordinary naturalist, yet the old tradition of wonder was too strong in him to be more than temporarily obscured. Unfortunately, his occasional faults have become in some of his recent imitators the staple of their talent; but Thoreau was preeminently the poet and philosopher of his school, and I cannot do better than close these desultory notes with the quotation of a passage which seems to me to convey most vividly his sensitiveness to the solemn mystery of the deep forest.

"We heard," he writes in his Chesuncook, "come faintly echoing, or creeping from afar, through the moss-clad aisles, a dull, dry, rushing sound, with a solid core to it, yet as if half smothered under the grasp of the luxuriant and fungus-like forest, like the shutting of a door in some distant entry of the damp and shaggy wilderness. If we had not been there, no mortal had heard it. When we asked Joe [the Indian guide] in a whisper what it was, he answered,—'Tree fall.'"

—Paul Elmer More, "A Hermit's Notes
on Thoreau," *Atlantic,* June 1901,
pp. 857–864

WORKS

Almost all the pieces in this section focus on *Walden*. This is not surprising since nineteenth-century and early-twentieth-century critics of Thoreau neglected his only other book-length work, *A Week on the Concord and Merrimack Rivers* (1849). Only with Thoreau's accession to the American literary canon in the 1930s did his other works, including his essays, receive critical attention. *Walden* was Thoreau's most successful work. Written almost entirely during the two years that its author spent by Walden Pond near Concord (1845–1847), the book went through a lengthy process of corrections and rewriting. It was finally published in 1854 in 2,000 copies. This first edition sold out by 1856, and the second edition was published a few weeks after the author's death in 1862. This was a very limited success, but *Walden* fared much better than Thoreau's previous book, *A Week on the Concord and Merrimack Rivers,* which only sold about 200 of its original 1,000 copies.

Thoreau's contemporaries split between being supporters and detractors of *Walden.* New England critics generally reviewed the book favorably, although some were angered by the author's sharp judgments on the recent developments in American society. *Walden* aimed to show to its readers how little people needed to live and decidedly refused the consumerist mind that was taking hold of American and New England way of life. According to F.O. Matthiessen, this is clear from the opening chapter, "Economy," which Thoreau conceived "as an antidote for the 'lives of quiet desperation' that he saw the mass of men leading." In it, Thoreau provides a pessimistic answer to the question "why do we work?" Capitalist culture induces people to accept its fundamental principle without properly questioning them. The result is that people lead alienated existences and become, with the environment that surrounds them, instruments rather than ends.

The natural descriptions in *Walden* also earned Thoreau the title "worshipper of nature." The book does not offer scientific explanation for natural phenomena but, in accordance with Thoreau's transcendentalism, mingles an objective and a subjective approach. As Fannie Hardy Eckstorm points out in the only essay in this section not to focus on *Walden* but on Thoreau's Maine writings, "It was not as an observer that Thoreau surpassed other men, but as an interpreter."

WALDEN

Andrew Preston Peabody (1854)

The economical details and calculations in this book are more curious than useful; for the author's life in the woods was on too narrow a scale to find imitators. But in describing his hermitage and his forest life, he says so many pithy and brilliant things, and offers so many piquant, and, we may add, so many just, comments on society as it is, that his book is well worth the reading, both for its actual contents and its suggestive capacity.

—Andrew Preston Peabody, *North American
Review,* October 1854, p. 536

George William Curtis (1862)

This book, the record of his residence, his thoughts, and observations during the time he lived in the woods upon the shore of Walden Pond, in Concord, Massachusetts, is of the very best of its kind in any literature.

—George William Curtis,
"Editor's Easy Chair,"
Harper's New Monthly Magazine,
July 1862, p. 270

William Dean Howells "My First Visit to New England" (1894)

The main American supporter of literary realism, William Dean Howells (1837–1920) grew up in Ohio and initially began a career as a journalist. Thanks to his campaign biography of Abraham Lincoln, Howells was able to finance a trip to New England where he was introduced to the literary establishment of the day. When Lincoln won the presidency, he rewarded his biographer with a consulship in Venice (1861–65). When Howells returned to the United States he became assistant editor and, from 1871, editor of the *Atlantic Monthly*, a position that he held for the next ten years. Howells's own reviews and articles on American writers show that he was an acute critic of his contemporary literary scene. In this short excerpt, Howells compares *Walden* favorably to Tolstoy's books for its portrayal of the hopelessness of life in a materialist world.

He is an author who has fallen into that abeyance, awaiting all authors, great or small, at some time or another; but I think that with him, at least in regard to his most important book, it can be only transitory. I have not read the story of his hermitage beside Walden Pond since the year 1858, but I have a fancy that if I should take it up now, I should think it a wiser and truer conception of the world than I thought it then. It is no solution of the problem; men are not going to answer the riddle of the painful earth by building themselves shanties and living upon beans and watching ant-fights; but I do not believe Tolstoy himself has more clearly shown the hollowness, the hopelessness, the unworthiness of the life of the world than Thoreau did in that book. If it were newly written it could not fail of a far vaster acceptance than it had then, when to those who thought and felt seriously it seemed that if slavery could only be controlled, all things else would come right of themselves with us.

—William Dean Howells, "My First Visit
to New England," 1894, *Literary Friends
and Acquaintance,* 1900

THEODORE F. WOLFE
"THE CONCORD PILGRIMAGE" (1895)

Some one has said, "Thoreau experienced Nature as other men experience religion." Certainly the life at Walden, which he depicted in one of the most fascinating of books, was in all its details—whether he was ecstatically hoeing beans in his field or dreaming on his door-step, floating on the lake or rambling in forest and field—that of an ascetic and devout worshipper of Nature in all her moods.

—Theodore F. Wolfe, "The Concord Pilgrimage,"
Literary Shrines, 1895, p. 71

FRED LEWIS PATTEE (1896)

Walden, which contains a minute account of the two years at Walden Pond, is Thoreau's best book. It is full of the wild aroma of the woods. In no other book can one come so close to Nature's heart. We hear in it the weird cry of the loons over the water; we watch the frolics of the squirrels; we observe the thousand phenomena of the wonderful little lake; we listen to the forest sounds by day and by night; we study the tell-tale snow; we watch, with bated breath, a battle to the death between two armies of ants. For minute and loving descriptions of the woods and fields, *Walden* has had no rival.

—Fred Lewis Pattee, *A History of*
American Literature, 1896, pp. 224–225

Fannie Hardy Eckstorm
"Thoreau's 'Maine Woods'" (1908)

Although most of Thoreau's writings focus on the nature and scenery of New England, particularly around the Concord area, the posthumous volume *The Maine Woods* documents the author's travels to Maine. These represent those rare occasions in which Thoreau ventured to more remote parts of New England. *The Maine Woods* contain an important piece on nature such as "Ktaadn and the Maine Woods," an appeal for a closer contact between human beings and the natural world. Fannie Hardy Eckstorm was the daughter of a lumberman who was a friend of George Thatcher, Thoreau's companion on his trip through the Maine woods.

It is more than half a century since Henry D. Thoreau made his last visit to Maine. And now the forest which he came to see has all but vanished, and in its place stands a new forest with new customs. No one should expect to find here precisely what Thoreau found; therefore, before all recollection of the old days has passed away, it is fitting that some one who knew their traditions should bear witness to Thoreau's interpretation of the Maine woods.

We hardly appreciate how great are the changes of the last fifty years; how the steamboat, the motor-boat, the locomotive, and even the automobile, have invaded regions which twenty years ago could be reached only by the lumberman's batteau and the hunter's canoe; how cities have arisen, and more are being projected, on the same ground where Thoreau says that "the best shod travel for the most part with wet feet," and that "melons, squashes, sweet-corn, tomatoes, beans, and many other vegetables, could not be ripened," because the forest was so dense and moist.

Less than twenty years since there was not a sporting camp in any part of the northern Maine wilderness; now who may number them? Yet, even before the nineties, when one could travel for days and meet no one, the pine tree was gone; the red-shirted lumberman was gone; the axe was about to give place to the saw; and soon, almost upon the clearing where Thoreau reported the elder Fowler, the remotest settler, as wholly content in his solitude and thinking that "neighbors, even the best, were only trouble and expense," was to rise one of the largest pulp mills in the world, catching the logs midway their passage down the river and grinding them into paper. And the pine tree, of which Thoreau made so much? Native to the state and long accustomed to its woods, I cannot remember ever having seen a perfect, old-growth white pine tree; it is doubtful if there is one standing in the state to-day.

So the hamadryad has fled before the demand for ship-timber and Sunday editions, and the unblemished forest has passed beyond recall. There are woods enough still; there is game enough,—more of some kinds than in the old days; there are fish enough; there seems to be room enough for all who come; but the man who has lived here long realizes that the woods are being "camped to death;" and the man who is old enough to remember days departed rustles the leaves of Thoreau's book when he would listen again to the pine tree soughing in the wind.

What is it that *The Maine Woods* brings to us besides? The moods and music of the forest; the vision of white tents beside still waters; of canoes drawn out on pebbly beaches; of camp-fires flickering across rippling rapids; the voice of the red squirrels, "spruce and fine;" the melancholy laughter of the loon, and the mysterious "night warbler," always pursued and never apprehended. Most of all it introduces us to Thoreau himself.

It must be admitted in the beginning that *The Maine Woods* is not a masterpiece. Robert Louis Stevenson discards it as not literature. It is, however, a very good substitute, and had Robert Louis worn it next to the skin he might perhaps have absorbed enough of the spirit of the American forest to avoid the gaudy melodrama which closes *The Master of Ballantrae*. *The Maine Woods* is of another world. Literature it may not be, nor one of "the three books of his that will be read with much pleasure;" but it is the Maine woods. Since Thoreau's day, whoever has looked at these woods to advantage has to some extent seen them through Thoreau's eyes. Certain it is that no other man has ever put the coniferous forest between the leaves of a book.

For that he came—for that and the Indian. Open it where you will—and the little old first edition is by all odds to be chosen if one is fastidious about the printed page, to get the full savor of it; open where you will and these two speak to you. He finds water "too civilizing;" he wishes to become "selvaggia;" he turns woodworm in his metamorphosis, and loves to hear himself crunching nearer and nearer to the heart of the tree. He is tireless in his efforts to wrench their secrets from the woods; and, in every trial, he endeavors, not to talk *about* them, but to flash them with lightning vividness into the mind of the reader. "It was the opportunity to be ignorant that I improved. It suggested to me that there was something to be seen if one had eyes. It made a believer of me more than before. I believed that the woods were not tenantless, but choke-full of honest spirits as good as myself any day."

It is sometimes the advantage of a second-rate book that it endears the writer to us. The Thoreau of *Walden*, with his housekeeping all opened up for inspection, refusing the gift of a rug rather than shake it, throwing away his paperweight to avoid dusting it—where's the woman believes he *would* have dusted it?—parades his economies priggishly, like some pious anchoret with a business eye fixed on Heaven. But when he tells us in the appendix to the *Woods* that for a cruise three men need only one large knife and one iron spoon (for all), a four-quart tin pail for kettle, two tin dippers, three tin plates and a fry pan, his economy, if extreme, is manly and convincing. We meet him here among men whom we have known ourselves; we see how he treated them and how they treated him, and he appears to better advantage than when skied among the lesser gods of Concord.

Here is Joe Polis, whose judgment of a man would be as shrewd as any mere literary fellow's, and Joe talks freely, which in those days an Indian rarely did with whites. Here is the late Hiram L. Leonard, "the gentlemanly hunter of the stage," known to all anglers by his famous fishing rods. Those who remember his retiring ways will not doubt that it was Thoreau who prolonged the conversation. Here is Deacon George A. Thatcher, the "companion" of the first two trips. That second invitation and the deacon's cordial appreciation of "Henry" bespeak agreeable relations outside those of kinship. The Thoreau whom we meet here smiles at us. We see him, a shortish, squarish, brown-bearded, blue-eyed man, in a check shirt, with a black string tie, thick waistcoat, thick trousers, an old Kossuth hat,—for the costume that he recommends for woods wear must needs have been his own,—and over all a brown linen sack, on which, indelible, is the ugly smutch that he got when he hugged the sooty kettle to his side as he raced Polis across Grindstone Carry.

To every man his own Thoreau! But why is not this laughing runner, scattering boots and tinware, as true to life as any? Brusque, rude, repellant no doubt he often was, and beyond the degree excusable; affecting an unnecessary disdain of the comfortable, harmless goods of life; more proud, like Socrates, of the holes in his pockets than young Alcibiades of his whole, new coat; wrong very often, and most wrong upon his points of pride; yet he still had his southerly side, more open to the sun than to the wind. It is not easy to travel an unstaked course, against the advice and wishes and in the teeth of the prophecies of all one's friends, when it would be sweet and easy to win their approval—and, Himmel! to stop their mouths!—by burning one's faggot. A fighting faith, sleeping on its arms, often has to be stubborn and ungenial. What Henry Thoreau needed was to be believed in through thick and thin, and then let alone; and the very crabbedness, so often complained of, indicates that, like his own wild apples, in order to get a chance to grow, he had to protect himself by thorny underbrush from his too solicitous friends.

There is a popular notion that Thoreau was a great woodsman, able to go anywhere by dark or daylight, without path or guide; that he knew all the secrets of the pioneer and the hunter; that he was unequaled as an observer, and almost inerrant in judgment, being able to determine at a glance weight, measure, distance, area, or cubic contents. The odd thing about these popular opinions is that they are not true. Thoreau was not a woodsman; he was not infallible; he was not a scientific observer; he was not a scientist at all. He could do many things better than most men; but the sum of many excellencies is not perfection.

For the over-estimate of Thoreau's abilities, Emerson is chiefly responsible. His noble eulogy of Thoreau has been misconstrued in a way which shows the alarming aptitude of the human mind for making stupid blunders. We all have a way of taking hold of a striking detail—which Mr. Emerson was a rare one for perceiving—and making of it the whole story. We might name it *the fallacy of the significant detail*. Do we not always see Hawthorne, the youth, walking by night? Who thinks of it as any less habitual than eating his dinner? And because Stevenson, in an unguarded moment, confessed that "he had played the sedulous ape" to certain authors, no writer, out of respect to our weariness, has ever forborne to remind us of that pleasant monkey trick of Stevenson's youth. Nor are we ever allowed to forget that Thoreau "saw as with microscope, heard as with ear-trumpet," and that "his power of observation seemed to indicate additional senses." It is because the majority of mankind see no difference in values between facts aglow with poetic fervor and facts preserved in the cold storage of census reports, that Emerson's splendid eulogy of his friend, with its vivid, personal characterizations rising like the swift bubbles of a boiling spring all through it, has created the unfortunate impression that Thoreau made no blunders.

Emerson himself did not distinguish between the habitual and the accidental; between a clever trick, like that of lifting breams guarding their nests, and the power to handle any kind of fish. He even ran short of available facts, and grouped those of unequal value. To be able to grasp an even dozen of pencils requires but little training; to be able to estimate the weight of a pig, or the cordwood in a tree, needs no more than a fairly good judgment; but that "he could pace sixteen rods more accurately than another man could measure them with rod and chain,"—that is nonsense, for it puts at naught the whole science of surveying. Emerson's data being unequal in rank and kind, the whole sketch is a little out of focus, and consequently the effect is agreeably artistic.

Nor is the matter mended by misquotation. Emerson says, "He could find his path in the woods at night, he said, better by his feet than his eyes." There is nothing remarkable in this. How does any one keep the path across his own lawn on a black dark night? But even so careful a man as Stevenson paraphrases thus: "He could guide himself about the woods on the darkest night by the touch of his feet." Here we have a different matter altogether. By taking out that "path," a very ordinary accomplishment is turned into one quite impossible. Because Emerson lacked woods learning, the least variation from his exact words is likely to result in something as absurd or as exaggerated as this.

Thoreau's abilities have been overrated. *The Maine Woods* contains errors in the estimates of distance, area, speed, and the like, too numerous to mention in detail. No Penobscot boatman can run a batteau over falls at the rate of fifteen miles an hour, as Thoreau says; no canoeman can make a hundred miles a day, even on the St. John River. The best records I can discover fall far short of Thoreau's estimate for an average good day's run. Even when he says that his surveyor's eye thrice enabled him to detect the slope of the current, he magnifies his office. Any woman who can tell when a picture hangs straight can see the slant of the river in all those places. . . .

It was not as an observer that Thoreau surpassed other men, but as an interpreter. He had the art—and how much of an art it is no one can realize until he has seated himself before an oak or a pine tree and has tried by the hour to write out its equation in terms of humanity—he had the art to see the human values of natural objects, to perceive the ideal elements of unreasoning nature and the service of those ideals to the soul of man. . . .

Yet because Thoreau does not measure up to the standard of the woodsman born and bred, it would be wrong to infer that the average city man could have done as well in his place. Well done for an amateur is often not creditable for a professional; but Thoreau's friends demand the honors of a professional. On the other hand, because he made some mistakes in unimportant details, he must not be accused of being unreliable. How trustworthy Thoreau is may be known by this,—that fifty years after he left the state forever, I can trace out and call by name almost every man whom he even passed while in the woods. He did not know the names of some of them; possibly he did not speak to them; but they can be identified after half a century. And that cannot be done with a slip-shod record of events. The wonder is, not that Thoreau did so little here, but that in three brief visits, a stranger, temperamentally alien to these great wildernesses, he got at the heart of so many matters.

Almost any one can see superficial differences; but to perceive the essence of even familiar surroundings requires something akin to genius. To be sure, he was helped by all the books he could obtain, especially by Springer's *Forest Life and Forest Trees*, to which he was indebted for both matter and manner; from which he learned to narrow his field of observation to the woods and the Indian, leaving other topics of interest unexamined. But how did he know, unless he discerned it in Springer's account of them, that these remote woods farms, in his day (not now), were "winter quarters"? How did he understand (and this he surely did not get from Springer) that it is the moose, and not the bear nor the beaver, which is "primeval man"? How came he to perceive the Homeric quality of the men of the woods? Hardly would the chance tourist see so much. And he can explain the Homeric times by these: "I have no doubt that they lived pretty much the same sort of life in the Homeric age, for men have always thought more of eating than of fighting; then, as now, their minds ran chiefly on 'hot bread and sweet cakes;' and the fur and lumber trade is an old story to Asia and Europe." And, with a sudden illumination, "I doubt if men ever made a trade of heroism. In the days of Achilles, even, they delighted in big barns, and perchance in pressed hay, and he who possessed the most valuable team was the best fellow."

So, though he was neither woodsman nor scientist, Thoreau stood at the gateway of the woods and opened them to all future comers with the key of poetic insight. And after the woods shall have passed away, the vision of them as he saw them will remain. In all that was best in him Thoreau was a poet. The finest passages in this book are poetical, and he is continually striking out some glowing phrase, like a spark out of flint. The logs in the camp are "tuned to each other with the axe." "For beauty give me trees with the fur on." The pines are for the poet, "who loves them like his own shadow in the air." Of the fall of a tree in the forest, he says, "It was a dull, dry, rushing sound, with a solid core to it, like the shutting of a door in some distant entry of the damp and shaggy wilderness." Katahdin is "a permanent shadow." And upon it, "rocks, gray, silent rocks, were the silent flocks and herds that pastured, chewing a rocky cud at sunset. They looked at me with hard gray eyes, without a bleat or low." I have seen the rocks on many granite hills, but that belongs only to the top of Katahdin.

Indeed, this whole description of Katahdin is unequaled. "Chesuncook" is the best paper of the three, taken as a whole, but these few pages on

Katahdin are incomparable. Happily he knew the traditions of the place, the awe and veneration with which the Indians regarded it as the dwelling-place of Pamola, their god of thunder, who was angry at any invasion of his home and resented it in fogs and sudden storms. ("He very angry when you gone up there; you heard him gone oo-oo-oo over top of gun-barrel," they used to say.) Thoreau's Katahdin was a realm of his own, in which for a few hours he lived in primeval solitude above the clouds, invading the throne of Pamola the Thunderer, as Prometheus harried Zeus of his lightnings. The gloomy grandeur of Æschylus rises before him to give him countenance, and he speaks himself as if he wore the buskin. But it is not windy declamation. He does not explode into exclamation points. Katahdin is a strange, lone, savage hill, unlike all others,—a very Indian among mountains. It does not need superlatives to set it off. Better by far is Thoreau's grim humor, his calling it a "cloud factory," where they made their bed "in the nest of a young whirlwind," and lined it with "feathers plucked from the live tree." Had he been one of the Stonish men, those giants with flinty eyebrows, fabled to dwell within the granite vitals of Katahdin, he could not have dealt more stout-heartedly by the home of the Thunder-God.

The best of Thoreau's utterances in this volume are like these, tuned to the rapid and high vibration of the poetic string, but not resolved into rhythm. It is poetry, but not verse. Thoreau's prose stands in a class by itself. There is an honest hardness about it. We may accept or deny Buffon's dictum that the style is the man; but the man of soft and slippery make-up would strive in vain to acquire the granitic integrity of structure which marks Thoreau's writing. It is not poetical prose in the ordinary scope of that flowery term; but, as the granite rock is rifted and threaded with veins of glistening quartz, this prose is fused at white heat with poetical insights and interpretations. Judged by ordinary standards, he was a poet who failed. He had no grace at metres; he had no æsthetic softness; his sense always overruled the sound of his stanzas. The fragments of verse which litter his workshop remind one of the chips of flint about an Indian encampment. They might have been the heads of arrows, flying high and singing in their flight, but that the stone was obdurate or the maker's hand was unequal to the shaping of it. But the waste is nothing; there is behind them the Kineo that they came from, this prose of his, a whole mountain of the same stuff every bit capable of being wrought to ideal uses.

—Fannie Hardy Eckstorm, "Thoreau's
'Maine Woods'," *Atlantic Monthly*, CII,
August 1908, pp. 242–250

Chronology

1817   David Henry Thoreau born on July 12 at Concord, Massachusetts; he later switched his first and middle names.

1828   Enters Concord Academy.

1833   Enters Harvard College.

1837   Graduates from Harvard. Begins teaching in the Concord School but resigns when required to administer corporal punishment. Meets Emerson and begins writing his *Journal.*

1838   Starts a private school with his brother John. Gives his first public lecture at the Concord Lyceum.

1839   Takes a canoe trip on the Concord and Merrimack rivers with John, which is described in *A Week on the Concord and Merrimack Rivers.*

1840   Publishes in *The Dial,* the newly started transcendentalist magazine.

1841   Takes up residence at Emerson's home, serving as tutor and handyman.

1842   Thoreau's brother John dies of lockjaw after cutting his finger.

1843   Serves as a tutor for the family of Emerson's brother William, on Staten Island.

1844   Returns home, working at the family's pencil-making business.

1845   Begins building a house on the shore of Walden Pond.

1846   Takes his first camping trip to the Maine woods. Arrested in Concord and jailed overnight for refusing to pay the poll tax to a government that supported slavery and waged an imperialist war against Mexico.

1847 Leaves Walden Pond and moves back in with the Emersons.

1849 Moves back to his father's house. *A Week on the Concord and Merrimack Rivers* and "Civil Disobedience" are published. He makes his first trip to Cape Cod.

1850 Travels again to Cape Cod and then to Canada.

1853 Makes a second trip to Maine.

1854 Publishes *Walden; or, Life in the Woods*. Delivers the lecture "Slavery in Massachusetts."

1855 Takes a third trip to Cape Cod.

1856 Meets Walt Whitman in New York.

1857 A fourth visit to Cape Cod, followed by a third trip to the Maine woods. Meets the abolitionist John Brown, who was hanged after a raid on Harpers Ferry.

1859 Delivers "A Plea for Captain John Brown."

1860 Takes his last camping trip to Monadnock.

1861 Travels to Minnesota due to his failing health.

1862 Dies of tuberculosis on May 6.

1874 Thoreau's body is moved from Concord to Author's Ridge at the cemetery in Sleepy Hollow, New York.

Index